P9-CMM-158

"Few Americans realize how radical the ACLU has become and the threat it poses to liberty. This well-researched and documented book pulls the veil away and exposes the ACLU's true agenda."
— Bill O'Reilly, Author and
   Host of Fox News' *O'Reilly Factor*

"Perhaps no organization has done more to remove America from its Judeo-Christian moorings than the ACLU—whom I often call the 'Anti-Christian Litigation Union.' Alan Sears and Craig Osten have done a major service to the Body of Christ and to Americans of goodwill by exposing this evil organization in their new book. I recommend it!"
— D. James Kennedy, Ph.D., Founder and President of
   Coral Ridge Ministries; Senior Minister, Coral
   Ridge Presbyterian Church, Ft. Lauderdale, Florida

"Alliance Defense Fund is doing a wonderful work in defending religious liberty and preserving the rights of Christian people."
— James Dobson, Founder, Focus on the Family

THE
ACLU
VS
AMERICA

KENTUCKY CHRISTIAN EDUCATORS ASSOCIATION

KCEA is a Network
Affiliate of

Christian Educators
Association Int'l
www.ceai.org

For additional information please visit our Christian
Educators Resource Page at **www.psst.com/KCEA**
or email us at KCEA1@earthlink.net

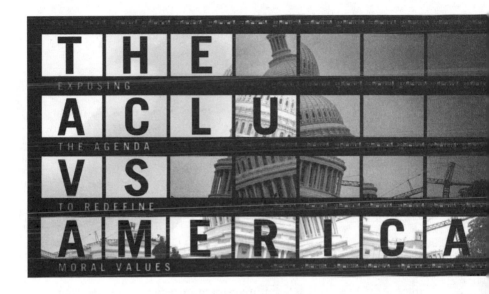

THE ACLU VS AMERICA

EXPOSING THE AGENDA TO REDEFINE MORAL VALUES

ALAN SEARS AND **CRAIG OSTEN**

BROADMAN
&HOLMAN
PUBLISHERS

NASHVILLE, TENNESSEE

© 2005 by Alliance Defense Fund, Alan Sears, and Craig Osten
All rights reserved
Printed in the United States of America

13-digit ISBN: 978-0-8054-4045-4
10-digit ISBN: 0-8054-4045-3

Published by Broadman & Holman Publishers,
Nashville, Tennessee

Dewey Decimal Classification: 261
Subject Headings: AMERICAN CIVIL LIBERTIES UNION
                  UNITED STATES—RELIGION
                  CHRISTIANITY AND CURRENT ISSUES

Unless otherwise noted, Scripture quotations have been taken from the
Holman Christian Standard Bible®, © 1999, 2000, 2002, 2003 by Holman Bible Publishers.

1 2 3 4 5 6 7 8 9 10 09 08 07 06 05

THIS BOOK IS DEDICATED TO

the founding members of the Alliance Defense Fund,
including the late Dr. Bill Bright, the late Larry
Burkett, the late Marlin Maddoux, the late William Pew,
Dr. James C. Dobson, and Dr. D. James Kennedy.

Contents

Acknowledgments

The authors want to thank the following people whose assistance and expertise made this book possible: Elizabeth Murray, Al Janssen, Christina Nichols, Ashley Kyle, and John Perrodin.

Each made important contributions to the finished product, and we are grateful for their wisdom and service in helping to bring this work to completion. We also thank our wives for their encouragement and sacrifices. Finally, we give thanks to Almighty God, who is the source of all wisdom, knowledge, and strength.

—Alan Sears and Craig Osten

SPECIAL ACKNOWLEDGMENT

The authors also wish to thank Bill O'Reilly (who asked Alan the question on air that caused us to write chap. 1), Sean Hannity, Laura Ingraham, John Leo, Dennis Prager, and Lou Dobbs for using their national media platform to help educate Americans about the ACLU and its real agenda for their future. We appreciate their efforts to take a stand for the truth.

Introduction

Can you imagine this scenario? Well-known evangelical leaders Dr. James Dobson of Focus on the Family, Dr. D. James Kennedy of Coral Ridge Ministries, and Steve Douglass of Campus Crusade for Christ, joined by a conservative Roman Catholic bishop and an Orthodox Jewish rabbi, fly to several Midwestern towns with teams of Christian lawyers. They descend on the local courts and file multi-million-dollar lawsuits—demanding that the local public schools and governments immediately cease the recognition and celebration of two-hundred-year-old (or two-thousand-year-old) cultural and historical traditions, remove all historic documents from building walls, and stop all teaching or even mentioning certain subjects to students because they violate "the separation of church and state."

These leaders then discover some government employees and public school students are Muslim. They demand that Muslims quit wearing anything that would identify their faith and that all government recognition or protection of their religious liberty, including their use of public property, be halted immediately.

Could you imagine the reaction of the national secular media if such a scenario occurred? Dobson, Kennedy, Douglass, and the others would be vilified, ridiculed, and mocked for their actions. They would be labeled "intolerant" by the secular Left and called the American Taliban, here to create a theocracy.

This scenario has *never* happened and it won't. But a substantially similar one is played out regularly across America. The perpetrator? The American Civil Liberties Union, better known as the ACLU. And many in the same secular media hail the ACLU and its members as heroes.

1

For eight decades, the ACLU has been America's leading religious censor, waging a largely uncontested (until recently) war against America's core values—all not only without protest but with the support of much of the media—cloaking its war in the name of liberty.

The result of this conflict is that Americans find themselves living in a country that, with each passing day, resembles less of what our nation's Founding Fathers intended when they came to these shores. We now live in a country where our traditional Christian and Jewish faith and religion—civilizing forces in any society—are openly mocked and increasingly pushed to the margins. We live in a country where parental authority is undermined and children have less protection from pornography, violent crime, and the promotion of dangerous and selfish sexual behaviors. We live in a country where the value of human life has been cheapened—from the moment and manner of conception to natural or unnatural death.

These seismic shifts did not happen overnight or by accident. Many are the result of a persistent, deliberate legal strategy by the ACLU and its allies to reshape America to conform to their vision. We know the ACLU did not advance its agenda in a vacuum, but it is for other writers to discuss that part of the story.

While the ACLU positions itself as the great defender of freedom, it is actively striving to eliminate the freedoms of millions of Americans. The ACLU is *against the freedom* of parents to pass their faith and values along to their children. It is *against the freedom* of organizations such as the Boy Scouts to set standard rules of conduct for their leaders. It is *against the freedom* of churches to publicly teach and proclaim the uncensored Word of God in the public square. It is *against many of the freedoms* and our nation's sovereignty that our forefathers fought and died for in the American Revolution and the many wars that followed. The ACLU and its allies work for much of what our forefathers opposed through the advocacy of international law to interpret the U.S. Constitution.

Most Americans are unaware of the most extreme positions of the ACLU. Many believe either the ACLU exists to stick up for the little guy, or it was an organization with noble beginnings but took a wrong turn somewhere along the way. This book will demonstrate neither view is the full story.

One needs only to look through one of the policy guides of the ACLU, listen to their founders and the speeches by their leaders, or go to its Web site and read actual documents it has filed in court, to get a clearer picture of the ACLU agenda. Consider these ACLU positions and imagine what America would be like if these dreams were fulfilled:

- All legal prohibitions on the distribution of obscene material— *including child pornography*—are unconstitutional.[1]
- Pornographic outlets can locate wherever they please— whether next to churches or day-care centers or near residential neighborhoods.[2]
- Tax-funded libraries should not restrict access of children to pornography on the Internet.[3]
- Parents should have no legal recourse when it comes to shielding their children from exposure to hard-core pornography.[4]
- The military cannot enforce even the most basic codes of conduct—such as discipline for disrespectful behavior toward a superior officer.[5]
- The military cannot stop open displays of homosexual behavior within its ranks.[6]
- Parents cannot limit their children's exposure to, or participation in public school classes and assemblies, any topic—except Orthodox Jewish or Christian teachings—that violates the family's core religious and moral beliefs.[7]
- Public schools cannot observe recognized religious, historical, and cultural holidays such as Christmas, Easter, or Hanukkah, despite hundreds of years of American tradition.[8]
- All legislative, military, and prison chaplaincy programs should be abolished.[9]
- All criminal and civil laws that *prohibit polygamy* (having multiple wives)[10] and same-sex "marriage" should be done away with.[11]

For eight decades, not only has the ACLU advocated for these and many other extreme positions, but through a legal and educational campaign of "fear, intimidation, and disinformation," it has been successful in turning many of them either into the law of the land or what Americans perceive to be the law of the land. In its quest to mold

American law as it desires through judicial activism, the ACLU also looks to force *international law* (at least their selective view of international law) on the American people—with complete disregard for American sovereignty and the U.S. Constitution.

In great part because of the ACLU's philosophy and actions, America the Beautiful has become America the Litigious. The so-called trial lawyers take much of their lead from the environment created by the ACLU's actions. "Rights" trump personal responsibility. "Alternative lifestyles" have replaced Mom and Dad. The U.S. Constitution has become an unrecognizable "living, breathing document" with "emanations from penumbras,"*[12] including a bizarre interpretation that has led to the deaths of more than 46 million of our nation's children.[13] The vibrant shield of protection the First Amendment was meant to provide for religious freedom, freedom that millions fled other countries to enjoy, has now become a sword to use against people of faith. The Founding Fathers could have never imagined this.

Unfortunately, until recently much of the ACLU's eight-decade war on the values of most Americans has largely gone unopposed. With an annual budget of $45 million and an endowment of $41 million,[14] the ACLU has used its army of at least sixty full-time attorneys, three hundred chapters, more than one thousand volunteer attorneys, and three hundred staff members[15]—as well as sympathetic members of the judiciary, the faculties of law schools, and the media—to engage in an ongoing campaign of legal intimidation, misinformation, and fear.

To provide an idea of the vast resources at the ACLU's disposal, according to guidestar.org, which tracks financial information on nonprofit organizations, the ACLU Foundation had net assets of $175,909,869 as of May 31, 2004.[16] In addition, the ACLU received an $8-million gift in 2003 from ACLU member Peter B. Lewis, chairman of Progressive Insurance, the largest individual donation ever received by the ACLU.[17] The Ford Foundation provided a $7-million grant (though the ACLU and the Ford Foundation have more recently dis-

---

*According to Webster's dictionary, a *penumbra* is "a partial shadow, as in an eclipse of the moon, between regions of complete shadow and complete illumination."

agreed over grant terms) in 1999, which Lewis matched with another $7 million to bring the total to $14 million.[18]

The ACLU's goal is a secularized "tolerant" America where religious speech is not only silenced but punished; where unwanted human life is quickly and easily discarded, hopefully at taxpayer expense; where the God-ordained institution of marriage and the family is on its way to becoming a distant memory, and where their "tolerance" is the silence of many others.

The ACLU has accomplished many of its goals by bringing lawsuit after lawsuit, threatening to bring often cripplingly expensive lawsuits, even on claims it would admit had little or no merit, to exhaust the will, resources, and strength of those who stand for religious freedom, the sanctity of human life, and traditional values. The ACLU has done this, in many cases, by finding activist judges who agree with its demands to re-create the law in the ACLU's image. In many instances, the ACLU and its allies have won by *default* because no one with a real stake in the outcome showed up to legally confront their demands. The effect has been court decisions in lieu of constitutional conventions—either through the Supreme Court rewriting what the Founding Fathers did more than two hundred years ago or by one pushy ACLU lawyer forcing a school system to change its rules, with the religious freedom of tens of thousands of Americans negatively affected.

But the tables are beginning to turn.

In 1993, after years without adequate legal resources to match the ACLU and its allies, a group of more than thirty Christian leaders finally said, "Enough!" They came together to discuss what could be done to slow and stop the ACLU and its allies' seemingly unopposed assault on America's freedoms. They recognized that many dedicated Christian lawyers had sought to slow and stop the ACLU but didn't have enough resources to succeed. Out of this, a new organization was formed—the Alliance Defense Fund (ADF). While ADF's resources are still dwarfed by those available to the ACLU and its many legal allies, ADF and its allies have quickly grown to become a formidable opponent and has been successful with a growing legal army of allies through strategy, training, funding, and litigation to defeat the ACLU and its allies several times in courtrooms and in the battle for minds across the nation.

This book will expose some aspects of the ACLU's war on American values, America's law and Constitution, and our national sovereignty. We will shed light on the ACLU's extreme positions and refute the assertion that the ACLU was once a good organization that took a wrong turn. We will discuss how God is allowing ADF to confront the ACLU in case after case. ADF's goal is to surpass the ACLU's vast manpower and financial resources to shape a future in which the values of religious freedom, the sanctity of human life, traditional marriage, and the family are strongly affirmed and protected.

With God's grace, we are confident we can not only reclaim America's judicial system and values from the ACLU and its allies but also protect our nation from present legal attacks. We can return our country to the original vision of the liberty framed by the Founding Fathers and fought for by generations of Americans on battlefields from Yorktown to Gettysburg to Omaha Beach to the sands of the Middle East. It will take prayers, perseverance, and great financial resources to do so, but we will win.

(Note: Portions of quotations that appear in italics indicate the authors' emphasis is added.)

CHAPTER 1

The ACLU: Against America from the Beginning

I am for socialism, disarmament, and ultimately for abolishing the state itself as an instrument of violence and compulsion. I seek social ownership of property, the abolition of the propertied class, and sole control by those who produce wealth. Communism is the goal.[1]
—ACLU founder Roger Baldwin

The American Civil Liberties Union is Roger Baldwin.[2]
—former ACLU counsel Arthur Garfield Hays

One of the great myths of the twentieth century and now the twenty-first century is that the ACLU started out as a good, pro-America, proliberty organization that somehow got off the track.

When we look closely at the ACLU's roots, the evidence shows something else. From the very start, the ACLU wanted to destroy from within the America our founders intended, with the use of lawyers and the courts as the chief weapons.

The ACLU was founded in 1920 by Roger Baldwin, an agnostic and socialist who demonstrated Communist leanings.[3]* Baldwin described himself as an "affluent, Harvard-educated Bostonian" whose ancestors included Mayflower pilgrims.[4] His grandfather, William Henry Baldwin, was described as an "iconoclastic and non-conformist anti-Christian crusader."[5] His aunt Ruth was a member of the Socialist

---

*Eight months before his death, at the age of ninety-six in 1981, Baldwin was given the Medal of Freedom, the highest civilian honor of our country, by President Jimmy Carter.

Party. Baldwin said of her, "My almost saintly Aunt Ruth was an endless source of comfort and inspiration to me. She was wise, selfless, and sensitive. She shared my radicalism, but in her own more respectable way."[6]

Baldwin claimed that his grandfather and aunt played a major role in his upbringing and the shaping of his worldview.[7] His family was mostly Unitarians, generally social liberals who rejected the deity of Christ.[8] When asked late in life to give his definition of religion, Baldwin said, "It's something you accept because you believe that somebody had a very close contact with the Deity. Moses revealed religion with the Ten Commandments. And Jesus was supposed to have had some connection with headquarters. God gave his only son to redeem us for our sins. And it's possible that the Mormons who got their religion out of some brass plate left on a mountain by Mr. Smith—it's possible they had some tie-in too with God. Anyway they said they had."[9]

Baldwin was then asked, "Don't they all say they have?" He replied, "That's it, sure they do. That's how they get followers. Otherwise, it wouldn't be revealed, I guess."[10]

In the book *Trial and Error: The American Civil Liberties Union and Its Impact on Your Family*, the author noted, "He [Baldwin] followed his grandfather into a life-long moralistic rebellion against the church."[11] Baldwin discussed this contempt quite candidly, when he said, "We Unitarians knew we were very advanced people and that the other churches were backward."[12]

Baldwin's type of thought also fed the elitist mind-set that permeated much of the ACLU—the view that only a small group of intellectuals has the capability of understanding and dictating what everyone else should believe.[13] Former ACLU president Norman Dorsen explained, "Baldwin thought of the ACLU as a group of elitists, of highly educated people, a few thousand at most throughout the country, who would be the vanguard of a movement to protect individual rights in this society."[14]

This mind-set, that the ACLU knows what's best for the great unwashed masses, drives the ACLU's disdain for the will of the people. This mind-set also is behind its use of the judiciary, rather than the electorate, to implement its agenda. In addition, the promotion of "individual rights" ultimately results in a society in which the rights of individuals drastically outweigh the collective responsibility individuals should have to society or the concept of a higher law or duty individuals are responsible to follow. The result is a modernistic, media-driven, self-centered society that has evolved to "all about me" instead of "all about us," a nation that no longer, in too many instances, lives up to the challenge of our late President John F. Kennedy: "Ask not what your country can do for you, ask what you can do for your country."[15]

Baldwin counted among his friends Margaret Sanger,[16] a eugenicist[17] who founded Planned Parenthood, establishing the early link between the ACLU and abortionists.[18]* Although abortion can be an extremely financially lucrative practice today, in its early days it was primarily pushed by eugenicists, individuals who study and promote proposed ways of improving the human species through selective breeding. Eugenics was practiced by the Nazis in Germany in pursuit of their goal of a "master race" by suppressing the birthrate of "inferiors" such as the poor, the handicapped, and racial minorities.[19] In fact, Adolf Hitler admired Sanger.[20] And Baldwin spoke almost glowingly of her: "She was a frail, beautiful, unassuming woman. She never thought of herself as important, even on the public platform, but she always had a quiet insistence on the rightness of what she was doing."[21] Sanger's role in forming the foundations of the Baldwin–ACLU philosophy is unquestionable.

Another one of Baldwin's early friends was the radical anarchist Emma Goldman, whom he considered a mentor.[22] Goldman has been described as a consistent promoter of anarchism, radical education, free love, and birth control.[23] Her advocacy of these causes led to her nickname "Red Emma."[24] She conspired to kill Henry Clay Frick of Carnegie Steel,[25] founded the anarchist *Mother Earth* magazine,[26] and was eventually deported to Russia in 1919.[27] According to the online exhibit of Goldman's papers, her ideas led to the "founding of the American Civil Liberties Union,"[28] and her career served as an inspiration for Baldwin.[29]

---

*Many resources document the ACLU–Planned Parenthood link. Both organizations often work together to strike down any legal restriction on abortion.

Baldwin said, "Emma was on tour around the country talking to her working-class followers in obscure halls. . . . I was quite overcome by the range and depth of her speech."[30] Afterward, according to Peggy Lamson, Baldwin's biographer, Baldwin approached Goldman and later arranged an opportunity to introduce her to his friends.

Baldwin recalled,

I gave quite a party for Emma—at the Planter Hotel.
I remember very well where it was. I had the intellectual
elite there to meet her—social workers, lawyers, edi-
tors—some twenty of them. She was a bit uneasy with such
strange company, but she hit it off with charm, wit and such
subdued good sense in answering their questions that the
"Red Queen of Anarchy" [as Goldman was also called] was
nowhere to be seen or heard. . . . Then I got my lady friends
to hold an evening for her at the Wednesday Club, which
was the swankiest women's club in town. . . . Nowhere was
there a word of violence and hardly a mention of revolution
though it was implicit in everything she championed. From
that first visit I became a friend for life.[31]

Goldman's biographer Robert Drinnon wrote, "Baldwin made numerous acknowledgements of his great intellectual and moral debt to Emma Goldman. He wrote in one of his letters to her, for instance, 'you always remain one of the chief inspirations of my life, for you aroused in me a sense of what freedom really means.'"[32]

Baldwin added, "Emma Goldman opened up not only an entirely new literature to me but new people as well, some of whom called themselves anarchists, some libertarians, some freedom lovers, and some had no label—like me. They ranged far and wide in time and place, bound together by one principle—freedom from coercion. The State, since it was the supreme form of coercion, was their prime target philosophically. Most anarchists I read or knew accepted nonviolence; they were in fact and thought philosophical anarchists."[33]

Baldwin's philosophy still permeates the ACLU today, as it advocates that people can do virtually anything at anytime and no individual, no religion or its God, and no government entity has the legitimate power to stop them (except they have no objection to using the power of the state—through agreeable activist judges to crush opposition to their anti-"coercive" legal agendas). Understanding this mind-set helps to make sense of some of the ACLU's actions, such as supporting the efforts of the mayor of San Francisco when he directed the city and county clerk to defy state law and issue thousands of same-sex "marriage" licenses in the spring of 2004.*

Goldman's friendship with Baldwin served as his introduction to her mentor—Prince Peter Alexeevich Kropotkin, a Russian revolutionary. Lamson wrote, "His [Kropotkin's] espousal of anarchism was based on his belief that true cooperation between human beings would make government rule superfluous. His utopia would come into being, he believed, when neither private property nor the church nor the state exercised control over the individual spontaneity of men." Lamson added, "It was natural, therefore, that as Roger came under Emma's influence he tended to adopt the philosophy of her mentor."[34]

These statements from Baldwin, Drinnon, and Lamson are quite telling. What Baldwin also learned from Goldman was how to mask his true agenda and disguise it in a way to get the elites on his side. This would be a strategy Baldwin and the ACLU would use repeatedly to gain access to funding from the wealthy, while at the same time working to destroy many of the core values of the free enterprise system that led to the creation of their wealth. It also explains the ACLU's continued advancement of a society in which anything goes, and individual "spontaneity," advocated by Kropotkin, is paramount over individual responsibility.

In part, because of Goldman's influence, Baldwin, along with the other ACLU founders, was a committed pacifist and conscientious objector to World War I.[35] The genesis of the ACLU dates to 1914 when Baldwin replaced the female pacifist Crystal Eastman as a committee member of the American Union against Militarism (AUAM) to oppose U.S. entry into the war.[36] When war did come, the AUAM became an avenue for those who wished to avoid the draft but did not have faith-based conscientious objector reasons to do so.[37]

---

*For a current example, the goal of many ACLU allies is to abolish marriage entirely as a government-ordained institution, and to make marriage whatever any group of consenting adults (and perhaps beyond consenting adults to interspecies relationships) wants it to be. All current legal posturing and most litigation are couched in terms of "equality," "fairness," and "tolerance" for same-sex "marriages."

When Baldwin was ordered to register for the draft in 1918, he wrote the following to the Selective Service, which administered the draft,

Gentlemen: In registering today under the Selective Service Act, I desire to make the following statement as to my attitude towards conscription. I am opposed to the use of force to accomplish any ends, however good. I am, therefore, opposed to participation to this, or any other war. My opposition is not only to direct military service, but to any service whatever designed to help the war. I am furthermore opposed to the principle of conscription in time of war and peace, for any purpose whatsoever. I will decline to perform any service under compulsion, regardless of its character. I am advising you of my views so that you may record my record with your board to show from the start where I stand.[38]

When Baldwin refused to report for a physical examination, he was arrested for resisting the draft.[39] Eventually many of his colleagues were arrested too. After the trial, at which he was found guilty, Baldwin was sentenced to incarceration for one year. During his time in prison, Baldwin corresponded with the committed Communist Anna Louise Strong (to whom he was once engaged);[40] his then girlfriend and future wife, Madeleine Doty, a committed feminist with socialist leanings;[41] and Scott Nearing, a prominent Socialist of the era.[42]

When he left prison in 1919 after the war was over, Baldwin married Doty in an unconventional ceremony that vividly illustrated his (and the ACLU's future) contempt for the institution of marriage. There was no formal dress, bridal veil, and no ring. Both Doty and Baldwin shared during the ceremony what marriage meant to them. Here is what Baldwin read to Doty:

To us who passionately cherish the vision of a free human society, the present institution of marriage among us is a grim mockery of essential freedom. Here we have the most intimate, most sacred, the most creative relationship shackled in the deadening grip of private property and essentially holding the woman subservient to the man. . . .

We deny without reservation the moral right of state or church to bind by the force of law a relationship that cannot be maintained by the power of love alone. We submit to the form of law only because it seems a matter of too little importance to resist or ignore. . . .

The highest relationship between a man and a woman is that which welcomes and understands each other's loves. Without a sense of possession there can be no exclusions, no jealousies. The creative life demands many friendships, many loves shared together openly, honestly, and joyously. . . . [polyamory]*

My primary interest and joy is the great revolutionary struggle for human freedom today, so intense, so full of promise. I regard our union only as contributing to that cause, making us both serve it more passionately, the more devotedly.[43]

Later, as an elderly man, Baldwin dismissed these vows in an interview with Peggy Lamson as "pretentious and idealistic." He stated at the time he made the remarks he was "quite elevated."[44] Regardless of his later repudiation of these remarks, they reveal how Baldwin viewed marriage during the founding era of the ACLU. And that mind-set set the tone for the ACLU's policies toward and attempts to redefine marriage later.

When World War I ended, the organization that Baldwin and his colleagues had founded seemed to have lost its public sense of purpose. As someone noted, it was like a disease prevention charity frustrated that a cure was found for its cause, so the members discussed how they could perpetuate its existence. The result was its reinvention in 1920 as the American Civil Liberties Union.[45]

Baldwin was clear about his goals and purposes. In his thirtieth-anniversary Harvard University classbook he wrote, "I am for Socialism, disarmament, and ultimately the abolishing of the state itself as an instrument of violence and compulsion. I seek social ownership of property, the abolition of the propertied class, and sole control by those who produce wealth. Communism is the goal."[46]

---

*[Polyamory is a form of open marriage, in which several individuals (male and female) can be married to each other and openly and indiscriminately engage in sexual relations with their multiple partners.]

In 1920, Baldwin also created three other organizations, including the International Committee for Political Prisoners to aid deported aliens, which he would later describe as "a network of correspondents in the various countries, and we had contacts with the Communist movement and with the Socialist International in New York, plus a very strong committee." When asked by his biographer Peggy Lamson if this committee included ACLU members, Baldwin replied, "Yes, a lot of the same crowd."[47] Another organization, the Mutual Aid Society, was designed "to help radicals who were in trouble, who couldn't get jobs, or who needed bail; or defense money and lawyers." When asked about the Mutual Aid Society, he replied that the members were "leftist intellectuals, trade unionists, the radical fringe."[48] This philosophy of the Left has continued to this day to find jobs for radicals in trouble.

In its first year, the ACLU also supported the Communist[49] Industrial Workers of the World movement.[50] In the very next year, 1921, the ACLU would call itself a "militant, central bureau in the labor movement for legal aid, defense strategy, information, and propaganda." In addition, the ACLU asserted that it worked side by side with the International Workers of the World movement and the Communist Party to be a "center of resistance."[51] According to Earl Browder, general secretary of the American Communist Party, the ACLU served as a "transmission belt" for the party.[52] Baldwin acknowledged this, stating to Lamson that he was a member of a number of "united front" groups, which were in his words, "recruiting centers [for the Communist Party where] lists could be taken, sympathizers spotted and enrolled and if the treasurer happened to be a party member, funds could be siphoned off for party purposes." He added, "I joined. I don't regret being a part of the Communist tactic which increased the effectiveness of a good cause. I knew what I was doing; I was not the innocent liberal. . . . I wanted what the Communists wanted and I traveled the United Front road—not the party road—to get it."[53]

Besides Baldwin, other early ACLU board members showed clear Communist sympathies. Robert W. Dunn, a board member and founder of the New England ACLU chapter, made two trips to the Soviet Union to assist Communists there.[54]

In 1924, Baldwin, who organized and traveled with the International Committee for Political Prisoners to the Soviet Union, wrote, "Many of the members of the Committee for Political Prisoners as individuals regard the Russian Revolution as the greatest and most daring experiment yet undertaken to recreate society in terms of human values. . . . Many of them look upon Russia today as a great laboratory of social experiment of incalculable value to the development of the world."[55]

Many Americans have forgotten that during this period of Russian, and then Soviet, history, so admired by Baldwin, as many as two million people were relocated, had their property seized, or were killed as a result of Marxism and Communism.[56]

William Donohue, president of the Catholic League for Religious and Civil Rights and an expert on ACLU history,* writes in his book *The Politics of the American Civil Liberties Union:*

Baldwin, the father of American civil liberties, not only failed to question the abuses of freedom in Russia but actually defended the repressive regime. In 1928 he published his glowing account of Russia in *Liberty under the Soviets.* In it he confessed that he held a favorable bias toward the Soviet Union, as the title of his work conveys. Economic freedom, i.e., the abolition of class privilege, was more important than civil liberties. Anticipating the charge that he was engaging in duplicity, Baldwin frankly acknowledged that "repressions in western democracies are violations of professed constitutional liberties, and I condemn them as such. Repressions in Soviet Russia are weapons of struggle in a transition period to socialism."[57]

The ACLU quickly found resistance to this radical message and knew it would need to soften its rhetoric and repackage its image to the American public if it was to succeed. In 1920, a joint committee of the New York State Legislature described the ACLU as "a supporter of all subversive movements; and its propaganda is detrimental to the interests of the state. It attempts not only to protect crime, but to encourage attacks upon our institutions in every form."[58]

---

*Donohue conducted extensive interviews with Baldwin before Baldwin's death in 1981.

Baldwin had already thought through how he would "sell" the ACLU to the American public. In a 1917 letter to one of his supporters (when he was heading the AUAM and before the ACLU was officially formed), he explained this dilemma and how the ACLU could solve its image problem and convince the American people they had no cause for alarm. He wrote, "Do steer away from making it [the organization] look like a Socialist enterprise. Too many people have gotten the idea that it is nine-tenths a Socialist movement. We want also to look like patriots in everything we do. We want to get a good lot of flags, talk a good deal about the Constitution and what our forefathers wanted to make of this country, and to show that we are really the folks that stand for the spirit of our institutions." William Donohue wrote, "By wrapping themselves in the flag, then, civil libertarians could pursue their political objectives while feigning loyalty to the nation."[59]

The ACLU of today still carries out Baldwin's marching orders. Until a recent redesign, its Web site (www.aclu.org) was draped in red, white, and blue, with the Statue of Liberty prominently displayed on most pages. The rhetoric claims fervent loyalty to America, certain Jeffersonian ideas (we will discuss in a later chapter), and the Constitution, ignoring, of course, the nation's founders' writings, ideals, and purposes. But from the very start, as we will see, the ACLU *was not* about America. At least not the America our nation's founders envisioned as they stepped onto the *Speedwell* and *Mayflower* to cross the icy North Atlantic and later founded what became the Ivy League universities. These new Americans fought the most powerful nation on earth for liberty, and their leaders would gather in Philadelphia to write the Declaration of Independence, then the U.S. Constitution, and finally, during the first session of Congress, the Bill of Rights. The ACLU was about the promotion of the ideas behind Socialism and Communism and reordering America to fit its agenda.

While presenting itself to be a "patriotic" organization, its definition of "patriotism" is also very different from that of the average American's. Baldwin pushed an agenda that would systematically weaken America. Its policy was to say one thing, then do another. In the late 1920s, Baldwin laid out his agenda for the ACLU. It included opposition to the use of military or naval forces of the United States, as he said it, to "control weaker nations as a violation of their civil liberties."[60]

In addition, Baldwin developed the strategy—still used today—to occasionally defend a conservative to illustrate it was nonpartisan. And, as in the early days, the ACLU has a few associates who not only espouse a broad support of free speech, but will actually take steps, in a few times and places, to defend speech they personally disagree with. Yet the ACLU's infrequent, even rare, defense of conservatives or orthodox and traditional persons of faith is often just a tactic to advance its agenda for left-wing causes.* As Baldwin noted in 1934, "If I aid the reactionaries to get free speech now and then, if I go outside the class struggle to fight against censorship, it is only because those liberties help to create a more hospitable atmosphere for working class liberties."⁶¹ William Donohue commented, "In other words, the occasional defense of right wing extremists opens up the courts, thereby making it easier for the ACLU to defend its ideological kinfolk on the left."⁶²

Throughout the 1920s and '30s, the ACLU had prominent Communist Party members such as Harry F. Ward, Louis Budenz, Elizabeth Gurley Flynn, William Z. Foster, Robert W. Dunn, Anna Rochester, A. J. Isserman, and Mary Van Kleeck among its leadership.⁶³ William Donohue's research disclosed that the ACLU loaned money and provided bail for many Communist Party members and Communist front organizations.⁶⁴ For example, in 1930, the ACLU provided bail for five Communist textile workers, who then immediately jumped bail and fled to the Soviet Union.⁶⁵

While Baldwin held Communist/Socialist sympathies to the end of his life, eventually, like many U.S. Communist sympathizers, he became disenchanted with the Soviet version of Communism only after the Nazi-Soviet NonAggression Pact of 1939,⁶⁶ which allowed Adolf Hitler and the Nazi Party to take over much of Eastern Europe. Later in life, he said, "Anti-communism was much more of a menace to civil liberties. Communism never affected our civil liberties very much. And the Communist party in the United States was certainly never strong enough to be a menace at any time or in

---

*An example of this is the ACLU of Virginia's recent threat to sue the Fredericksburg–Stafford (Virginia) Park Authority for prohibiting baptisms by a local Baptist church in a river bordering the park. After the ACLU threat, the park authority backed down and allowed the baptisms. See "Following Threat of ACLU of Virginia Lawsuit, Officials to Agree Not to Ban Baptisms in Public Parks," http://www.aclu.org/news/NewsPrint.cfm?ID=15897&c=141.

any way.* The only menace was the people who believed in a Communist dictatorship, which is a denial of civil liberties. They did not belong with us in a leadership position."[67]

Baldwin rid the ACLU board of overt Communists because of his anger about the Nazi-Soviet pact, establishing a policy that read, in part: "The Board of Directors and the National Committee of the American Civil Liberties Union . . . hold it inappropriate for any person to serve on the governing committees of the Union or its staff, who is a member of any political organization which supports totalitarian dictatorship in any country, or who by his public declarations indicates his support of such a principle."[68]

Baldwin gave this reason for purging those he perceived to be Soviet-style Communists from ACLU leadership: "The ACLU is a private organization. . . . And a private organization is like a church. You don't take nonbelievers into the church. We are a church; we have a creed and only true believers should lead us."[69] He claimed that privilege for the ACLU, but decades later in legal arguments, the ACLU would attempt to deny other private organizations, such as the Boy Scouts, the same privilege of exclusivity in defining a standard of conduct for their leaders. But as we will see in succeeding chapters, the ACLU has no problem with using, or others using, the courts to force other private organizations (and religious ministries such as Catholic Charities)[70] to accept individuals as leaders or adopt policies that violate the organizations' core beliefs.

The Scopes Monkey Trial

One of the first targets of the ACLU in its effort to undermine the America our founders intended was organized religion—at least religious entities that believed in the inerrancy and authority of the Bible. This was consistent with Baldwin's intellectual disdain for the church. In 1925, the ACLU advertised for a teacher who would be willing to challenge the state of Tennessee's Butler Act, which prohibited teaching the theory of evolution in state public schools and

---

*Much of the American Communist Party was directly funded from Moscow. See H. Klehr, J. E. Haynes. K. M. Anderson, eds., *The Soviet World of American Communism* (New Haven, CT, and London: Yale University Press, 1998).

universities.[71] This would be the first prominent example, of many, of how the ACLU would use events to advance its agenda.

Peggy Lamson wrote, "By all odds the most important 'manipulated test case' of the 1920s was, of course, the Scopes Monkey Trial, which the ACLU literally originated by creating a confrontation between an individual and the state in which he lived. . . . The fact is that it was the Scopes case that largely won for the American Civil Liberties Union the national renown it has enjoyed ever since."[72]

The Butler Act had first come to the attention of ACLU member Lucille Milner, who saw a news item about it in the newspaper. She took the article to Baldwin, who in turn, brought it up at the ACLU board meeting. The board then authorized a special fund to finance the defense case of any teacher who would defy the law, with the goal to get the case before the U.S. Supreme Court.[73] The ACLU found John Thomas Scopes, a high school football coach and substitute science teacher in Rhea County, Tennessee. Recent scholarship shows that the regular science teacher at the school would have nothing to do with the scheme.[74]

Scopes was brought to the attention of the ACLU by a man named G. W. Rappelyea, who had heard about the scheme. He sent a telegram: "J. T. Scopes, teacher of science, Rhea Central High School, Dayton, will be arrested, charged with teaching evolution . . . for test case to be defended by you. Wire me collect if you wish to cooperate and arrest will follow."[75]

Scopes defied the law and was subsequently arrested.[76] Baldwin immediately saw the trial as an opportunity to pursue his personal anti-religion agenda, writing, "It was immediately apparent what kind of a trial it would be: the Good Book against Darwin, bigotry against science, or, as popularly put, God against the monkeys."[77]

The Scopes Monkey Trial has been written about endlessly and has been made into a play and the movie *Inherit the Wind*.* Even though the foreword of the play denies it is the Scopes case in the story, virtually every adult American who has read, seen, or heard

---

*Alan served as legal counsel at a hearing conducted in the historic Rhea County courtroom where the Scopes trial took place. His opposing counsel was a descendent of one of the participants in the Scopes trial, who spent a few hours proudly telling Alan the oral history of his family's role in the events surrounding the trial.

the play knows of its parallel to Scopes. Our purpose here is not to discuss the creation–evolution debate or other events in the trial.* The importance of the Scopes trial was that it was an early use of the ACLU's tactics of intimidation, misinformation, and fear to advance its agenda.

Throughout the trial, Clarence Darrow, one of the attorneys defending Scopes, attempted to undermine the biblical account of creation and mocked the religious beliefs of William Jennings Bryan, former three-time Democratic candidate for U.S. president, who had joined the prosecution team.† He did this at the expense of focusing on the facts and the Tennessee statute at issue. In his relentless questioning of Bryan, and in his arguments, it was evident that the agenda of Darrow and the ACLU was not primarily to defend Scopes but to publicly discredit traditional religious beliefs. On that account, they succeeded.‡ Additionally, it was one of the first attempts by the ACLU to prove the superiority of its intellectual elitism over the ignorant faith of the masses.

The best example of this was Darrow's argument that the law was unconstitutional. Nowhere in this argument did he mention the law specifically or examine its text under constitutional requirements. Instead, he engaged in what would later become typical ACLU rhetoric to demonize its opponents, play upon human emotion, and evade the real issue at hand. Darrow asserted:

> If today you can take a thing like evolution and make it
> a crime to teach it in the public school, tomorrow you can
> make it a crime to teach it in the private schools, and the next
> year you can make it a crime to teach it to the hustings or in
> the church. At the next session you may ban books and the
> newspapers. Soon you may set Catholic against Protestant
> and Protestant against Protestant, and try to foist your own

---

*The Tennessee Supreme Court would eventually dismiss the charges against Scopes, who was initially found guilty and fined $100. The Tennessee Supreme Court also upheld the constitutionality of the statute.

†According to Lamson, there was a great deal of debate within ACLU circles whether or not to challenge the Butler Act on constitutional grounds or to turn the trial into an opportunity to discredit religious belief. When Bryan became part of the prosecution team, Clarence Darrow stepped forward for the opportunity to use the trial as a forum to debate Bryan's religious beliefs. With this development, the ACLU's strategy became clear.

‡The most comprehensive Web site to read the trial transcripts is http://www.law.umkc.edu/faculty/projects/ftrials/scopes/scopes.htm.

religion upon the minds of men. If you can do one you can
do the other. Ignorance and fanaticism is ever busy and needs
feeding. Always it is feeding and gloating for more. Today it is
the public school teachers, tomorrow the private. The next day
the preachers and the lectures, the magazines, the books, the
newspapers. After awhile, your honor, it is the setting of man
against man and creed against creed until with flying banners
and beating drums we are marching backward to the glorious
ages of the sixteenth century when bigots lighted fagots [pieces
of wood] to burn the men who dared to bring any intelligence
and enlightenment and culture to the human mind.[78]

While Darrow was not the first choice of the ACLU board
(which was split over who should serve as lead counsel), and Baldwin was ambivalent about his involvement,[79] Darrow's rhetoric was
symbolic of the type of speech the ACLU has used for eighty years
to accomplish its agenda. This rhetoric, disguised as legal arguments,
deemphasizes or ignores the real constitutional or legal issues and
facts of the case. Instead, the ACLU appeals to people's emotions
and worst fears, while attacking religious believers and others who
oppose its agenda.

The ACLU's Unlucky Thirteen

For the first several decades of its existence, the ACLU had some
victories at various courts, including the U.S. Supreme Court level, but
none that seemed to have a particularly significant impact on American
society at large. However, while their early legal victories were sparse,
they were actively laying the groundwork through their growing connections in academia, the media, and the judiciary to change America's
understanding of the U.S. Constitution and religious freedom. The
ACLU engaged in what some call "building precept on precept" (setting
legal precedent) to eventually lead to a tidal wave of decisions in its favor.
(ADF is utilizing a somewhat similar strategy to reclaim our nation's
legal system from the years of damage inflicted by the ACLU.)

Starting in the late 1940s, the foundation the ACLU had been
building for the previous two decades began to pay dividends. In
what was seemingly the blink of an eye, the ACLU established a tremendous momentum of legal decisions that would be used to limit

religious freedom, to remove legal protections for the unborn and infirm, and to undermine marriage and the family.

To understand how the ACLU built legal precedent to advance its agenda, let's visit thirteen U.S. Supreme Court decisions the ACLU used to help reshape America. While the ACLU or its direct allies were not parties in every one of these cases, they served as building blocks for the ACLU's agenda.

Many of these and similar victories came about because most of those who opposed the ACLU's agenda essentially sat on the sidelines. Sometimes when the opposition did appear, it was often too underfunded or ill equipped to put up much of a struggle. These Supreme Court decisions, along with numerous others at all court levels (combined with the relentless use of legal demand letters), have played a pivotal role in moving our society to where it is today.[80]

- *Everson vs. Board of Education* (1947): This case involved a New Jersey law that allowed reimbursements of money to parents who sent their children to school on buses operated by the public transportation system. Children who attended Catholic schools also qualified for the transportation subsidy. While the Court held the specific law was not enacted in violation of the Constitution, Justice Hugo Black, a former Ku Klux Klan member who wrote the opinion for the court, stated, "First Amendment has erected a wall between church and state. That wall must be kept high and impregnable."[81]* Even though that wording is found *nowhere* in the U.S. Constitution or the First Amendment, this phrase, which was proposed to the court in the ACLU's friend-of-the-court brief filed in the case, would be used by the ACLU in many cases to whittle away our religious freedoms.†

- *Engel vs. Vitale* (1962): In this case the Supreme Court built on the church and state language from the *Everson* decision. The court held that public school teachers could not open

---

*Amazingly, Hugo Black tried to re-create history by suggesting that Thomas Jefferson played a leading role in drafting and adopting the First Amendment, even though Jefferson was serving as minister to France at the time. (See *Everson vs. Board of Education of Ewing Township*, 330 U.S. 1 (1947) at 15.

†We will discuss the ACLU's misuse of the term "separation of church and state" in depth in chapter 6.

class with a prayer, even when the prayer was nonsectarian and even if the schools did not compel a student to join in prayer over his, or his parents', objection.[82] The whittling away of our religious freedom continued.

- *School District of Abington Township vs. Schempp* (1963): Just one year later, the *Engel* precedent was used to successfully support the Supreme Court's holding that the state could not require the recitation of the Lord's Prayer and the reading of Scripture in public school classrooms, even when students had the right to opt out from these activities.[83] The whittling continued.

- *Epperson vs. Arkansas* (1968): The Court once again relied on previous ACLU-supported legal precedents—this time applying them to prohibiting the teaching of evolution in public schools. The Court held that the prohibitions against teaching evolution were motivated by religious beliefs and therefore violated the First Amendment.[84] More whittling occurred.

- *Wallace vs. Jaffree* (1985): Not content with silencing public prayer, the ACLU even went after moments of silence for voluntary prayer or meditation at the beginning of public school classes. The Supreme Court again agreed with the ACLU and ruled that the statute was unconstitutional because it was intended "to convey a message of state approval of prayer activities in public schools."[85] The whittling away of the right to publicly express one's faith—even in silence—continued.

- *Lee vs. Weisman* (1992): Continuing its assault on the public expression of faith, the ACLU was successful in arguing that nonsectarian prayers delivered by ministers and rabbis at public high school graduation ceremonies violated the Establishment Clause of the First Amendment.[86]

The ACLU has also used Supreme Court precedent to systematically remove legal protections for the unborn:

- *Griswold vs. Connecticut* (1965): The ACLU backed this case, which challenged a Connecticut statute that prohibited the use of contraceptives and forbade assisting or counseling individuals to use contraceptives. The Court used this case to craft a new constitutional "right of privacy" for married couples. The Court wrote, "The 'right' of privacy is based

on the Bill of Rights [which] have penumbras, formed by
emanations from those guarantees that help give them life
and substance."[87]

- *Eisenstadt vs. Baird* (1972): The Court once again relied on
  the right of privacy in holding that states could no longer
  prohibit the distribution of contraceptives to even unmar-
  ried persons. *Griswold* and *Eisenstadt* were just small trem-
  ors compared to the nation-altering legal, cultural, and moral
  earthquake that would follow the next year.[88]

- *Roe vs. Wade* (1973): *Griswold* and *Eisenstadt* set the stage
  for the ACLU and its allies' big prize, *Roe vs. Wade*, which
  essentially "legalized" abortion up to the moment of birth.[89]
  The judicially crafted right of privacy was now extended to
  the killing of unborn children. The result of this decision is
  that more than 46 million Americans—more than the entire
  population of California or the nation of Canada—have been
  legally killed since 1973.[90*]

- *Planned Parenthood vs. Casey* (1992): Nineteen years later,
  pro-life groups thought they finally had the case (and the
  ideological makeup of the Court) to overturn *Roe vs. Wade*.
  In this case, Robert Casey, the pro-life Democratic governor of Pennsylvania, had been successful in getting the state
  legislature to place some reasonable restrictions on abortion.
  In spite of the courageous efforts of Casey and others, the
  ACLU, Planned Parenthood, and other groups were successful when the Court reaffirmed *Roe vs. Wade* and established a new test to evaluate abortion regulations. This new
  test prohibits regulations that place an "undue burden" on
  a woman's "right" to get an abortion. Still, the Court did
  uphold some of Pennsylvania's restrictions on abortion.[91]

  The ACLU and its allies were also successful in getting
  the court to inject the "mystery" clause—language that reads:
  "Abortion is a 14th amendment right, not just an applied
  right of privacy, but a 14th amendment protected liberty—at

---

*The trimester-based analysis of *Roe*, on its face, left some room for states to regulate abortion
but included the "health of the mother" provision which essentially "legalized" abortion up to the
moment of live birth.

the heart of liberty is the right to define one's own concept of existence, of meaning, of the universe, and of the mystery of life."[92] This phrase would also be used in the Court's decision in *Lawrence vs. Texas*, which struck down state laws regulating the practice of same-sex sodomy. This statement—to define "one's own concept of existence"—now elevated to national policy, comes directly from the philosophies of Emma Goldman and Roger Baldwin.[93]

The ACLU has also used Supreme Court precedent to support the distribution of pornography and obscene material, desensitize society, and undermine marriage and the family:

- *Jacobellis vs. Ohio* (1964): The ACLU participated in this case in which the Supreme Court overturned the conviction of a theater manager for violating a state obscenity law by showing a film. According to the Supreme Court, the film was not obscene, so it was protected by the First Amendment.[94]* Fortunately, the ACLU has not gotten nearly all it has asked the Supreme Court to do. As early as 1982, in *New York vs. Ferber*, the ACLU asked the justices to decree that child pornography was protected by the Constitution. The Court rejected the argument.[95]†

- *Romer vs. Evans* (1996): Working with advocates of homosexual behavior, the ACLU has relentlessly pushed the homosexual legal agenda through our nation's judicial system, bypassing the often very express will of the people to the contrary. The result has been the continued erosion of religious freedom, as any speech or action that mentions the spiritual, emotional, and physical destructiveness of homosexual behavior is increasingly restricted by courts or public officials cowered by what they fear courts would otherwise order them to do. When the voters of Colorado overwhelmingly passed an amendment to the Colorado Constitution in

---

*The Court applied a test that asked "whether to the average person, applying contemporary community standards, the dominant theme of the material taken as a whole appeals to the prurient interest." *Jacobellis vs. Ohio*, 378 U.S. 184 (1964).

†In 2004, in *Ashcroft vs. ACLU*, the Supreme Court prevented the implementation of the Child Online Protection Act (COPA), which was designed to protect minors from obscene material on the Internet. The Court remanded (returned) the case to the lower court for further argument.

1993 to ensure that those who practice homosexual behavior would not receive special legal rights and privileges beyond that of ordinary citizens, the ACLU and homosexual activists sued the governor, state attorney general, and the state. The U.S. Supreme Court ruled that the Colorado amendment had violated the Equal Protection Clause of the Fourteenth Amendment. Justice Anthony Kennedy also took a jab at Colorado voters, stating that the amendment displayed "animus" (prejudiced ill will) for homosexuals when they adopted the initiative.[96] This decision further encouraged the ACLU and its allies who advocate for homosexual behavior to further bypass the will of the people time and again and to force their radical agenda through our nation's judicial system.

- *Lawrence vs. Texas* (2003): *Romer vs. Evans* and *Planned Parenthood vs. Casey* were part of the groundwork for this decision, which was based in part on international law (and more creative twisting of the Constitution and the Fourteenth Amendment), extending the right of privacy to provide constitutional protections to homosexual sodomy.[97] This decision now serves as a major linchpin for the ACLU and its homosexual activist allies to press for legal recognition of same-sex "marriages" and other demands for special privileges and public funding for their cause and for pornographers to increase their profits.[98]

The *Lawrence* decision had several alarming elements. First, it opened the door for radical homosexual activists—despite a contrary sentence in the decision—(and the ACLU) to further use the judicial system to try to force same-sex and polygamous "marriage" on America. Second, the Court's reference to international law in its decision (see chap. 8 for further discussion about the ACLU's advocacy of international law) may well undermine American sovereignty and many principles of our forefathers.

But there is good news on *Lawrence*. So far, ADF and its allies have been successful in holding back the demands of homosexual activists and the ACLU for judicially decreed marriage in many states, except Massachusetts. Courts have not yet shown a propensity to extend the *Lawrence* decision to create a new constitutional right for such unions. In fact, the Indiana Court of Appeals and Arizona Supreme Court have both rejected *Lawrence* as a framework to grant marital rights to same-sex couples.

Through the ACLU's relentless legal campaign—in the courts and by activist judges—to conform America to its agenda, our nation has gone from one that affirmed the role of God and Judeo-Christian values to one now often hostile to God and those values.

The ACLU's Ultimate Agenda

The impact of all these ACLU victories is an America vastly different from what the Founding Fathers intended. To contrast the ACLU's vision for America with that of the Founding Fathers, consider the following words from John Quincy Adams, the sixth president of the United States:*

> When the children of Israel, after forty years of wanderings in the wilderness, were about to enter the promised land, their leader, Moses . . . commanded that when the Lord their God should have brought them into the land, they should put the curse upon Mount Ebal, and the blessing upon Mount Gerizim. This injunction was faithfully fulfilled by his successor Joshua. Immediately after they had taken possession of the land, Joshua built an altar to the Lord, of whole stones, upon Mount Ebal. And there he wrote upon the stones a copy of the law of Moses, which he had written in the presence of the children of Israel. . . .
>
> Fellow citizens, the ark of your covenant is the Declaration of Independence.
>
> Your Mount Ebal, is the confederacy of separate state sovereignties, and your Mount Gerizim is the Constitution of the United States. . . .
>
> Lay up these principles, then, in your hearts, and in your souls . . . teach them to your children . . . cling to them as to the issues of life—adhere to them as to the cords of your

---

*John Quincy Adams, who served as a foreign minister and secretary of state, and was nominated for but declined appointment to the U.S. Supreme Court, was son of the second president John Adams, one of principal framers of the Declaration of Independence. Between the two men, they were involved in the formation and government of America for seventy-three years (1775–1848).

eternal salvation. So may your children's children . . .
[celebrate the] Constitution . . . in full enjoyment of all
blessings recognized by you in the commemoration of this
day, and of all the blessings promised to the children of
Israel upon Mount Gerizim, as the reward of obedience to
the law of God.[99]

Adams knew America's future depended on how the succeeding generations adhered to what the founders intended, although the
ACLU would probably argue that those intentions are irrelevant.
Yet, in a short amount of time, the ACLU and its allies have twisted
the Constitution and its First Amendment—meant to be a shield for
people of faith—into a sword to be used against them. Courts that
once dared not violate the laws of God—and enforced rules against
blasphemy—now openly mock His name. Thanks to the ACLU's
relentless attacks on religious expression, many courts, instead of allowing religion to flourish, help suppress and punish people and organizations of faith.

Through the ACLU's continued attacks on the sanctity of human
life, *all* human life has been cheapened, and the legal door has been
opened to many aspects of social Darwinism, assisted suicide, cloning,
and a general disregard for the welfare of our fellow human beings.

The ACLU's advocacy has led to the legal undermining of
marriage and the family, including the weakening of parental authority. Marriage, an institution that civilizes society and promotes mutual
respect between the sexes and the nurturing environment children
need to develop and thrive, is now used to promote a social agenda
that elevates self-gratification above mutual commitment.

For instance, the ACLU has constantly sought to redefine the
First Amendment's protections of press and speech* to include the
most foul and perverse hard core and child pornography imaginable.
They have publicly cloaked their efforts to undermine any effort by
the government to enforce obscenity laws, or by parents to protect
their children from obscene material, as combating "censorship."

---

*The First Amendment to the U.S. Constitution reads: *"Congress shall make no law respect-
ing an establishment of religion, or prohibiting the free exercise thereof; or abridging the freedom
of speech, or of the press, or the right of the people to peaceably assemble, and to petition the
Government for a redress of grievances."*

However, the First Amendment was *never* intended to protect obscene material. Obscenity is outside the scope of the First Amendment and is not considered to be "speech" as defined in the Constitution.[100] In fact, the First Amendment calls for self-restraint and for individuals to be held responsible for their actions.

Numerous states have echoed this theme and have put equivalent speech protections in their constitutions. For example, the Constitution of the state of Washington reads: "Every person may freely speak, write, and publish on all subjects, being responsible for the abuse of that right."[101] Other states, such as Arizona, have similar language.[102] From the beginning of our republic, and in every state, long before cameras, there were laws relating to and proscribing what is now called obscenity, including what is now commonly called hardcore and child pornography.[103] Such material was no more considered "protected speech" by the authors of the U.S. Constitution than was defamation (libel and slander, excluding some public officials), criminal conspiracy, fighting words, incitement, and certain acts of espionage.

This is an important point to understand when the ACLU accuses concerned people of faith of "censorship" when they engage in educational campaigns, urge boycotts to oppose the sale of pornography in their community or insist on law enforcement efforts against pornographers who distribute obscene materials, or who violate zoning and other regulations relating to the time, place, and manner of distribution of even non-obscene material. Such law enforcement and private speech efforts to protect the community and children are not censorship, which, properly defined, is an act of a government agent selecting what materials or portions of materials can be published in advance.

These attempts to protect children (and communities) from obscene materials are radically different from the ACLU's efforts to eliminate from the public square any public expression of religious faith. Religious communications—including prayer and proselytization—are considered to be the essence of liberty by the drafters of the First Amendment, *not* hard-core and/or child pornography. They considered the right to publicly express or exercise one's faith to be so important that they listed it first on the list of the limits imposed on the federal government in the amendment.

This also illustrates the ridiculousness of the ACLU's claim that a *voluntary* public prayer made by a high school valedictorian, selected on absolutely neutral grounds, or the posting of a Ten Commandments memorial by the American Legion with private funds on a public courthouse lawn, violates the Establishment Clause of the First Amendment.* By no stretch of the imagination are either of these actions, or numerous others, either done by Congress nor are such actions "laws" to establish religion. Because of the ACLU's misinterpretation of the Establishment Clause, no other section in the U.S. Constitution has faced more abuse in terms of its clear and original text being completely reconfigured and misapplied than these ten words.

Dennis Prager, a well-known columnist and radio host, perhaps best expressed the ACLU's worldview (and that of its allies) and its antagonism toward American values, when he wrote the following:

> To understand the worldwide ideological battle—especially the one between America and Western Europe and within America itself—one must understand the vast differences between leftist and rightest worldviews and between secular and religious (specifically Judeo-Christian) values.
>
> One of the most important of these differences is their attitudes toward law. Generally speaking, the Left and the secularists venerate, if not worship, law. They put their faith in law—both national and international. For most on the Left, "Is it legal?" is usually the question that determines whether an action is right or wrong. . . .
>
> To the Left, legality matters most, while to the Right, legality matters far less than morality. To the Right and to the religious, the law, when it is doing its job, is only a vehicle to morality, never a moral end in itself. Even the Left has to acknowledge this. When Rosa Parks refused to give up her seat to a white man on a Montgomery, Alabama, bus in 1955, she violated the law. Therefore, anyone who thinks she did the right thing is acknowledging that law must be subservient to morality. . . .

---

*The Establishment Clause states: *"Congress shall make no law respecting an establishment of religion."*

And why is the Left so enamored of law?

First, the Left, which is largely secular, regards morality not as absolute, but as relative. This inevitability leads to moral confusion, and no one likes to be morally confused. So instead of moral absolutes, the Left holds legal absolutes. "Legal" for the Left is what "moral" is for the Right. The religious have a belief in a God-based moral law, and the Left believes in man-made law as the moral law.

Second, whereas they cannot change God's laws, those on the Left can and do make many of society's laws. In fact, the Left is intoxicated with law-making. It gives them the power to mold society just as Judeo-Christian values did in the past. Unless one understands that leftist ideals function as a religion, one cannot understand the Left.

Laws are the Left's vehicles to earthly salvation. Virtually all human problems have a legal solution. Some men harass women? Pass laws banning virtually every flirtatious action a man might engage in vis-a-vis a woman. Flood legislatures with laws preventing the creation of a "hostile work environment." Whereas the religious world has always worked to teach men how to act toward women, the secular world, lacking these religious values, passes laws to control men.

In fact, since it lacks the self-control apparatus that is a major part of religion, the Left passes more and more laws to control people. That is why there is a direct link between the decline in Judeo-Christian religion and the increase in governmental laws controlling human behavior.

Of course, the more laws that are passed, the less liberty society enjoys. But to the Left, which elevates any number of values above liberty—e.g. compassion, equality, fairness—this presents little problem.

All this helps to explain the Left's preoccupation with controlling courts; passing laws; producing, enriching and empowering lawyers; filing lawsuits; and naming judges. Laws and the makers of laws will produce heaven on earth.

And that's one reason why the Left hates the America ... [that] says morality is higher than man-made law.[104]

The ACLU's vision for America is radically different from that of most Americans—people who still believe man is subject to a higher law that comes from God and not to man's latest or most "enlightened" fad. The ACLU's vision is of an America that looks like much of modern-day Europe—secularized, with little or no public vestige left of religious faith and the traditional family. The ACLU's legal demands, as we will see in subsequent chapters, have already and will further affect the futures of our children and grandchildren. Gone unchecked, America will slide from "a shining city upon a hill" to a nation that sees all values as relative, with no moral absolutes. This type of thinking leads to totalitarian societies that the ACLU and its leftist allies say they oppose but Roger Baldwin admired during their "struggle in a transition period to Socialism." When society exalts individual rights over collective responsibility, then speech or actions seen as interfering with the right of the individual must be silenced. When law, instead of God, is seen as the salvation of mankind, more and more restrictive laws are passed to ultimately limit freedom, rather than expand it.

Robert Bork has written:

Law is the key element of every Western nation's culture, particularly as we turn more to litigation than to moral consensus as the means of determining social control.

Activist judges are those who decide cases in ways that have no plausible connection to the law they purport to be applying, or who stretch or even contradict the meaning of that law. They arrive at results by announcing principles that were never contemplated by those who wrote and voted for the law.

Though judges rule in the name of a constitution and their authority is accepted as legitimate only because they are regarded as keepers of a sacred text in a civic religion, there is no guarantee that the results actually come from that constitution.[105]

That is exactly what is happening. Through the ACLU's use of the law to shape mankind in its image, it is constantly restricting liberty, not enlarging it. They are censoring speech rather than protecting it. Public school officials are afraid to say, "Merry Christmas," to acknowledge our nation's faith history or celebrate Christmas, for fear of an ACLU lawsuit. Many people are afraid to talk openly and publicly about their sincerely held religious beliefs in their workplaces because of fear of legal action against them. The list goes on and on.

Left unchallenged, the ACLU will create an America that is far from the country to which our ancestors fled so they might breathe the sweet air of freedom. Instead, it will become more and more like the countries they fled from.

But there is hope. In the past decade, with God's grace, ADF and its allies have been successful in slowing the advance or even turning the tide on numerous issues against the ACLU. On some legal fronts, there is clearly more religious liberty than there was a decade ago. We can still win, but it will take hard work, endurance, and perseverance if we are to do so. The ACLU has been slowly eroding American freedoms for more than eighty years. But those freedoms can be reclaimed, protected, and preserved for future generations if Americans stand together and say, "Enough!" to the ACLU's agenda. That is ADF's mission.

CHAPTER 2

The ACLU vs. Marriage

Today's results prove that certain fundamental issues should not be left up to a majority vote.[1]
—Former ACLU Executive Director Ira Glasser after Alaskan voters overwhelmingly passed a constitutional amendment that protected marriage between one man and one woman

No large organization can long continue without a strong element of authority and respect for authority.[2]
—Sir Winston Churchill, 1938

On February 12, 2004, Gavin Newsom, the new mayor of San Francisco, and the city and county clerk disregarded the rule of law and started issuing marriage licenses to same-sex couples. Newsom took this action despite the fact that California voters, in 2000, had overwhelmingly voted to adopt Proposition 22, which declared that California would recognize only marriages between one man and one woman.

When Mayor Newsom made his decision to openly defy state law, the ACLU was standing right beside him. Tamara Lange, an ACLU staff attorney, said, "We are eager to take on this historic opportunity to end marriage discrimination in California. Marriage is a commitment. It is about sharing, love, trust, and compromise. Two adults who make this personal choice to form a lifelong commitment should not be denied the right to marry just because they are gay and lesbian."[3]

Dorothy Ehrlich, executive director of the Northern California ACLU, added, "Just as we told the state in 1974 when they passed a statute [California Family Code 300, previous to Proposition 22] limiting marriage to a man and a woman, that kind of discrimination against same-sex couples violates the California constitution's promise of equality. . . ."[4]

In 1986, the ACLU became, as it stated, "the first mainstream organization to seek the legal recognition of same-sex marriage."[5] When advocates of homosexual behavior finally found a state whose highest court (Massachusetts) would creatively construct a constitutional right to marriage in 2003, the ACLU pounced on the decision to try to expand its impact to legally force same-sex "marriage" on the rest of the American public—this despite the fact that when voters were allowed to cast a vote on this issue, same-sex "marriage" was soundly defeated in every instance.*

But that didn't matter to the ACLU. Former ACLU Executive Director Ira Glasser had already shown his organization's contempt for the will of the people and the democratic process, when he said in an ACLU press release after Alaskan voters enacted a constitutional amendment—by a nearly 2–1 vote—preserving the traditional definition of marriage, "Today's results prove that certain fundamental issues should not be left up to a majority vote."[6]

When the mayor of San Francisco took his unlawful action, the ACLU called for other public authorities across America to ignore the law and start issuing marriage licenses to same-sex couples. When the mayor of New Paltz, New York, followed Mayor Newsom's lead, the executive director of the New York chapter of the ACLU said, "Bravo, bravo for the mayor. Equal rights for gay couples are long overdue. They are entitled to equal treatment under the law, including the right to marry and the family protections enjoyed by heterosexual couples."[7]

What the ACLU and these public officials did once again was to advocate social anarchy and a total breakdown of the rule of law in society. By encouraging public officials to blatantly ignore fully constitutional state and federal laws—regardless of what they are—the ACLU created a climate for *all* valid laws to be openly defied. For

---

*In 2004, voters in thirteen states passed constitutional amendments affirming marriage "between one man and woman" by overwhelming margins in thirteen of thirteen states the issue was on the ballot. At press time for this book, eighteen state constitutions have been amended to prevent judicial activism from redefining marriage in their boundaries.

instance, what would happen if a public official decided he did not like gun control laws restricting automatic weapons and issued machine gun permits to citizens? What if a city official decided that forcing vehicles to stop at red lights was an infringement on an individual's choice to stop or not stop for traffic? These scenarios might sound outrageous, but if one takes the ACLU's position to its logical conclusion, they are indeed plausible.

That is why these words of Winston Churchill are so ominous: "No large organization can long continue without a strong element of authority and respect for authority."[8] When Newsom and the ACLU defied state law in California, the ability to maintain order in society was at stake.

ADF immediately went to court to stop Newsom, the ACLU, and its allies. On August 12, 2004, the California State Supreme Court ruled 7–0 that the mayor exceeded his authority in having the clerk issue the licenses and 5–2 that the licenses were invalid. ADF senior counsel Jordan Lorence successfully defended the rule of law before the California Supreme Court, with much assistance from the ADF legal team.

This was a big victory, but there are many more battles to come. The ACLU filed a lawsuit in California challenging Proposition 22 and the definition of marriage on behalf of six homosexual couples, arguing that "denying same-sex couples the right to marry violates the California Constitution."[9]

Five of the couples had their appointments to be married canceled after the State Supreme Court issued its directive that the city and county of San Francisco immediately cease issuing the marriage licenses.[10]

In Oregon, the ACLU issued a press release announcing a lawsuit against state officials to require the state to allow same-sex couples to marry. Officials in Multnomah County proceeded to do just that. Also, in Oregon, an ACLU board president and chapter cochairs testified before county commissioners before a vote on whether to begin issuing marriage licenses to same-sex couples. In its press release, the ACLU compared the "plight" of homosexual activists to that of Japanese-American war veterans who had been unjustly prohibited from owning land![11] Working with radical advocates of homosexual behavior, the ACLU started to file, promote, or support lawsuits around the country to impose same-sex "marriage" by judicial fiat, regardless of the will of the people on the issue.[12]

The good news is that the ACLU's efforts failed in Oregon, as ADF staff and allied attorneys successfully argued before the Oregon Supreme Court that the nearly three thousand "marriage" licenses issued by the county in the days after the ACLU's actions and that of the mayor of San Francisco should be declared invalid. On April 14, 2005, in a unanimous decision, the Oregon Supreme Court agreed with ADF and against the ACLU.[13]

The homosexual newspaper the *Washington Blade* wrote, "The American Civil Liberties Union recently moved to center stage in the national gay marriage debate after filing its fourth lawsuit challenging state laws prohibiting gay unions. . . . With these four recent actions by the ACLU's Lesbian and Gay Rights Project, the legal group moves to the forefront of the same-sex marriage legal battle."[14]

The ACLU has also played an active role in either seeking to block public votes on same-sex "marriage" or to overturn the will of the people through filing lawsuits to stop the implementation of state constitutional amendments and other laws that define marriage as between one man and one woman. The ACLU filed lawsuits (unsuccessfully) in Alaska,[15] Hawaii,[16] Louisiana,[17] Arkansas,[18] Georgia,[19] and Oklahoma[20] to circumvent the will of the people by trying to put up legal roadblocks to voter initiatives on same-sex "marriage." In Mississippi, the ACLU also supported homosexual groups in their efforts to defeat a marriage amendment to that state's constitution.[21]

In January 2005, after nearly 80 percent of voters had passed a constitutional amendment to affirm marriage, ACLU allies tried to use the courts to nullify the vote. The Louisiana Supreme Court unanimously denied all challenges to the vote in that state. ADF counsel Mike Johnson defended the will of the state legislature and the people to affirm marriage between one man and one woman from the legal attack by the ACLU and its allies.[22]

The ACLU has also gone on the offensive before the state's voters have had a chance to express their will with regard to same-sex "marriage." In Maryland, the ACLU has filed a lawsuit challenging the state's "law defining marriage as solely between a man and a woman."[23]

Just as this book was going to press, the ACLU obtained a victory (for now) in its ongoing battle to undermine democracy and overturn the will of the people. The ACLU and its allies had filed a lawsuit challenging Nebraska's constitutional amendment—passed by more than *70 percent* of the voters—that legally protected traditional marriage.[24] In a decision that will be appealed, U.S. District Court Judge Joseph Bataillon (appointed by President Bill Clinton in 1996) struck down the amendment—basing his decision on *Lawrence vs. Texas*. This one lone judge overruled the overwhelming majority of voters in the Cornhusker State in their effort to protect marriage, all because of the ACLU.

In his decision, the judge wrote that the amendment "amounts to punishment" and that "the institution of marriage is difficult to define and/or describe."[25]

Amy Miller of the ACLU Nebraska proudly proclaimed: "The judge was clear that states can't enact amendments that bar gay people from the democratic process."[26] The ACLU's action was clear that it believes that the democratic process is only a one-way street—in their direction.

But it is not just contempt for America's democratic process that those in the ACLU have shown when it comes to this issue. They have also openly mocked the sincerely held religious beliefs of those who oppose same-sex "marriage." After the U.S. Supreme Court rendered its decision in *Lawrence vs. Texas*, the ACLU issued the following statement, "Since our [homosexual] relationships are protected by the Constitution, the state will need to have an explanation for why it treats them differently. And states should not be allowed to get by with words alone. . . . In most cases this will be all we need. For virtually all of the 'explanations' for preferring heterosexuals over gay people are based on beliefs that have nothing to do with reality."[27]

That last sentence illustrates the ACLU's elitist attitude toward the religious beliefs of many Americans because these beliefs "have nothing to do with reality." However, if a person's religious beliefs allow for same-sex "marriage," then suddenly the ACLU feels that such beliefs are now relevant for discussion.

In Chicago, the ACLU held an event called "Blocking the Way to the Altar." One of the panelists was Rev. Stacey Edwards of the Trinity United Church of Christ's Same Gender Loving Ministry. Edwards implied that religious objections to same-sex "marriage" were caused by those who have "interpreted the Scriptures out of context" and by "some religious leaders having their pockets filled by the [current Bush] administration."[28]

In the same paper that mocked the sincerely held religious beliefs of those who support traditional marriage, the ACLU openly talked about how it would use the *Lawrence* decision as a battering ram to destroy marriage as we know it and God ordained it. The ACLU stated, "Will *Lawrence* help bring down 'don't ask, don't tell' [in the military] and bans on same-sex marriage? In time, yes, although how much time will depend. *Lawrence* largely erodes the underpinning of both. . . . Defenders of heterosexual marriage will insist they are defending not a moral precept, but a tradition that goes back thousands of years. But that isn't much of a defense for keeping all the legal consequences society has attached to marriage exclusive to heterosexuals."[29]

The ACLU then crowed about a related accomplishment: "The ACLU is very proud of its work in helping to get rid of sodomy laws. . . . We helped to strike down or repeal sodomy laws in California, Georgia, Kentucky, Maryland, Minnesota, Montana, Nevada, New York, Tennessee . . . you get the picture. Along with Lambda Legal, we've worked for eight years to get a same-sex intimacy case to the Supreme Court. . . . After this, who knows what we can do and when. Here at the ACLU, we've already got some ideas. . . ."[30] This all despite the serious risk to public health and safety posed by sodomy. ADF attorneys submitted a legal brief to the Supreme Court in the *Lawrence* case on behalf of the Christian Medical and Dental Society and Catholic Mental and Dental Society, that spells out in detail the public health risk and costs by this not-so-private behavior. And if the ACLU has more ideas, it means that the future of marriage and the family will continue to find itself in increasing jeopardy in the years ahead.

In 1993, Franklin E. Kameny, who was a board member of the Washington, D.C., ACLU, said, "The First Amendment creates an inescapable moral relativism, societal and cultural, for our nation taken as a whole. For example, I view homosexual sexual activity as

not only not immoral, or sinful, or wrong, or undesirable, but as affir-
matively moral, and virtuous, and right, and desirable."[31] This would
shock those who wrote the First Amendment and were charged with
upholding it. As John Adams, our second president, noted: "Our
Constitution was made only for a moral and religious people. It is
wholly inadequate for the government of any other."[32]

In November 2004, the ACLU announced the release of a new
CD titled *Marry Me*, featuring semi-nude homosexual and lesbian
couples on the cover. The ACLU's press statement announcing the
release of the CD proudly proclaimed:

"*Marry Me*, a new album from Figjam Records, brings together a diverse group of musicians to celebrate love and support
the American Civil Liberties Union's efforts to secure the rights
of same-sex couples to marry . . . . The ACLU Lesbian and Gay
Rights and AIDS Project will receive 50 percent of the proceeds
from the wholesale price of the *Marry Me* compilation . . . . The
projects hold a key role in the current movement for marriage, with
ongoing cases in New York, Oregon, Maryland, and California.

Last spring, performer and drag legend Hedda Lettuce [yes,
that's her name—the authors] approached Figjam's Jack Chen
about the struggle for marriage. Hedda and other artists wanted
to use music to explain to the world why marriage for same-sex
couples was a matter of fairness . . . ."[33]

Just before this book went to press, the ACLU announced their
launch of a national campaign to educate Americans on the "need"
for same-sex "marriage." The ACLU press release announcing this
effort said, "Among other public education efforts, the campaign will
offer assistance to local campaigns fighting constitutional amendments (i.e., the will of the people) that seek to ban gay people from
marriage and other family protections."[34]

In Alabama, the ACLU tried to get the courts to create a new
"right" that would protect the sale of "sex toys" at pornographic outlets. The ACLU had asked the United States Court of Appeals for the
Eleventh Circuit to add "a right to sexual privacy" as a "fundamental
right" under the U.S. Constitution and strike down the state's statute
prohibiting the sale of such objects. This time, the Eleventh Circuit

saw through the ACLU's agenda, upheld the statute, and wrote in its opinion:

The proper analysis for evaluating this question turns on whether the right asserted by the ACLU falls within the parameters of any presently recognized fundamental right or whether it instead requires us to recognize a hitherto unarticulated fundamental right. . . . The ACLU invokes "privacy" and "personal autonomy" as if such phrases were constitutional talismans. In the abstract, however, there is no fundamental right to either. . . . Hunting expeditions that seek trophy game in the fundamental-rights forest must heed the maxim "look before you shoot." Such excursions, if embarked upon recklessly, endanger the very ecosystem in which such liberties thrive—our republican democracy. Once elevated to constitutional status, a right is effectively removed from the hands of the people and placed into the guardianship of unelected judges.[35]

That last statement sums up exactly what the ACLU wants to do when it comes to the issue of marriage and the other demands for the homosexual agenda—to take the decision out of the hands of the people and remake America via judicial fiat. This is the brave new world of the ACLU.

Why Preserving Marriage Is Important

The present battle over marriage between the ACLU and its allies and those who believe in marriage between one man and one woman is all about the future of America's children. Should marriage and family be viewed as a form of obtaining instant gratification and fulfillment of the self—what can be called the "all about me" theology (the ACLU's vision)—or should it be seen as others centered, a God-ordained relationship that is the best environment for raising and nurturing children and the transmission of our culture?

To see where the ACLU's vision of marriage would lead us, we need look no further than Scandinavia. In countries such as Norway, Sweden, Iceland, and Denmark, it has been decades since many children have known any semblance of a traditional family.[36] The result has been the well-documented rise in social alienation and sexual confusion, which has now reached our shores as well.

In Sweden, 54 percent of all children are born to unwed mothers. In Norway, that number is 49 percent, while 46 percent of Danish children and 65 percent of children in Iceland are birthed outside marriage.[37] In Nordland, a county in Norway, the illegitimacy problem is so bad that in 2002 an incredible 82.27 percent of first-born children (and 67.29 percent of all children) were born to single-parent homes.[38] In America, the figure of children in one-parent homes continues to rise at an alarming rate; at least half of all children born in the United States will live in a single-parent home sometime during their childhood years.[39]

When marriage is redefined, as the ACLU and its activist allies seek to do, the result is the eventual destruction of marriage and societal chaos as advocates for other forms of "marriage," such as polygamy and polyamory, start to press for their right to marry. Stanley Kurtz, research fellow for the Hoover Institute, wrote in the *National Review*: "The National Swedish Social Insurance Board recently convened a panel in which two legal experts recommended changes in Swedish family law. One invoked same-sex parenting to argue for legal recognition of three- and even four-parent families. . . . Polyamory has reached Sweden, and there are now Swedes who would seize on triple or quadruple parenting to usher in legalized polyamory. . . . With so many dissolved cohabiters and gay parents, why not do away with the two-parent standard altogether?"[40]

Social commentator Gene Edward Veith, professor of English at Concordia University in Wisconsin, echoed this thought: "Under the emerging framework, there will be no difference between a married couple, a homosexual couple, or a couple in a temporary sexual relationship."[41]

When marriage is changed to merely fit the selfish whims of adults who treat children as if they are merely along for the ride, it does not take long to realize that marriage, which God ordained from the beginning of time for the raising and nurturing of children, becomes irrelevant.*

---

*See Genesis 2:24: "This is why a man leaves his father and mother and bonds with his wife, and they become one flesh."

In chapter 8, we will look at the ACLU's embrace and advocacy of international law to reshape America and undermine the Constitution. It is important to note here, however, that the ACLU and its allies plan to use international law as one of the weapons to legally undermine marriage and the family.

At a conference at King's College in London titled "Legal Recognition of Same-sex Marriage: A Conference on National European and International Law," one of the topics was whether marriage should exist at all. Strategies were presented on how legal activists, like the ACLU and Lambda Legal, could circumvent the democratic process through the judicial system to force governments to sanction same-sex "marriage." But it did not end there. Those attending went a step further and talked about the abolishment of marriage altogether so that adults could be free to pursue any sexual relationship they wanted, with no legal restrictions and little or no regard for children.[42]

Finally, there are the public health consequences of sexual behaviors outside marriage between one man and one woman. (The following section contains graphic content.)

The Centers for Disease Control and Prevention (CDC) estimates, "In the United States, more than 65 million people are currently living with an incurable sexually transmitted disease (STD). An additional 15 million people become infected with one or more STDs each year, roughly half of whom contract lifelong infections."[43] The CDC has determined that men who engage in anal sex or sodomy are among the groups "most vulnerable to STDs and their consequences."[44]

In addition, those who engage in sodomy can suffer from what is known as "gay bowel syndrome." According to Dr. Thomas C. Quinn, writing in *The American Journal of Medicine*, infections such as hepatitis A, shigella, entamoeba histolytica, giardia lamblia, enterobious vermicularis, and in some cases salmonella have become increasingly apparent in homosexual men.[45]

Dr. Neil E. Reiner concurred in *The Annals of Internal Medicine*. He wrote, "Serologic surveys of groups of homosexual men have shown that 50% to 75% have evidence of previous or current infection with HBV [hepatitis B virus], and it has been estimated that in the United [S]tates alone more than 100,000 homosexual men are carriers of hepatitis B surface antigen HbsAg. . . . Prevalence rates for homosexual men exceed those for heterosexual partners of HbsAg-positive persons, suggesting that the sexual activities of homosexual men lead to a greater frequency of exposure to infectious virus or provide more efficient routes of transmission."[46]

The CDC reported that 18 percent of acute hepatitis B cases were associated with homosexual activity.[47] This is huge in view of the fact that men who engaged in homosexual acts account for no more than 1 to 2 percent of the population.[48]

The bottom line is that when groups such as the ACLU and its allies in the homosexual activist movement start to tinker with the legal definition of marriage, there are high private and public prices our society must pay.

The ACLU's Brave New World

The ultimate plan by the ACLU and its allies to extend marriage far beyond same-sex "marriage" is revealed in the ACLU policy guide: "The ACLU believes that criminal and civil laws prohibiting or penalizing the practice of plural marriage [polygamy or polyamory] violate constitutional protections of freedom of expression and association, freedom of religion, and privacy for personal relationships among consenting adults."[49]

At first, the ACLU denied that there was a slippery slope leading to polygamy or polyamory. After the Vermont Supreme Court decision that created civil unions for homosexual couples, ACLU Director Matt Coles said, "I think the idea that there is some kind of slippery slope [to polyamory or group marriage] is silly."[50] But once again, what the ACLU says to the mainstream press differs from its actions and intent.

In Utah, a civil rights attorney filed a lawsuit challenging Utah's ban on polygamy (which the state abandoned when it sought statehood).[51] The challenge was brought after the ACLU-supported victory in *Lawrence vs. Texas*. While the ACLU was not a party to the Utah polygamy case, its Utah Executive Director Dani Eyer expressed support for those seeking to redefine marriage to include polygamy, saying the state will "have to step up to prove that a polygamous relationship is detrimental to society. There's no denying that thousands and thousands are doing that here and will maintain that it's healthy. The model of the nuclear family as we know it in the immediate past is unique, and may not necessarily be the best model. Maybe it's time to have this discussion."[52]

Fortunately, a federal judge dismissed the polygamy case on February 16, 2005, but appeals are pending as this book goes to press.[53]

However, the ACLU did back a group of Utah polygamists back in 1999 when they attempted to challenge the state's polygamy law. In an ACLU press release, Stephen Clark, the ACLU's Salt Lake City legal director, said, "Talking to Utah polygamists is like talking to gays and lesbians who really want the right to live our lives, and not in fear because of whom they love. So certainly that kind of privacy expectation is something the ACLU is committed to protecting."[54]

These are not only "loose cannon" ACLU executive and legal directors espousing this view. Art Spitzer, with the ACLU of the National Capital Area, added that the ACLU-supported victory in *Lawrence* had opened the door for other forms of marriage. Spitzer said, "Yes, I think *[Lawrence]* would give a lawyer a foothold to argue such a case [for the legalization of polygamy]. The general framework of that case, that states can't make it a crime to engage in private consensual intimate relationships, is a strong argument."[55]

Michele Parish-Pixler, the former Utah executive director of the ACLU, has said, "I can't see that there's any rational justification for prohibiting it [polygamy]. As long as it is between consenting adults, it ought to be permitted."[56]

And Nadine Strossen, ACLU president, when asked about polygamous relationships during a talk at Yale Law School in 2005, said, "We have defended the right for individuals to engage in polygamy. We defend the freedom of choice for mature, consenting individuals."[57]

According to constitutional law experts Bruce Fein and William Bradford Reynolds, the ACLU has a larger agenda in mind when it advocates for the legal recognition of other forms of marriage. They wrote in 1989, "Its real game is to secure . . . a veritable constitutional juggernaut that can topple a host of laws on the books in numerous states—for instance, prohibitions on homosexual sodomy, obscenity, indecency. . . ."[58]

Professor George W. Dent Jr., writing in the *Journal of Law and Politics*, said once same-sex "marriage" is legalized, other forms of marriage, such as polygamy, endogamy (the marriage of blood relatives), polyamory, bestiality, and child marriage will soon be legalized as well.[59] As in all other areas, the ACLU's anything-goes mentality when it comes to personal behavior applies to marriage as well.

For instance, polyamorists, as we have mentioned earlier, have started to clamor for their right to be married. In the April 20, 2004, edition of the *San Francisco Chronicle*, Jasmine Walston, president of Unitarian Universalists for Polyamory Awareness, said, "We're where the gay rights movement was 30 years ago."[60] Polyamorists even sent a letter to San Francisco Mayor Gavin Newsom after he directed the city clerk to start issuing same-sex "marriage" licenses, which asked, "What possible reason could you find for discriminating against or denying equal access to threesomes, foursomes, etc.?"[61]

When Hawaiian voters passed a constitutional amendment allowing the legislature to protect marriage as between one man and one woman on November 4, 1998, the same day Alaskan voters amended their constitution (after a bitter court battle for their right to vote at all), the ACLU showed not only its disregard for the will of the people in that state, but also stated where it wants to go with marriage in a press release: "We believe that marriage is a personal choice as well as a basic human right and should be available to all Americans who are in deeply committed relationships."[62]

Notice the ACLU's carefully parsed language. It is not confining the extension of marriage merely to homosexual couples but wants to extend it to "all Americans who are in deeply committed relationships." This loose definition of marriage could be broadened to include more than same-sex "marriage" and polygamy, but many other forms as well. Many, if not most, of the laws and local ordinances ACLU lawyers have supported use the term "sexual orientation" with *no* definition for the phrase. The laxity of this language is exactly what the ACLU and others in alternative lifestyles are seeking. Based on the ACLU's comments, someone could make the logical argument that you could marry your long-time pet because the two are presumably in a deeply committed relationship.

In fact, some academics and lawyers are already on the edges of that argument. Peter Singer, chair of Princeton University's Center for Human Values, wrote an article titled *Heavy Petting*, which defends bestiality (sexual relations between humans and animals). He wrote, "We are all animals, indeed more specifically, we are great apes. This does not make sex across the species barrier normal, or natural, whatever those much-misused words may mean, but it does imply that it ceases to be an offense to our status and dignity as human beings."[63]*

The Federal Marriage Amendment

The ACLU has come out with both barrels blazing against the Federal Marriage Amendment (FMA)—also known as the Marriage Protection Amendment. The amendment, submitted for Senate passage in 2004, simply states, "Marriage in the United States shall consist only of the union of a man and a woman. Neither this Constitution, nor the constitution of any State, shall be construed to require that marriage or the legal incidents thereof be conferred upon any union other than the union of a man and a woman."

The ACLU and its allies know that they will not be able to implement their agenda to redefine and perhaps abolish marriage if this or a similar amendment is added to the federal Constitution. All of a sudden, the ACLU, which has had no problem with other proposed constitutional amendments, like the so-called Equal Rights Amendment, giving eighteen-year-olds the right to vote, or state "Blaine" amendments that were based on racial and religious bigotry, now warns that amending the Constitution to protect marriage from activist judges "is an extreme act."[64] Perhaps the ACLU thinks that the abolishment of slavery (accomplished by the Thirteenth Amendment) was an extreme act as well. Does it believe extending the right to vote to women (the Nineteenth Amendment) was an extreme act? Or is it because the amendment is contrary to their agenda?

---

*Peter Singer, saying disabled babies are not persons and can be killed, wrote, "When the death of a disabled infant will lead to the birth of another infant with better prospects of a happy life, the total amount of happiness will be greater if the disabled infant is killed. Killing a disabled infant is not morally equivalent to killing a person. Often, it is not wrong at all." (See Peter Singer, *Practical Ethics* (Cambridge University'Press, 1979).

Objecting to the FMA, the ACLU stated, "We are not asking people to change their religious beliefs. There are many things about modern society that religious organizations do not endorse. For example, we did not ask the Catholic Church or other religions to accept divorce or birth control when they became legal in this country."[65] In chapter 6, we will expose the ACLU's duplicity because, in fact, it is trying to force religious organizations, including Catholic Charities and the Salvation Army, to violate their core beliefs when it comes to birth control, marriage, and homosexual behavior.*

The ACLU continued, "The U.S. Constitution is not the place to change morality every time someone in Congress has an idea about what morality should be."[66] Taking this argument to its logical conclusion, we ask does the ACLU mean that Congress should not have taken action on issues such as slavery and voting rights simply because certain individuals became convinced these practices were wrong? We suspect the ACLU believes such changes should be made by judges in cases they support.

In yet another example of ACLU duplicity, it claimed the FMA was not needed and that the issue should be settled at the state level.[67] Then the ACLU turned around and sued states to demand that courts overrule the democratic process when citizen petitions or legislatures have put the issue before the voters. And, as we have discussed earlier, the ACLU has little or no regard for the rights of voters who have said no several times to this issue.

For example, the ACLU helped recruit former Congressman Bob Barr of Georgia, the author of the Federal Defense of Marriage Act, to testify against the Federal Marriage Amendment. Barr said the DOMA law "allowed [state] legislatures the latitude to decide how to deal with marriage rights themselves, but ensured that no one state could force another to recognize marriages of same-sex couples."[68]

---

*A number of legal scholars and church leaders believe the ACLU and its allies will use the same-sex "marriage" issue as a form of legal extortion to force them to perform same-sex "marriage" ceremonies or have their tax-exempt, nonprofit status revoked on discrimination grounds. The legal precedence for this was already set by the ACLU and its allies more than twenty years ago; see *Bob Jones Univs. vs. U.S.*, 461 U.S. 574 (1983) and Robert B. Bluey, "Marriage Changes May Shake Churches' Tax Exemptions," CNSNews.com., February 23, 2004, and Alan Sears and Craig Osten, *The Homosexual Agenda: Exposing the Principal Threat to Religious Freedom Today*, (Nashville, TN: Broadman and Holman, 2003), pp. 228–30.

In a position paper on its Web site, the ACLU said something quite the opposite:

Neither the U.S. Constitution nor any state constitution explicitly mentions a constitutional right to marry. Most courts have said that the right to marry is understood to be part of the due process clause that is found in the U.S. Constitution and most state Constitutions. To decide what rights are implicitly protected by due process, courts typically look to see whether society has historically treated the right as something the government could not take away. The problem here is that our opponents will say that traditionally, we [homosexuals] never had a right to marry. We have a good argument that a history of excluding some people from a right is not relevant. As with equality, we should do well in courts that hear a lot of due process cases, or courts that are truly open to claims from gay people. . . . Moreover, even after we have convinced most states to change their laws and stop excluding same-sex couples from marriage, to get marriage for same-sex couples everywhere we'll eventually need to have the federal courts insist that the remaining states can't refuse to recognize same-sex marriages.[69]

That obviously means overruling DOMA.

The ACLU is well aware that when state legislatures or the people vote on this issue, same-sex "marriage" loses. Whenever it has come up for a vote, traditional marriage is soundly affirmed and same-sex "marriage" has been overwhelmingly defeated by the people* and their elected officials.† So the ACLU and its allies use the courts to circumvent the democratic process to force same-sex "marriage" on the states. When one radical court, by a 4–3 margin, ignored the will of the people in Massachusetts through the Massachusetts Supreme Judicial Court's imposition of same-sex "marriage" on the commonwealth,

---

*Constitutional amendments that define marriage as between one man and one woman have been passed by voters in Hawaii, Alaska, Nevada, Louisiana, Nebraska, Missouri, Arkansas, Georgia, Kansas, Kentucky, Michigan, Mississippi, Montana, North Dakota, Oregon, Ohio, Oklahoma, and Utah.

†More than forty states have passed defense of marriage acts since 1994. See http://www.domawatch.org.

the ACLU and its allies have used that decision to file lawsuits to attempt to force same-sex "marriage" on others. The ACLU supports
litigation against the very DOMA laws it says "protect" marriage and
should prevent the need for the FMA!

It is also important to note that the ACLU pulled out all stops to
defeat the federal DOMA that was signed into law in 1996. In a letter to former U.S. Representative Charles Canady, one of the federal
DOMA sponsors, the ACLU said, "This bill is bad constitutional
law and bad policy. . . . Apart from being an unmistakable violation
of the Constitution, it is a deplorable act of hostility unworthy of the
United States Congress."[70] Now, in the ACLU's revision of history,
the DOMA—the "unmistakable violation" of the Constitution—is
being used by the ACLU to disingenuously argue against the FMA.

The ACLU knows a constitutional amendment would put the
brakes on its anti-marriage agenda. It noted this in a question-and-
answer paper to homosexual activists who would have been "married" in Massachusetts after the state Supreme Judicial Court ruled
in favor of same-sex "marriage" in November 2003. The ACLU
wrote, "Before you begin any kind of case about your marriage, you
should contact the ACLU or one of the other LGBT [lesbian, gay, bisexual, transgender] legal organizations. You may have a good claim
that should be brought, but it's also possible to do serious harm by
suing. In 1997, an Alaskan couple sued the state for the right to marry.
After they won a preliminary hearing, the state, with a 71% majority,
passed a constitutional amendment, banning same-sex marriage. That
ended the case. It also prevents any state court or the state legislature
from ever allowing same-sex marriage until the people vote to change
the state constitution again."[71]

The reason the ACLU opposes the FMA is the same reason ADF,
Focus on the Family, Family Research Council, Coral Ridge Ministries, and numerous other Christian organizations strongly support
the FMA (see www.domawatch.org). It is the only guaranteed way to
firmly stop the ACLU's anti-marriage juggernaut.

While ADF and its allies have been successful in several states in
defending state DOMAs (most recently in Arizona and Indiana), we
cannot be assured that the federal DOMA will stand once it comes
under review by the U.S. Supreme Court. After the February 2004

actions of the mayor of San Francisco, thirteen states (including nine in Fall 2004) swept marriage protection amendments into their constitutions, and yet, Matt Coles, director of the ACLU's Lesbian and Gay Rights Project, said, "Lawsuits to end the exclusion [of same-sex marriage] will go forward. We will continue to fight for equal treatment through the courts. . . . Same-sex couples will marry, and become fully a part of the American landscape."[72]

The battle to adopt the FMA may well take years of perseverance as the ACLU and its allies in the homosexual activist movement make every effort to defeat it. They know the stakes: If marriage and the family fall, the door will be swung wide open for the advancement of their agenda to reorder American society.

That is why ADF, Focus on the Family, Family Research Council, and countless other pro-family allies, are dedicated to a long-term and costly battle to defend marriage between one man and one woman. It is essential that this institution be protected for the sake of our children, their children, and all future generations.

The Effect on Future Generations

We have already discussed how the gradual weakening of traditional marriage in Europe has led to skyrocketing illegitimacy rates, particularly in Scandinavia.

Studies examining the weakening of traditional marriage in Sweden (perhaps the most socially liberal of all the Scandinavian countries) have found that boys living with single, separated, or divorced mothers had high rates of emotional impairment once they hit the adolescent years.[73] A recent study by Gunilla Ringback Weitoft and others showed that children of single parents in Sweden have more than double the rates of mortality, severe morbidity, and injury than children in two-parent households, regardless of demographic and socioeconomic circumstances.[74]

When one examines the ACLU's legal attacks on marriage combined with its legal attacks on religion, one can see how its legal assaults on both of these institutions work together in order to advance its revisionary agenda. The Scandinavian countries are by far the most secular in Europe and have the most non-traditional laws when it comes to same-sex "marriage." Those countries that have a stronger religious influence have stronger marriage and family structures.* They also have the least number of out-of-wedlock births.[75] Therefore, for the ACLU to achieve its agenda on marriage, it has to create a legal climate in the United States that is hostile to both institutions.

The ACLU has not only consistently supported laws that weaken marriage but has also opposed legal efforts to *strengthen* marriage. The ACLU has long been an advocate of no-fault divorce, which was promoted as a cultural peacemaker and problem solver but led to skyrocketing divorce rates during the past three decades.[76] The ACLU has opposed purely voluntary, optional "covenant marriages," which would make it more difficult to obtain a divorce, even if a couple willingly chooses this option when they get married or later. The ACLU calls these marriages, based on a joint interest to be enduring, "emotional blackmail."[77]

Many studies have shown children do best in a traditional, two-parent home. The no-fault divorce movement has contributed to dysfunctional relationships that are affecting future generations, leading to increased premarital sex,[78] out-of-wedlock births,[79] and early marriage and divorce.[80] In contrast, children who grow up in well-grounded two-parent, traditional families with involved parents are far more likely to have higher grades[81] and be less prone to substance abuse.[82] Same-sex "marriage," over time, would reduce marriage to just another right rather than the God-ordained institution for raising and nurturing children and strengthening how males and females complement each other. Same-sex "marriage" also weakens the civilizing influence of traditional marriage on society as a whole. When the ACLU and its allies legally attack marriage, it is the children who ultimately face the consequences of decisions made for selfish and not selfless reasons.†

For example, one of the reasons that polygamy initially was outlawed was because the practice often resulted in subservience for women and poverty for both women and children.[83] This is certainly

---

*Stanley Kurtz, a fellow at the Hoover Institute at Stanford University, has also noted a 2002 study by the Max Plank Institute that found the countries with the lowest rates of family dissolution and out-of-wedlock births were strongly dominated by the Catholic confession. In countries with high levels of family dissolution, religion had little influence.

†For more information on this topic and the detrimental effects of same-sex parenting on children, please contact ADF and request the book, "No Basis: What the Studies Don't Tell Us About Same-Sex Parenting," by Robert Lerner, Ph.D., and Althea Nagai, Ph.D.

the impact today where this is practiced. Yet, here is the ACLU, who also claims that they unabashedly supports women's rights, advocating a practice that would return us to an era when women were treated with far less than the equality God intended in marriage. The consequences for our future daughters and granddaughters are clear if the ACLU's anti-marriage legal crusade succeeds.*

In addition, if the ACLU's disdain for the rule of law, as witnessed by its encouragement to public officials to openly defy state and federal marriage laws, is taken to its logical conclusion, the result is a total breakdown of society, or social anarchy. We must stand up to the ACLU's efforts to undermine marriage laws, otherwise all laws, and the rule of law under our Constitution, essential to the social order and our nation's future are in jeopardy.

As we ponder the ACLU's agenda for the future of marriage, we ask the following questions:

- What are the overwhelming cultural and economic implications that would result from the redefinition and ultimate abolition of marriage?

- What must be taught in the public schools about various forms of sexual behavior if the government has decreed all equal?

- What will the financial costs—long term and short term—be for social programs, insurance, and Social Security?

- What will the legal implications and punishment ultimately be for those who make public objections to alternative forms of marriage?

- What will a generation of children raised in such a legal environment be like?

- Will tax exemptions be denied to colleges, ministries, and even churches that do not recognize, assist with, or subsidize radical legal revisions of marriage and the family?

Perhaps more than with any other area, the battle over marriage is truly about what tomorrow will look like in America. If the ACLU

---

*We have both, one through personal experience and the other through an immediate family member's experience, known the pain, shame, and the sorrow when God's plan for the traditional family has been broken by divorce. Only by God's grace, forgiveness, restoration, and healing in our lives do our own families today experience the richness of His model lifestyle.

and its allies win, families will continue to disintegrate, selfishness will trump sacrifice, and our children and grandchildren will ultimately be the losers.

In the next chapter, we will examine how the ACLU has extended its war against marriage to the undermining of parental authority, another front in the ACLU's war to undermine the family and, ultimately, America.

CHAPTER 3

The ACLU vs. Mom and Dad

When the state forces parents to be involved, the consequences are often catastrophic.[1]
—Howard Simon, ACLU of Florida

It was a seemingly typical day at an elementary school in Novato, California, a community north of San Francisco. The students, some as young as seven years old, were summoned to a mandatory assembly featuring a program called "Cootie Shots."

But this was not an innocuous program. It was blatant propaganda presented by a homosexual activist theater troop, and none of the parents had an inkling about what their children were exposed to.

One of the skits featured a young boy dressing up in his mother's high heels so he could share cross-dressing with his classmates during show-and-tell. The young boy launched into a poem before the captive room of elementary-age students:

In Mommy's high heels the world is beautiful,
Let the peasants choke way down below.
I'm standing high above the crowds,
My head is breaking through the clouds.
In Mommy's high heels, I'm ten feet tall!
In Mommy's high heels life's a fantasy;
Ev'ry wish I make is a decree!
Let Sissy keep her shrunken heads,
Let Mary walk her dog who's dead,
In Mommy's high heels I have it all!
Here the world is beautiful:

Forests of coat racks and shoe trees
A land of hope and shopping sprees!!
When I grow up I'll have the cash
To go out and buy a bag to match!
So let them say that I'm like a girl!
What's wrong with being like a girl?!
And let them jump and jeer and whirl—
They are swine, I am the pearl!
And let them laugh and let them scream!
They'll be beheaded when I'm queen!
When I rule the world! When I rule the world!
When I rule the word, in my mommy's high heels![2]

When a group of parents learned their children had been subject to this presentation without parental authority or knowledge, they were rightfully outraged. In fact, Norma Bowles, the coauthor of the play, acknowledged the group wanted to isolate children from their parents regarding the assembly. She stated, "Children in a group are different than children alone. They look to a group to help them decide how they should feel and act, so what we try to do is to make it cool to do the right thing."[3]

The parents filed a lawsuit against the school but quickly found themselves facing the tremendous financial and manpower resources of the ACLU, which helped to defend the school district and the group that presented the play. While the parents hung on gallantly for two years, they finally gave up, having been outgunned by the ACLU. Once again, the ACLU had undermined parental authority and was proud of it. Julia Harumi, a Massachusetts staff attorney for the ACLU, said, "The plaintiffs' decision to walk away at this stage of the case ... sends a message throughout the state [of California] that schools have the authority to require mandatory attendance in tolerance-building and diversity education programs."[4]

The ACLU, which positions itself as the great defender of rights, is *against* the right of parents to not allow their children (or for that matter the children's own desire) to participate in assemblies and curricula that actively undermine, and in this instance ridicule, their religious beliefs.

That doesn't appear to matter to the ACLU. In their eyes, a child should not be required to salute the American flag, recite the Pledge of Allegiance,[5] or even hear a Christmas carol, but parents do not have the right to remove their children from assemblies such as "Cootie Shots."

This type of legal opposition to parents (in particular to Orthodox Jewish and Christian parents) is typical of the ACLU. Just as the ACLU has displayed contempt for the will of the people, it has also shown complete disregard for the rights of parents to raise their children to embrace their values and faith. In fact, the ACLU has stated, "The United States Constitution does not mention the right of parents to direct the upbringing of their children."[6]* It is important to note, however, that the U.S. Constitution also does not mention sodomy, same-sex "marriage," abortion, the use of international law in domestic cases, euthanasia, or the right to be free from all religion in public, but that has not deterred the ACLU from demanding courts create and then vigorously enforce legal "rights" in these areas. Nor has the ACLU been hesitant to demand strong financial sanctions and other punishments for those who disagree with their vision for America.

But contrary to the ACLU viewpoint, the Supreme Court has recognized that the Constitution and the laws of the United States allow parents to direct the moral upbringing of their children. For instance, in 1944, the Supreme Court, emphasized the importance of parents: "It is cardinal with us that the custody, care and nurture of the child reside first in the parents, whose primary functions and freedom include preparation for obligations the state can neither supply nor hinder."[7]

This principle was reaffirmed years later by the Supreme Court in *Wisconsin vs. Yoder* (1972) when it noted, "The primary role of the parents in the upbringing of their children is now established beyond debate as an enduring American tradition."[8]

---

*In *Pierce vs. Society of the Sisters of the Holy Names of Jesus etal.*, the U.S. Supreme Court, in a 9–0 decision that reaffirmed parental rights, stated, "The child is not the mere creature of the state." The court noted that the state of Oregon (by forcing parents to place their children in public school) "unreasonably interfere[d] with the liberty of parents and guardians to direct the upbringing of their children under their control."

In numerous other cases, the Supreme Court, along with lower federal and state courts, have recognized that parents have the right to provide and guide their children's religious instruction and to encourage them in the practice of religious beliefs,[9] to direct the education of their children,[10] and to make medical decisions for their children, and other basic decisions for their care and upbringing.[11]

But like almost all the ACLU's public posturings, there is "flexibility." If something advances the ACLU's agenda, then all of a sudden the ACLU says parents *do have a right* to direct the upbringing of their children.

In Virginia, the ACLU filed a lawsuit against a state law that made it illegal for teens to attend a nudist camp without parental accompaniment. Virginia lawmakers had a legitimate concern that the camp could possibly attract potential pedophiles* so they passed a law outlawing nudist camps where juveniles are not accompanied by a parent, grandparent, or legal guardian.[12] The nudist camp, Camp White Tail, countered that the law "discriminated" against "nude teens."

The camp manager, Bob Roche, complained, "There's a whole bunch of kids that won't be able to come without their parents. . . . [This law] singles them out—a church group that lets students take nude showers doesn't need parents there."[13] Of course, we doubt many churches allow naked male and female teenagers to shower together, but that's beside the point.

Rebecca Glenberg, legal director of the ACLU of Virginia, said, "If there was a law requiring a parent to accompany every child to Boy Scout or Girl Scout camp, you can see what a burden that would be."[14] Again, the last time we checked, there were no co-ed Scout nudist camps either. But while defending teenage nudist camps, the ACLU has been actively fighting to effectively shut down, or at least defund, Boy Scout troops across the nation.

But Glenberg went on, "By denying children the opportunity to go to this summer camp and by denying parents the right to choose where to send their children during the summer, the state is trampling

---

*Pedophiles are generally defined as persons who have a sexual preference for pre-pubescent children. See generally: American Psychiatric Association, "Diagnostic and Statistical Manual of Mental Disorders," DSM-IV-TR, Fourth Edition, No. 302.2, p. 571.

on their right to privacy and the rights of parents to direct the upbringing of their children."[15]

Amazingly, the ACLU has become the great defender of the right
of parents to direct the upbringing of their children, after arguing
just the opposite in "Cootie Shots" and other cases! Another case of
ACLU "flexibility"! In the ACLU's mind, it is OK for parents to
permit their teens to play naked in front of their opposite-sex peers,
but it is wrong if parents object to their children's learning about how
to perform homosexual behavior or, as we will see later, having an
abortion without parental knowledge or approval.

The Virginia law was upheld by a federal judge, but as it does in
many other matters, the ACLU will continue to persist for this new
"right." It quickly announced it would likely appeal the ruling.[16]

Another example of how the ACLU attacks the moral beliefs of
parents occurred in the infamous *Hot, Sexy, and Safer Productions
Inc.* case in Chelmsford, Massachusetts. As in "Cootie Shots," students (this time high schoolers) were told that they had to attend an
assembly called "Hot, Sexy, and Safer" presented by AIDS "educator" Suzi Landolphi. Also, like "Cootie Shots," parents were *not* no-
tified about this assembly or the graphic sexual information that their
children would receive.

Landolphi started the assembly by telling the students, "What
we're going to do is we're going to have a group sexual experience here
today. How's that? Is that good? With audience participation!"[17]

Unfortunately, it went downhill from there. In the *Washington
Times*, Cheryl Wetzstein described the rest of Landolphi's "performance": "She giggled and strutted. They cheered and they laughed—especially when Dr. David Evans [of the American Medical Student Asso-
ciation] blew the condom on his head into King Kong proportions."[18]

Landolphi went on to give a shockingly lewd performance, and
other speakers discussed homosexual and premarital heterosexual
conduct by minors, used profanity, described oral and anal sex, and
had students act out sexual activities.

Wetzstein continued, "For example, Miss Landolphi asked a student to participate in a demonstration, and, holding a condom on
one hand, she handed another condom to him. She slowly licked her
condom and asked him to do the same. Then, saying, 'I don't want to

waste this condom,' she invited a teen-age girl to come down. Miss Landolphi told the boy to kneel and instructed the girl to take the condom and place it over the boy's head."[19]

When parents heard about this assembly, there were justifiably upset. ADF provided financial and legal assistance for an appeal of the lawsuit that was filed by offended students (and their parents) against the school, claiming that the right of parents to direct the upbringing and education of their children had been violated. Guess who showed up to fight the parents in court? Yes, the ACLU. When it comes to teenage nudity, parents have the right to direct the upbringing of their children, but if parents object to their children being exposed to graphic sexual information or Internet pornography in a public library (as we will discuss later), the ACLU feigns ignorance or even comes to the defense of those who distribute such material.

Unfortunately, going against the war chest of the ACLU, the students and the parents who were offended by the performance and who did not have adequate funding at the beginning of the case lost.[20]

It is not just in the area of sex education that the ACLU wages war against parents. That war extends to the issue of abortion as well.

Parental Rights

In the mid-1990s, the ACLU wrote then Senate Majority Leader Robert Dole to express its opposition to the Parental Rights and Responsibilities Act, which had been introduced by Senator Charles Grassley of Iowa and then Oklahoma Representative Steve Largent. In a letter to the senator, the ACLU wrote, "This legislation will make it extraordinarily difficult for the government to assist children in situations in which their health is endangered because of their parents' actions or inaction."[21]

In opposing this legislation, was the ACLU's reasoning because it was concerned that a child might die of a life-threatening illness because of parental neglect? No. What the ACLU was referring to was situations involving school counselors or other persons who have transported female minors across state lines to have an abortion, without complying with the parental involvement and judicial bypass laws in the minors' home states. Later, again showing its disregard for parents, the ACLU opposed the Child Custody Protection Act of 1999, which would have made it unlawful for individuals, such as school counselors, to do this.[22]

A public school guidance counselor in suburban Philadelphia made arrangements for a young girl to drive across state lines to have a second-trimester abortion, without her parents' knowledge or consent. She drove to New Jersey to avoid Pennsylvania's parental consent law. The counselor allegedly cashed checks from the girl's boyfriend using school district bank accounts, lied to the girl's teachers to get her out of class, and then drew her a map describing how to get to the clinic. When she told the counselor she was a Southern Baptist and that abortion was against her faith beliefs, the counselor reportedly said, "One day you're going to look back at this and laugh."[23]

When this came to light, ADF funded the case filed in the U.S. District Court in Philadelphia on behalf of the girl's parents. The case was finally settled when the school district established a policy that forbids school employees from encouraging or assisting students in getting abortions.[24] This is only one of many victories in which ADF has been able, with God's grace, to help parents stand up to the ACLU and its allies, and win.

A glimpse at the ACLU's true agenda shows in its fact sheet opposing parental rights legislation. It stated, "A significant new threat to reproductive rights [abortion] has emerged in the form of 'parental rights' legislation. . . . These bills would give parents such absolute control over their children's lives that, in some instances, the minors' own constitutional rights would be threatened and their health and well-being endangered."[25]

The fact sheet continued, "Depending on a bill's specific provisions, parents might bring a lawsuit . . . because a school provided sexuality education, a condom availability program, or a health clinic that gave students confidential services."[26]

The ACLU then spelled out its true agenda: "Although parental rights legislation threatens to undermine the rights and well-being of minors in many different ways, it particularly jeopardizes their access to sexuality education, birth control, and AIDS prevention services, testing and treatment for sexually transmitted diseases (STDs), pregnancy testing, prenatal care, and abortion services. Some states would severely limit minors' access in these areas by requiring parental notification or consent."[27]

The fact sheet neglected to mention that the U.S. Supreme Court has ruled, in a case where the ACLU was a participant, that any such laws must have a judicial bypass that allows girls to have an abortion without parental involvement notice in certain circumstances.[28]

To the ACLU and its allies, it appears any parental involvement that would discourage teenage sexual activity and abortion is a bad thing. To quote Howard Simon, executive director of the ACLU of Florida, "When the state forces parents to be involved, the consequences are often catastrophic."[29]

This contempt for parents surfaces in other ACLU communications attacking parental consent and notification laws. In a briefing, "Reproductive Freedom and the Rights of Minors," the ACLU wrote, "Although parents have interests in their children's well-being, in the case of pregnancy a teenager's privacy rights must be paramount."[30] (And, of course, as with all abortion issues, the right to life of the yet-to-be-delivered child is irrelevant.)

This statement comes from the same ACLU that believes when it comes to teenage nudist camps parents have the right to direct the upbringing of their children. When it comes to abortion, that interest, at least in the ACLU's eyes, is middling at best.

William Donohue commented, "For the ACLU, those who want to restore a measure of accountability are promoting 'chastity acts,' legislation that enfeebles the liberty of youngsters to make up their own rules of sexual behavior."[31]

In the letter mentioned earlier to former Senator Dole, the ACLU expressed its disdain for parental involvement in school curricula: "Providing every parent with a veto over every decision a school makes regarding his or her child could create chaos in our public schools." The letter continued, "Our schools should provide a wide range of ideas and a diversity of political viewpoints."[32] To the ACLU and its allies this means the promotion of sexual behavior, but not if a traditional Christian or Orthodox Jewish viewpoint is expressed. Those ideas and the "diversity" they provide are intolerable to the ACLU and its allies.

What was so insidious about the parental rights legislation for the ACLU to oppose it so fervently?

Section 4 of the parental rights bill basically reaffirmed previously cited language from *Wisconsin vs. Yoder* (1972) and *Pierce vs. Society of Sisters* (1925), stating: "No Federal, State, or local government, or any official of such a government acting under color of law, shall interfere with or usurp the right of a parent to direct the upbringing of the child of the parent."[33]

Section 3 stated that the parents' right to direct the upbringing of a child included the right to:

- Direct or provide for the education of the child;
- Make a health or mental health decision for the child, with exceptions;
- Discipline the child, including reasonable corporal punishment as already defined by the Supreme Court; and
- Direct or provide for the religious and moral foundation of the child.[34]

The ACLU's stated concern that "this legislation will make it extraordinarily difficult for the government to assist children in situations in which their health is endangered because of their parents' action or inaction" was just a smokescreen.[35] Analysts of the bill clearly noted that "the exceptions spelled out in section 2, part 3, subparagraph (b) of the bill are medical service or treatment that is necessary to prevent an imminent risk of serious harm or remedy serious harm to the child, or medically indicated service or treatment for a disabled infant with a life-threatening illness."[36]

The ACLU's fervor was not about parents' withholding medical care in emergency and life-threatening situations. Instead it was about keeping parents in the dark about decisions, such as abortion, that could have a detrimental effect on the long-term—even life-long—physical and emotional health of their daughters.

The other "straw man" that the ACLU used to argue against the parental rights legislation was the natural concern that this legislation would provide legal shelter to child abuse. The ACLU voiced this concern several times in public statements against the legislation. However, this was just another case of the ACLU using misinformation and fear to advance its agenda because the bill's sponsors clearly stated that child abuse was not a parental right and the bill would not protect such tragic conduct.[37] Patrick Fagan, a fellow at the Heritage Foundation, and Wade Horn, formerly of the National Fatherhood Initiative and currently assistant secretary for children and families for the U.S. Department of Health and Human Services, noted: "Over the years, widely scattered and repeated attacks on the fundamental rights of parents have come from state and local courts; from federal, state, and local government bureaucracies and officials; and from policy initiatives inspired by a number of the major professions dealing with children. Certain members of these professions seem more concerned with displacing parents than with aiding them. In fact, the bill is opposed by many liberal groups wishing to change the relationship between government and the family, including. . . the American Civil Liberties Union. . . ."[38]

Fagan and Horn nailed it on the head. The ACLU and its allies seek to strip parents of their right and authority to direct the upbringing of their children. If parents are denied this right, then children ultimately suffer, as eloquently stated by the bipartisan 1991 National Commission on Children, which wrote: "The family is and should remain society's primary institution for bringing children into the world and for supporting their growth and development throughout childhood. . . . Parents are the world's greatest experts on their own children. They are their children's first and most important caregivers, teachers, and providers. Parents are irreplaceable, and they should be respected and applauded by all parts of society for the work they do."[39]

Nevertheless, the ACLU and its allies were successful in staging their usual campaign of misinformation and fear to sink this much-needed legislation. The ACLU believes it is the expert when it comes to educating children.

Why has the ACLU been so fervent in pushing its sexual agenda for children, at the expense of parental rights? Part of the answer might be traced to the ACLU's anything-goes mind-set. Since the ACLU believes there should be *no* regulation of adult sexual activity such as prostitution[40] and the distribution of obscenity, then the sexual behaviors of children should not be curtailed either, even at the risk of their long-term physical and emotional health. Just like the adult male who keeps secrets from his spouse about his adultery with a prostitute, children, often with the ACLU's help, can keep their parents from knowing the truth about their sexual behavior and its costly consequences.

Defending Pornographers, Not Parents

Another example of the ACLU's agenda to undermine parents and strip them of recourse to protect their children is its war against reasonable prohibitions on the distribution of obscenity, or almost any form of pornography, *including child pornography*.[41]

In 1985–86, Alan served as executive director of the Attorney General's Commission on Pornography. ADF founder Dr. James Dobson was one of the eleven commissioners. From the very outset, the ACLU dogged the staff and research efforts of the commission, assigning its then legislative counsel Barry Lynn (now executive director of Americans United for the Separation of Church and State) and others to travel to and attend every commission hearing. In his testimony, the Reverend Lynn affirmed the ACLU's position that the U.S. Constitution protected distributors of child pornography from law enforcement. He added that it also prohibited legislatures from assisting parents in protecting children from exposure to hard-core pornography by barring obscenity.

The commission invited the ACLU and the nation's pornographers to produce witnesses to testify as to any positive impacts from child or hard-core pornography. At its adjournment in 1986, the commission had yet to hear from one such witness.

The ACLU has also opposed federal legislation that allowed parents to notify the post office if they did not wish to receive sexually oriented advertisements in the mail. It also opposed legislation that would have labeled pornographic mail as such so the post office would know not to deliver it to families who did not wish to receive it.[42]

In its policies, the ACLU placed the burden of keeping pornography out of the hands of children on parents and not on pornographers. They state, "The ACLU maintains that the burden of preventing exposure of children to offensive or pornographic material ultimately rests with parents."[43] Yet in typical ACLU duplicity, it opposes practically every avenue parents have to limit their children's exposure to pornography, such as reasonable time, place, and name regulation of pornography outlets; limits on sale of hard-core pornography; restrictions on cable television access; and laws restricting the sale of indecent material to minors. In addition, they oppose Internet filters in public libraries[44] and forcing online pornographers to provide access codes to adults to access their Web sites.[45]

The ACLU also opposed the "record keeping" amendment to the sexual exploitation of children prohibition, Title 18 U.S.C. sec. 2257, which merely requires those who produce any book, magazine, periodical, film, or videotape of actual sexually explicit conduct to obtain and maintain identity documents to determine if the performers are older than the age of eighteen. Records must be kept of the proof of age and true identity for a period of years and available for regulatory review.[46*] The statute was challenged in court by ACLU allies and upheld, but various challenges to regulations that have been enacted continue to this day. This would not be the last time the ACLU protected pornography. The ACLU believes it is too burdensome for those who want to film sexual acts to actually know the true identity and age of the people involved.

In *ACLU vs. Ashcroft* (2004), the ACLU sued the U.S. attorney general, challenging the Child Online Protection Act (COPA), which authorized fines of $50,000 and six months in prison for posting on the Internet material that was "harmful to minors" and could be accessed by children. COPA had been passed after the ACLU's victory in *Reno vs. ACLU*, one of the first attempts to provide protections for children from being exposed to Internet pornography. COPA also required the provision of adult access codes or some other form of registration to view pornographic material on the Internet to ensure that the users were adults. The bottom line: No one was restricting the right for so-called "consenting adults" to view online pornography if they wanted to see it. These were just common sense controls to protect children from this harmful material.

---

*Alan wrote the text for this section of the U.S. code and worked with the staffs of then-United States Senators Strom Thurmond and Dennis DeConcini for its passage. Alan testified on the bill before both Senate and House committees and met firsthand the ACLU's strong opposition to even this protection for young persons being exploited by pornographers, despite numerous, high profile, documented cases of underage performers.

From the ACLU's point of view, the right to unrestricted access to pornography trumps the need of parents to protect their children from it despite any contrary rhetoric.

This case was appealed to the U.S. Supreme Court. In a disappointing 5–4 decision, the Court affirmed a preliminary injunction against the enforcement of COPA and remanded the case back to the lower court to give the government an opportunity to argue that COPA was the least restrictive means to protect minors from sexually explicit materials on the Internet.[47] ADF funded a friend-of-the-court brief on behalf of the Family Research Council in defense of COPA.

After hearing the decision, Benjamin Bull, ADF's chief counsel, said, "For the time being, the U.S. Supreme Court's decision gives pornographers and their ACLU supporters a huge green light to push a pathetic, life-destroying trade without restriction or penalty."

So, while on one hand, the ACLU stated in its policy guide that it is the parents' responsibility to keep their children away from pornography,[48] it files or approves of lawsuits to take away the real and effective means for parents to do so! Parents are often left with little or no options in blocking their children's access to pornographic material. We will discuss the ACLU's battle against Internet filters at public libraries in a subsequent chapter.

The ACLU has also opposed efforts by the Federal Communications Commission (FCC) to enforce the most basic decency standards in light of the increasing coarseness on network and cable television, such as Janet Jackson's breast-baring Super Bowl performance. In one such incident, the rock star Bono of the group U2 used a blatantly profane word during a national television broadcast.* Chris Hansen of the ACLU said, "The FCC is now setting itself up as a national censorship board, seeking to impose its version of morality on the American public. What's worse, for the first time in television history, the FCC is declaring that tape delays of live broadcasts are necessary to protect us from so-called indecency and blasphemy. . . . As a result, broadcasters will self-censor, and we will lose both creative, challenging content and spontaneity." The ACLU then added

---

*Given the ACLU's role as America's foremost religious censor, we suspect they know what real censorship is, and is not.

its usual line mocking religion: "The move to include 'blasphemy' in the definition of profanity is particularly disturbing . . . because it injects the government into religious disputes in a way that violates the Constitution."[49]

The ACLU has also opposed the purely voluntary Motion Picture Association of America (MPAA) rating system that gives parents and theaters some information and guidance to determine films that are appropriate for children. The MPAA also provides guidelines to theaters with regard to what children should and should not be exposed to. The MPAA's policies are private agreements and not laws. According to William Donohue, "The ACLU opposes the Motion Picture Association of America because [the MPAA] does not allow parents to decide if their underage children should be allowed to see a pornographic film." The ACLU said, "The MPAA rating system, through its X and R [and now NC-17] ratings, interferes with the autonomy of the family. . . . Such restrictions on parents' freedom to raise their children as they see fit are particularly offensive."[50]

Or, rather, as the ACLU sees fit. The ACLU doesn't mention that even the very limited protections and information offered by the MPAA ratings are not compulsory. The ratings, the brainchild of former President Lyndon Johnson's aide Jack Valenti, to prevent government protective action, have no written standards and vary depending on decisions by a group of reviewers.[51] But to the ACLU, providing parents and theater owners with information for making choices limits a parents' freedom to raise their children as they seem fit. (But if a parent wants to pull a child from an offensive sex-ed program, they don't have the right to raise their child as they see fit in the ACLU's opinion.)

As we have seen, the ACLU is extremely concerned about the rights of parents to have their teenagers attend nudist camps or escape religion. At the same time, the ACLU fights to keep parents from having a say in whether their children are taught pro-homosexual propaganda in the public schools, receiving notice if their daughters plan to have an abortion, and protecting their children from pornography on the Internet or from inappropriate material at the local cinema or magazine vendor.

If the ACLU's demands are fully realized, the hardest of hard-core pornography will someday be broadcast on regular television channels at all hours of the day and night. It will be available to any-one and everyone who has a television set, and parental control will be impossible.

ACLU as Big Brother

In addition to working in the area of pornography, the ACLU actively works in other areas to make the job of being a parent—and raising children according to a family's morals and values—even harder through its strong advocacy of homosexual behavior in public schools.

The ACLU and its allies have threatened or sued school districts to force children to undergo "peer-to-peer" training sessions to force them to reject their parents' religious beliefs when it comes to sexual, including homosexual, conduct. This has happened in Morgan Hill, California; Visalia, California; and Boyd County, Kentucky, to men-tion a few places.

The danger of these training sessions is fairly obvious. During the teenage years, peer pressure is difficult for many young men and women. In many instances, teens desperately want to be accepted and to fit in. When teenagers train other teenagers to accept and affirm homosexual behavior, the pressure to reject parental and religious be-liefs can easily become too strong for many teens to resist.

In Morgan Hill, the ACLU won a settlement against the local school district for its alleged failure to protect six students who claimed to be homosexual from harassment.[52] While we agree that no child should undergo harassment in a public school, the ACLU takes advantages of these claims, whether real or imagined, to indoctrinate schoolchildren in the ACLU's totalitarian way.

One of the most alarming aspects of lawsuits such as this one is that the eventual settlement required school districts to provide man-datory training sessions for ninth-grade students.[53] To force acceptance of homosexual behavior makes it nearly impossible for parents to raise their children in accordance with their religious beliefs and values.

A similar settlement happened in Visalia after an ACLU lawsuit.[54] In addition, the ACLU's efforts are not limited to "gay friendly" areas like certain parts of California. Its latest victory occurred in the Appalachian mountain community of Boyd County, Kentucky.[55]

In this particular case, the ACLU was not hesitant to use a court order to force children in Boyd County to learn "tolerance." Working with advocates of homosexual behavior, they took what could have been a simple equal-access issue—allowing the gay-straight alliance club to have the same access to school facilities as everyone else—and expanded it to include the same type of anti-harassment training implemented in Morgan Hill and Visalia.[56]

The Boyd County case is particularly alarming. Students are *mandated* to attend. When hundreds of parents tried to "opt out" their children by keeping them home, the ACLU threatened to take legal action to force compliance—trying to make parents surrender their kids to well-organized "tolerance training" that can undercut their moral convictions.[57]

Now, ADF has taken action. On February 15, 2005, ADF filed a federal lawsuit on behalf of parents and students in Boyd County. The school handbook prohibits students from expressing opposition to homosexual behavior while in the training or anytime at school—a clear violation of their constitutional rights!

But under the ACLU's program entitled, *Every Student, Every School,* Boyd County is an example of where they want to take our children.

In an another amazing example of ACLU duplicity, the ACLU now seeks to intervene in ADF's lawsuit—claiming that the school district has gone too far to censor student speech—in the very training that they filed a lawsuit to get implemented into the school district!

These lawsuits are the result of the ACLU's partnership with GLSEN (the Gay, Lesbian, and Straight Educational Network). The ACLU published a manual (with GLSEN's assistance) audaciously titled *Making Schools Safe,* which is a blueprint for using the public schools to influence children to reject the values and beliefs of parents who oppose homosexual behavior.[58] GLSEN is also given a glowing endorsement in this manual. These cases prove beyond debate that the ACLU's view of tolerance and diversity is one way—their way.

In material to promote its "Day of Silence" (which encourages students to not speak all day at school in protest of alleged harassment against homosexual students), GLSEN has told children to "brainstorm" a list of people "who are likely to stand in your way" or "denied you their support in the past, or who've expressed bias against LGBT (lesbian, gay, bisexual, transgendered) people." The material said the list can include teachers, school board members, and *relatives*. The manual stated, "People who oppose your issue are known as, you guessed it, your opponents."[59]*

The primary lesson of the ACLU and its allies, such as GLSEN, to schoolchildren: Reject your pastors, your parents', your family's, and your church's beliefs, and if they stand in your way, treat them as the enemy.

And if parents want to remove their children from public schools or have access to charter schools or vouchers to avoid the ACLU's force-feeding of its agenda on their children? Well, they're out of luck there too. The ACLU—supposedly the defender of choice when it comes to religion, abortion, pornography, and homosexual behavior—has actively worked against parents having the right to use their hard-earned tax dollars to choose which school would be best for their children. School choice to the ACLU is evil, yet it constantly agitates for reproductive "choices."

In a position paper, the ACLU of Texas unwittingly put forth the exact reason why concerned parents should have the right to school choice. It wrote, "This generation of children will be the next generation of adult citizens who will make decisions on the directions this country will take. They will be molded by whatever education they receive."[60]

Couple this statement with the following by Deanna Duby of the ACLU's staunch ally, the National Education Association: "The fear of the Religious Right is that the schools of today are the governments of tomorrow. And you know what, they're right."[61] These two statements together show why the ACLU and its allies fight school choice so fervently. The ACLU and its allies know they have a captive audience in schoolchildren—an audience they can shape to reject their parents' beliefs.

---

*In 2005, ADF launched the "Day of Truth" to defend and protect the right of students to share God's love for their peers trapped in or being tempted by homosexual behavior. More than 1,100 students participated. For more information, go to www.telladf.org/truth.

The ACLU says in its arguments against school choice that it would hurt the poor, when exactly the opposite is true. Many poor parents in urban areas are clamoring for an escape from failed public schools that trap their children in the cycle of poverty.[62] In Cleveland, Ohio, for instance, the school choice program specifically targeted children in poor urban areas, where only 9 percent of ninth graders were able to pass the state's proficiency test.[63]

If that argument doesn't succeed, the ACLU brings out the old "separation of church and state" argument (which we will discuss later) to try to block parents from having a choice in where their children go to school and what they will learn, unless the curriculum opposes traditional values, patriotism, and religious faith.

To help empower poor families trapped in failing public schools (where the ACLU and its allies would keep them), ADF provided funding to assist in a number of school choice legal efforts, including a friend-of-the-court brief for state Representative Polly Williams, in a case in Milwaukee, Wisconsin (see *Jackson vs. Bensen*), and the Supreme Court case *Zelman vs. Simmons-Harris*, which dealt with the legality of the Ohio school choice plan. In the latter case, the Court dismissed the arguments by the ACLU (which filed a brief against the school choice program) and its allies claiming that the school voucher plan violated the Establishment Clause.[64] Still, the ACLU goes on undeterred, challenging virtually every attempt to allow parents to have a say in where their children go to school, and what they will learn once they get there.

The Effect on Parents

But for those with no choice in their schools or an ability to "opt out," how would the full implementation of the ACLU's agenda affect parents and their ability to raise their children? If the ACLU's dream agenda comes to its fruition:

1. Parents would have little or no legal recourse to shield their children from the vilest pornographic material possible.
2. Parents would be unable to call for criminal prosecution of child pornographers distributing pictures of their children.
3. Parents would have no say in dispensing contraceptives to their children or in monitoring their sexual behavior.

4. Parents would not be able to stop their minor daughters from having an abortion and perhaps would never know about it if they had.

5. Parents would have little or no say in their children's education, even if that education undermines the family's religious beliefs and values.

The world the ACLU wants is frightening to most American parents. It continues to wage a relentless campaign against the rights of parents to direct the upbringing of their children. In the ACLU's world, parents become little more than breeders or perhaps egg-sperm donors (unless they choose the ACLU-protected "right" to abort) for the ACLU and its allies, which will take the children and indoctrinate them in ACLU beliefs.

But there is much hope, with many recent victories against the ACLU's agenda, and we shouldn't assume the battle is over. It has only begun. ADF and its allies are battling the ACLU and its comrades across the nation in order to defend the legal rights of parents, and *not* the ACLU's, to direct the upbringing of their children. ADF funded a successful legal challenge by Connecticut parents to a GLSEN "pink triangle" program which encouraged teenagers to experiment with homosexual behavior. The school board discontinued the program.[65]

ADF continues to defend parental consent laws for abortion. In Arizona, it funded a successful effort to legally uphold much of the state's parental consent law.[66] Now parents, who must give consent to allow a school nurse to hand out an aspirin to a child, or allow a technician to pierce her ears, can actually have a say in a potentially life-and-death decision involving their teenage daughters.

While the ACLU constantly seeks to restrict the legal rights of parents to direct the moral upbringing of their children, ADF strives to empower parents to be actively involved in their children's lives, to the benefit of parents, children, and society as a whole. Parents now have a growing legal alliance and a growing list of legal precedents to help them stand up to the ACLU and its allies.

CHAPTER 4

The ACLU vs. Children

The ACLU is defending those who abuse children while attacking those who give them moral guidance. This contrast reveals the priorities of today's ACLU. . . . The ACLU has offered material support to those who openly preach pedophilia and arguably encourage kidnapping, rape, and murder.[1]
—Deroy Murdock

Warning: This chapter contains graphic and disturbing content.

Ten-year-old Jeffery Curley of Cambridge, Massachusetts, was just like any other fifth-grade boy who loved playing outside his home on a crisp fall day.[2]

But, unlike other ten-year-old boys who would grow up to be men, Jeffery would meet a tragic end.

On that fall day, two men, Salvatore Sicari and Charles Jaynes, drove by Jeffery's front yard and took him away.[3] They then drove to the public library and accessed a Web site for the North American Man/Boy Love Association (NAMBLA), which encourages sexual relations between adult men and young boys.[4]

After viewing the Web site's content, the two men attempted to sexually assault Jeffery, but the terrified young boy fought back. Not willing to give up, Sicari and Jaynes took a gasoline-soaked rag and choked Jeffery to death with it. Then, they took the boy's body across the state line to Jaynes's New Hampshire apartment. The two men then molested Jeffery's dead body and put his violated corpse in a cement-filled container. Then they drove to Maine and threw the corpse into a river. What was left of Jeffery's precious little body was recovered several days later and returned for burial to his broken-hearted parents.[5]

Sicari and Jaynes were caught and eventually convicted for their wicked crimes. They now are serving life imprisonment. But Jeffery's parents wanted to make sure other young boys did not meet the same gruesome fate as their young son. They filed a $200-million civil lawsuit against NAMBLA, claiming that their son might still be alive if not for the "man-boy love" organization and the content of its "educational" Web site. In addition, if the Curleys are successful, NAMBLA could be subject to damages from other families of children who had been molested by its members.[6] This case is still pending in our judicial system.

The family's attorney, Larry Frisoli, said that Jaynes wrote in a diary he had used NAMBLA's Web site for "psychological comfort" before he and Sicari killed and molested Jeffery. Jaynes also had been stalking Jeffery before the attack, and several NAMBLA materials were found in Jaynes's possession.[7] Frisoli said that NAMBLA is "not just publishing material that says it's OK to have sex with children and advocating changing the law. [It] is actively training their members how to rape children and get away with it. They distribute child pornography and trade live children among NAMBLA members with the purpose of having sex with them. . . . In his diary, Jaynes said he had reservations about having sex with children until he discovered NAMBLA. It's in his diary . . . , around the time he joined NAMBLA, one year before the death of Jeffery Curley."[8]

One of NAMBLA's publications is titled *The Survival Manual: The Man's Guide to Staying Alive in Man-Boy Sexual Relationships.* According to Frisoli, "Its chapters explain how to build relationships with children. How to gain the confidence of children's parents. Where to go to have sex with children so as not to get caught." Bill O'Reilly of Fox News added that the NAMBLA Web site "actually posted techniques designed to lure boys into having sex with men and also supplied information on what an adult should do if caught."[9]

The ACLU came to NAMBLA's defense, against the protection of young boys like Jeffery Curley.

Incredibly, the ACLU's Massachusetts executive director, John Roberts, said, "There was nothing in those publications [of NAMBLA] or Web site which advocated or incited the commission of any illegal acts, including murder or rape." ACLU Massachusetts Legal Director John Reinstein added, "Regardless of whether people agree with or abhor NAMBLA's views, holding the organization responsible for crimes committed by others who read their materials would gravely endanger important First Amendment freedoms."[10]

Then in an incredible leap of logic, Reinstein said, "The Supreme Court has made it clear that a speech or publication is protected under the First Amendment unless it is 'directed to inciting or producing imminent lawless action and is likely to incite or produce such action.' NAMBLA's materials are simply not in this category. While NAMBLA may extol conduct which is currently illegal, its materials fall far short of speech that may be prohibited."[11]

To most people, Web pages that provide advice on how to seduce and rape young boys would be enough evidence for a civil lawsuit that NAMBLA is encouraging and inducing its members to engage in lawless action. However, this does not seem to matter in the eyes of the ACLU, which claims to believe that what NAMBLA posts on its Web site has no link to the encouragement of criminal behavior.

An important distinction must be made here. Homosexual activists and their allies in the media and government, in the days after the murder of Matthew Shepard in Wyoming in 1998, tried to make a strong link between the murder and the speech by Christian conservative leaders who opposed homosexual behavior and shared the gospel of Jesus Christ. None of the Christian leaders cited by ACLU allies in the media, such as Dr. James Dobson, Gary Bauer, and Pat Robertson, have ever made public statements calling for the physical injury or murder of those who practice homosexual behavior.[12] On the other hand, the information on the NAMBLA Web site instructs those who visit with information to physically, not figuratively or emotionally, sexually assault young boys.

The ACLU's Reinstein turned to the victim strategy to defend NAMBLA, stating, "What they don't like is what NAMBLA stands for. They don't like their ideas or the notion that someone else would have accepted them."[13]

This sad story is another example of the ACLU's duplicity. On one hand, the ACLU states that NAMBLA cannot be held accountable for advocating sodomy of young boys on the Internet. Yet, after Shepard's murder by two thugs (who were neither Christian nor conservative), ACLU supporters have been among the many left-wing voices loudly calling for "hate-crimes" legislation[14] that could criminalize and punish speech that does not affirm homosexual behavior.* That type of speech, in the ACLU's view, is dangerous, and they have been strangely silent in many efforts across America to outlaw or silence various forms of speech.

NAMBLA, on the other hand, proudly posts materials on its Web site that advocate sexual relations with young boys. The ACLU believes that this material should be permitted and protected even though it openly promotes the sodomy with and rape of young boys. Yet, according to the ACLU, individuals such as the Christian leaders mentioned earlier, who do not promote or induce any form of violence, are responsible for the reprehensible actions of others.

The ACLU admits in one of its papers that "freedom of speech does not prevent punishing conduct that intimidates, harasses, or threatens another person, even if words are used."[15] Yet, the ACLU defends NAMBLA's "freedom of speech" that does just that. It looks like the ACLU is talking from both sides of its mouth.†

But cases such as the one involving NAMBLA and its support by the ACLU are happening not only in Massachusetts. At the time of this writing, the case is still pending in the Massachusetts court system. The ACLU has an established record of defending those that exploit children, at the expense of the safety of America's children.

---

*As we have seen in Canada, hate-crimes and similar legislation eventually leads to the suppression and criminalization of any speech critical of homosexual behavior, including sincerely held religious speech. On April 28, 2004, the Canadian Parliament passed Bill C-250, which could classify certain portions of the Bible that deal with homosexual behavior as "hate speech" with criminal penalties. The Canadian Bible Society put out repeated warnings that the bill could have a chilling effect on religious freedom and evangelism in Canada. Janet Epp of the Buckingham Evangelical Fellowship of Canada said, "Pastors are afraid. They're afraid to preach on this subject. Nobody wants to have the police come to the door." The bill, which added "sexual orientation" to Canada's hate-propaganda law, passed by a vote of 59–11. The bill reads, "Every one, who by communicating statements, other than in private conversation, willfully promotes hatred against an identifiable group, is guilty of an indictable offense and is liable to imprisonment for a term not exceeding two years." In addition, in Saskatchewan, Christians have *already been fined* for placing a newspaper ad presenting the biblical position on sexual behavior. The ACLU has been silent about the fines.

†The ACLU's absence from lawsuits challenging the Free Access to Clinics Entrances (FACE) legislation, used to curtail pro-life advocates from communicating the truth about abortion, is duly noted.

As discussed earlier, the ACLU opposes prosecution of those who distribute and sell child pornography. Alan, in his previous service as the director of the Attorney General's Commission on Pornography, has called child pornography "crime scene photos" because they cannot be produced without the actual sexual abuse of a child. He believes it is essential that Americans understand exactly what the ACLU seeks to "protect."

In Iowa, the ACLU played an instrumental role in striking down a law that prohibited convicted sex offenders from living within two thousand feet of schools and day-care centers.[16]

In Lafayette, Indiana, the ACLU defended an alleged pedophile convicted *three* times of molesting children! This was an active pedophile. After he had been released from jail the third time, the sex offender openly talked in a group therapy session about going to a local park to fantasize about having sex with the young children innocently playing there.[17]

The mayor of Lafayette, out of legitimate concern for the city's children, had the city attorney seek a restraining order to stop the convicted molester from "cruising" parks for life. Sure enough, the ACLU found a sympathetic court to agree that the actions of the mayor and the city attorney discriminated against the alleged pedophile. In a 2–1 decision, the Seventh Circuit Court of Appeals ruled that the city could not bar the offender from the public park, regardless of the potential endangerment to the children there. The ACLU attorney who opposed the city said, "These cases are symptomatic of what sort of discrimination follows people around."[18]

Paul Walfield, an attorney in California, expressed his dismay over the ACLU's actions: "Imagine that, convicted pedophiles who cruise city parks in search of children are 'discriminated' against because decent people who want to protect their children get a restraining order to stop one in particular who literally admitted to his vile intentions. . . . The ACLU decided that a pedophile's right to pursue his dreams was more important than the harm child molesters could cause to kindergartners."

Walfield continued, "If we don't look out for our kids now, their fates will be up to the likes of the ACLU. No one wants that. After all, how do you explain the court's ruling to the parents of the pedophile's next victim, let alone to the parents of little children who had been molested by him, that the monster is now free to 'cruise' playgrounds once again?"[19]

While our judicial system rightfully provides individuals, such as this convicted offender, with defense representation, the problem is the ACLU goes out of its way to protect this vile, damaging conduct—and in this case, enable and even perhaps agree with aspects of it. If the ACLU did not have a stake in defending such conduct, it would just allow the case to fall to a criminal defense attorney. This is another example of how the ACLU's view of autonomy is seemingly limitless.

The ACLU and the Boy Scouts

While the ACLU is defending sex offenders, pedophiles, and pedophilic organizations, it is legally attacking institutions such as the one-hundred-year-old Boy Scouts of America, whose goal and effective track record is to train boys to become mature, responsible citizens. As Deroy Murdock wrote in *National Review* online, "The ACLU has offered material support to those who openly preach pedophilia and arguably encourage kidnapping, rape, and murder. Yet this legal group is energetically hostile to an organization that tries to turn boys into men, with sex alien to the process."[20]

Here is a short list of famous Eagle Scouts (the highest rank attainable within the Boy Scout organization) to give an idea of how well the Scouts perform their mission to mold young boys into strong male leaders:

- Former U.S. Senator and Secretary of the Treasury Lloyd Bentsen Jr.
- Former U.S. Senator Bill Bradley
- Former NASA astronaut James Lovell
- U.S. Senator Richard Lugar
- Former U.S. Senator Sam Nunn
- Former President Gerald Ford
- Secretary of Defense Donald Rumsfeld
- Dr. William DeVries (the first man to transplant an artificial heart)[21]

That is quite an impressive (and bipartisan) list. As Scouts work toward the rank of Eagle, they must be involved in service projects, set goals, and show leadership skills—all things that develop young boys into responsible adults.[22]

So why has the ACLU attacked the Boy Scouts? Because the Scouts will not allow those who openly practice homosexual behavior to be Scoutmasters for teenage boys.[23] The Scouts oppose those who advocate sexual behavior between men from holding leadership positions and refuse to provide them an opportunity to advocate such behavior to impressionable preteen and teenage boys. And, despite claims to the contrary, there is a strong documented link between homosexual behavior and sexual abuse of underage boys and teenagers.* This link is evident to most people aware of the tragic incidents that occurred among a small, but very active, minority of priests within some Roman Catholic dioceses in America.

As it usually does, the ACLU has spun this discernment as discrimination. It is anything but that. Parents rely on the Boy Scouts to protect their young boys and to help mold them into young men of character and leadership. Therefore, it is common sense that the Boy Scouts have safeguards to keep young boys out of harm's way.

The Scouts are aware of this responsibility. Lee Sneath, a national spokesman for the Boy Scouts, said, "As an organization that stresses the values of the family, we believe that homosexuals do not provide the proper role model for youth membership" and added that the Scouts "provide a natural hunting ground for pedophiles."[24]

Columnist David Kupelian echoed this sentiment: "The Scouting folks know what everyone with half a brain understands: that adults interested in sexual contact with young people gravitate toward careers and volunteer positions allowing proximity to their prey, positions such as coaches, teachers, scoutmasters—and priests."[25]

NAMBLA actually wrote a letter to the national office of the Scouts asking them to "cease [their] discrimination against openly gay or lesbian persons in the appointment of its scoutmasters and

---

*A 1992 study by researchers K. Freud and R. I. Watson found that homosexual males are three times more likely than heterosexual males to engage in acts of sexual behavior with boys and that the average pedophile has sex with 20 to 150 boys before he is caught. (See K. Freud and R. I. Watson, "The Proportions of Heterosexual and Homosexual Pedophiles among Sex Offenders against Children: An Exploratory Study," *Journal of Marital Therapy*, vol. 34, 1992, 34–43.) A 1988 study found that 86 percent of pedophiles identified themselves as either homosexual or bisexual. (See W. D. Erickson and others, "Behavior Patterns of Child Molesters," *Archives of Sexual Behavior*, vol. 17, 1988.)

scouters and in its membership. This will permit scouts to be exposed to a variety of life styles and will permit more of those individuals who genuinely wish to serve boys to do so."[26]

Sadly, the Scouts have had to deal with some tragic real-life examples when those with less than pure motives become Scoutmasters. One of Craig's scoutmasters, for example, eventually confessed to sexually molesting young boys. In May 2005, it was revealed that the mayor of Spokane, Washington, Jim West, had allegedly used his position as a former sheriff's deputy, a Scout leader, and as mayor to obtain sexual relationships with boys and young men.[27]

One of the young boys that was allegedly molested, Richard Galliher, claimed in a court disposition that the mayor had molested him in the 1970s when West was a Boy Scout leader. A second man, Michael G. Grant Jr., also came forward with allegations that he had been abused by West at Boy Scout camp.[28] Another Scout leader in Spokane committed suicide after being alleged to have sexually abused young boys.[29]

Grant said, "Jim West came to where our camp was. He asked me to come back to his camper he had at the campgrounds. I told him I didn't want to go. He told me I need to come with him. He molested me in the camper. He sodomized me. I was told [by West] if I was to tell anybody, that he will kill my mom . . . that she would exist no more."[30]

West's alleged actions were finally uncovered when a forensic computer expert discovered that West had been using his position as mayor to entice and influence young men he met on a homosexual Web site. This matter was still pending as the book went to press.

Regardless of these tragic occurrences, the ACLU continues to use every legal method possible to punish and cripple the Scouts for not allowing practicing homosexuals to be Scoutmasters, while also attempting to rid the Scouts of any adherence to religious faith and a code of moral values.

The ACLU's legal war against the Boy Scouts has been going on for more than twenty years. In 1980, seventeen-year-old Scout Timothy Curran took a male "date" to the senior prom. After a photo of him with his date was printed in the *Oakland Tribune*, his local Boy Scout council told him he could not continue in Scouting because of the organization's policy that "homosexuality and Boy Scouting are not compatible." With the help of the ACLU, Curran sued the Boy Scouts, seeking an injunction to prevent them from taking away his membership and prohibiting him from being a troop leader.[31] The case went on for *seventeen years.*

After losing at the superior court level, the ACLU appealed the decision, and it was reversed.[32] The case went to the California Supreme Court, which agreed with the Boy Scouts and held that California's Civil Rights Act did not apply to membership decisions of the Boy Scouts.[33]

The ACLU was also involved in *Boy Scouts of America vs. Dale* (2000), by submitting a friend-of-the-court brief to the Supreme Court on behalf of a homosexual assistant Scoutmaster. In *Dale,* the Boy Scouts revoked the adult membership of assistant Scoutmaster James Dale, when in a published newspaper article he announced his involvement in homosexual behavior. In a 5–4 decision, the Supreme Court held that the First Amendment right of expressive association permitted the Boy Scouts to exclude the homosexual Scoutmaster.[34] But the ACLU warned ominously: "The days of the Boy Scouts' discriminatory policies are numbered."[35] These actions are from the organization whose founder Roger Baldwin stated, "The ACLU is a private organization. . . . And a private organization is like a church. You don't take nonbelievers into the church. We are a church; we have a creed and only true believers should lead us" (see p. 18). So much for equal treatment.

When the ACLU loses in court, in a case like *Dale,* it doesn't merely go away. It redoubles its efforts to demonize, intimidate, and silence those who do not succumb to its agenda.

Keeping those who engage in homosexual behavior from membership is strike 1 for the Boy Scouts in the ACLU's game. Strike 2 is not allowing girls to be members, even though they can join the Girl Scouts. (In 1991, the ACLU expressed interest in representing several girls from Quincy, California, who sought to join the Boy Scouts.)[36] Strike 3 is the Boy Scout oath and law that requires its members to believe in a supreme being.

The oath is as follows: "On my honor I will do my best to do my duty to God and my country and to obey the Scout Law; to help other people at all times; to keep myself physically strong, mentally awake, and morally straight."

The twelfth item in the Scout law states, "A Scout is reverent toward God. He is faithful in his religious duties. He respects the beliefs of others."[37]

The Boy Scout oath and law are nonsectarian. A Scout can be Christian, Jewish, or of another religion, but some form of religious belief in God is one of the basic tenets of Scouting. Of course, the ACLU believes this is discrimination against atheists and those who are nonreligious. Thus, the ACLU has legally attacked the Scouts on both fronts (homosexual behavior and religion) to force them to surrender their core beliefs and adhere to the ACLU's instead.

This legal attack has taken many forms. Here are a few examples:

In 1991, the ACLU filed a lawsuit against the Scouts on behalf of a father for his atheist twins because of the Scout oath.[38] The California Supreme Court eventually ruled in favor (on the same day as the *Curran* decision) of the Scouts.[39]

Since 1957, the Scouts have leased an eighteen-acre city parcel at Balboa Park in San Diego. The Scouts pay a nominal amount of money to the city for the parcel, and in return the Scouts have made numerous improvements to the property and have built an excellent campground site for all members of the community to use.[40] In 1987, the city leased another half-acre parcel to the Scouts at Mission Bay Park. The Scouts spent millions of dollars to build an aquatic center, which, again, is open to the public on a first-come, first-serve basis.

Then the ACLU got involved. It sued the city on behalf of a lesbian couple and an agnostic couple who had sons of Scouting age. Neither son (nor the parents) had been excluded from using the facilities. Moreover, the parents and the sons had not tried to become Scoutmasters or Scouts. Nevertheless, in July 2003, federal district court Judge Napoleon Jones ruled that the Boy Scouts "displays intolerance towards individuals who identify themselves as homosexual, agnostic, or atheist by denying them membership to or revoking the membership of gay and nonbelieving individuals. [The Scouts'] strongly held, private, discriminatory beliefs are at odds with values requiring tolerance and inclusion in the public realm."[41]

Peter Ferrara of the Scouting Legal Defense Fund said, "What the ACLU seeks now is something quite different. It is pursuing the vilification and marginalization of those who adhere to traditional morality."[42]

Hans Zeiger, a twenty-year-old Eagle Scout, added, "It is ironic that the ACLU is questioning the Scouts for practicing character and moral virtue on public lands, while the ACLU is occupying public courthouses around America, pulling down every vestige of decency in sight. One might say there is 'overwhelming and uncontradicted evidence' that the ACLU is destroying America, one Boy Scout camp at a time."[43]

Not only were the Scouts thrown out of the park when the city council caved, but the ACLU received an award of $950,000 of taxpayer dollars for legal fees and court costs from the city of San Diego. While the Boy Scouts are still appealing the decision to remove them from the park, the city basically has sold them out to the ACLU.[44] This came to the attention of Fox News talk-show host Bill O'Reilly, who had this to say:

Another big win for the American Civil Liberties Union. . . . The nation's most dangerous organization sued the city of San Diego for renting property to the Boy Scouts. The ACLU said the Scouts discriminated against gays and atheists, therefore the city cannot do business with them.

Even before any ruling in this absurd situation was made, the San Diego City Council voted 6–2 to throw the Scouts out. And they also agreed to give the ACLU a mil-
· lion bucks of taxpayer money.*

The mayor of San Diego, Dick Murphy, is outraged and we all should be. First of all, the Supreme Court has ruled the Scouts have a legal right to select membership based upon the scouting charter. So legally, the Scouts were in the right. But even if you disagree with the Supreme Court ruling, there are practical considerations.

---

*O'Reilly rounded the figure.

It would be impossible for the Boy Scouts or any children's organization to admit avowed homosexuals because of the potential liability. Say the Scouts put openly gay and straight kids together and some sexual activity occurred. Well, parents could sue for millions, same way parents could sue if the Scouts put boys and girls together and underaged sex occurred.

As far as the atheist issue is concerned, the Scouts say no specific belief in God is necessary, only an acknowledgement of a higher power. And that power could be nature. Come on. The whole discrimination thing is bogus.

What's really going on here is that the ACLU doesn't like the Boy Scouts and wants that organization damaged. And they've succeeded with the cowardice of the San Diego City Council.

Now the ACLU is free to come to your town and sue the heck out of it. And believe me, that organization will. The ACLU doesn't care about the law or the Constitution or what the people want. It's a fascist organization that uses lawyers instead of Panzers. It'll find a way to inflict financial damage on any concern that opposes its secular agenda and it's growing in power.

Right now, there's only one legal organization set up to fight the ACLU: the Alliance Defense Fund based in Phoenix, Arizona. Unless private citizens and lawyers in every state organize to counter this agenda driven machine, you'll see more San Diegos. This is just the beginning.

Once again, the American Civil Liberties Union is the most dangerous outfit in the USA today. Its defense of the North American Man/Boy Love Association in Massachusetts is all you need to know. . . . this is a freedom issue. And your freedom is in jeopardy.[45]

Later in the program, O'Reilly had ADF senior counsel Jordan Lorence on the program to discuss the San Diego case. Jordan reiterated that this was just another example of the ACLU's use of intimidation, disinformation, and fear to bully public officials and others into submission to its agenda. Lorence put it bluntly: "This decision allows the

ACLU to go to other cities and say you better cave in or we are going to sue."[46] That is exactly what the ACLU does—time and time again.

The ACLU has also gone after the Scouts for having a recruiting presentation in a Portland, Oregon, public school during school hours. Schools and state officials were ordered to pay $108,000—once again in taxpayer dollars—to the ACLU. ACLU attorneys argued that the "district discriminated against atheists by allowing the Boy Scouts to recruit during school hours."[47]

In Chicago, the ACLU filed a lawsuit against the city, demanding that it end public support for Scouting programs. The city caved in. Roger Leishman, director of the ACLU's Gay and Lesbian Rights Project, said, "All Chicago citizens benefit from the city's decision to drop its support for scouting programs rather than attempt to defend the Boy Scouts' discriminatory policies. We are hopeful that other state and local governments that support [the] BSA will take a cue from Chicago's action and end their sponsorship of these discriminatory programs."[48]

Is it really true, as the ACLU asserts, that all "citizens benefit" when the character-forming efforts of the Scouts are booted from public facilities? Perhaps the ACLU lawyers should pay a visit to the inner cities of our nation. They will see that it is children, specifically young boys, who lose in the ACLU's relentless campaign against the Scouts. The Scouts have been able to make a significant positive impact on troubled boys in poor urban neighborhoods.[49] When local governments cave into the ACLU, or the courts rule against the Scouts, these boys with few economic options lose one more opportunity for moral guidance and life skill training they so desperately need.

Jim Trageser, a columnist for the *North County Times* (a San Diego area newspaper), wrote about the Balboa Park case:

> [It's hard] to see how kicking the Scouts out of Balboa Park is going to help the kids—the many low-income (often minority) boys for whom the Scouts provide desperately needed leadership and growth opportunities. For many of these boys, a Scout camp may be their first interaction with nature. . . . It may be their first chance to be allowed to make decisions in a safe environment—to be allowed to make mistakes without any real-world repercussions. . . .

If the Scouts must go, then the rest of us—those of us concerned with the future of Latino and African-American men in our culture—ought to demand that the ACLU and its supporters help us provide an acceptable alternative. . . .

But the ACLU's record of championing the cause of black and Latino males isn't a pretty one. When Latino and black families try to break the grip of gangs on their neighborhoods, their families, and their own sons, the ACLU says no, gangs have rights, too. . . .

The Boy Scouts may not be perfect, but when it comes to investing in a positive future for minority and low-income boys, they're way ahead of the ACLU.[50]

But these contributions to the betterment of a community seemingly mean little to the ACLU. As Trageser said, the relentless demands of their agenda trumps the welfare of young boys. Rich Lowry wrote, "This squeeze [by the ACLU and its allies] on charitable giving [for the Scouts] will hurt most those poor urban kids who can't afford things like their own uniforms. Little do such kids know that in wanting to develop their character and skills, they are committing, by extension, alleged acts of bigotry. They are among the 1 million American boys who are collateral damage in the anti-Scout blitzkrieg."[51]

In San Luis Obispo, California, the ACLU went after the Scouts' leases of public facilities and government land. The ACLU press release said, "The ACLU believes that government should not subsidize organizations that exclude some youth and families—those who are religious non-believers, gay or lesbian, and also those who do not want their children to participate in an organization that teaches religious intolerance and homophobia."[52]

Ben Boychuk of the Claremont Institute summed up the ACLU's legal attacks succinctly: "The ACLU holds that the government should not 'help' the Boy Scouts. Under this logic, a Scout would be precluded from helping an old lady across the street because that street is supported by tax dollars."

He continued:

The ACLU will not stop its war against the Scouts until they interpret that oath the ACLU way, define diversity the

ACLU way, and accept as members those whom the ACLU
deems acceptable. Perhaps only when the ACLU creates
the merit badges will the campaign end. In a sense, though,
this campaign of legal harassment is just another step for an
ACLU that now marches more than symbolically with the
Nazis and the North American Man/Boy Love Association.
What it is doing is just an extension of its plastic self-serving
reading of the Constitution and American law. Only now,
the ACLU has moved from interpreting the Constitution
to serve its social engineering whims to working directly on
the beliefs of institutions that dare to think differently from
their politically correct lawyers.[53]

The latest salvos from the ACLU are a letter they sent to the
Boy Scouts, threatening to take legal action against any public school
or other taxpayer-funded government agency that charters a Scout
troop, and getting the Pentagon to agree to start warning military
bases not to sponsor Scout troops. The last action was the result of a
lawsuit that had been brought by the ACLU of Illinois.[54]

The Pentagon's decision to cave into the ACLU's demands raised
the ire of the American Legion, the nation's largest veteran's organization. In a letter to Secretary of Defense Donald Rumsfeld, American
Legion National Commander Thomas P. Cadmus wrote: "The idea
that sponsorship of Scouting by American military units is 'unconstitutional' goes beyond the absurd, even well past the point of stupidity."

He continued: "How is it the government can fund chapels on
military bases, and chaplains in the military [even though the ACLU
would like to go after those too—the authors], but not accommodate
Scouting? Why is it that the rank of Eagle Scout is an attribute highly
sought in candidates for military academies, but will soon become
unwelcome on military bases? How is it that Congress can sanction
Scouting by issuing them a federal charter, but the courts can declare
them outlaws? . . . Stand up to the ACLU. Find a way to give those
who serve our nation the chance to serve our children."[55]

Nat Hentoff, a former ACLU board member who became aghast
at much of what he saw, commented that the ACLU, which claims
to believe in the Constitution, has conveniently ignored the Supreme
Court precedent when it comes to the Scouts. He wrote:

The national ACLU, in one of its excursions into extreme political correctness, opposed the Boy Scouts when *Boy Scouts of America vs. Dale* (in which the U.S. Supreme Court held that the First Amendment right of expressive association permitted the Boy Scouts to exclude ["out of the closet"] homosexual scoutmasters) went before the Supreme Court. In doing so, the ACLU, which was founded to protect the First Amendment, ignored Supreme Court precedents. One such precedent states, "The First Amendment guarantees the . . . freedom to associate or not to associate." It is this "freedom to identify the people who constitute the association to those people only.". . . Should the NAACP be forced by the courts or by the ACLU to allow adherents of white racist organizations to take leadership positions in the NAACP? Should disability rights groups be compelled to have disciples of Dr. Jack Kevorkian in leadership roles?[56]

The ACLU's treatment of the Boy Scouts is only another example of how it is pushing to force all organizations, including the church, to ultimately bow to its ideological agenda. If an evangelical Christian, a devout Roman Catholic, or an Orthodox Jew who believes that homosexual behavior is sinful demanded a leadership position in a homosexual behavior advocacy group like the Human Rights Campaign, or a pro-life advocate had sued to be an officer in Planned Parenthood, or the ACLU itself, it is almost certain that the ACLU would either be silent or would defend the right of those organizations or itself to determine their leadership and members.

William Donohue, a longtime student of the ACLU, summed up the real agenda behind the ACLU's (and its allies) continued legal attack against the Scouts, writing:

Coercion is the means of choice of the cultural elite. It seeks to seize the legal arsenal of the state and impose on society a set of rules and regulations that run contrary to existing mores. Whether the issue is speech codes on college campuses, crèches on public property, racial quotas in the workplace, male-only clubs or mother-daughter dinners, the coercive thrust of political correctness is evident. Its motto is not "Inclusiveness or Bust," but "Inclusiveness or Else."

Since the rank-and-file that constitute the American public are not, like the elite, alienated from the traditional American culture—since, in fact, they are resistant to radical social change—the elite must work its will from the top down, using the club of the law. And no one knows better how to swing this club than the American Civil Liberties Union.[57]

This seems to flip on its head what Roger Baldwin learned from Emma Goldman in the founding days of the ACLU. Instead of freedom from coercion by the state,[58] the ACLU is now the master of using the state and its power-hungry courts to force coercion on those that do not agree with their agenda.

In another example of ACLU duplicity, Donohue mentioned that the ACLU had ejected a man named Ronald Long from one of its public meetings when he was identified as an off-duty police officer. According to Donohue, the ACLU was violating the very California statute about public accommodations that it used against the Boy Scouts. If the Boy Scouts physically remove someone who practices homosexual behavior or is an agnostic from one of their meetings, they can almost be assured the ACLU would be there with a lawsuit immediately.

This again illustrates how the ACLU wants one set of rules for itself and dictates other rules for everyone else. As Roger Baldwin acknowledged, he wanted only "true believers" to lead the ACLU.[59] Other private organizations, like the Boy Scouts, are merely asking to have that same right.

Donohue wrote, "The moral is clear: Because Mr. Long was not a member of a special group with special rights—whether criminals, atheists, homosexuals, or a racial or ethnic minority—he was judged by these 'civil libertarians' to have no rights."[60]

Ben Boychuk of the Claremont Institute agreed:

The ACLU does not tend to hire deeply religious Americans who believe that a prayer before a football game is a sign of free devotion. The ACLU excludes Americans who believe in the original intent and law of the Constitution. The ACLU actively discriminates against judges who oppose judicial activism. But under the Bill of Rights, that band of lawyers can gather based on their shared beliefs without fear of reprisal from the government—or from the Boy Scouts, as far as that goes. The Boy Scouts teach young men to respect the law, help the unfortunate, give to the community, and respect and preserve the nation's vast natural resources. Boy Scouts learn the consequences of their actions and the moral worth of teamwork. No matter. The ACLU wants all-out war. . . .[61]

Sadly, the victims of that war could be millions of young boys and men who will no longer have the opportunity to learn the strong moral values and life skill training that the Boy Scouts offer. The boys in the inner cities, who need positive role models and guidance, will suffer from the ACLU's war on the Boy Scouts. The ACLU will continue to trumpet its "wins" as "victories" for society. In the end, children will be the ones who pay the price of defeat if the ACLU wins its legal battle against the Scouts.

When it comes to children, the ACLU has no problem defending those who seek to sexually exploit children or profit from it—putting the children directly in harm's way—while denying organizations such as the Boy Scouts the opportunity to protect children from potential danger and raise them to be good citizens with strong morals and values.

Making America Safe for Pornographers and Dangerous for Children

As we discussed earlier, the ACLU has legally fought virtually all efforts to shield children from exposure to pornography at public libraries, through the U.S. mail, and through other outlets.

The ACLU has filed numerous lawsuits against parents who have fought to have Internet filtering software employed at local libraries to protect young children from being exposed to hard-core pornography. For the ACLU, the right to view pornography leaves no room for realistic, common sense actions taken to protect children from material that can harm them. As the NAMBLA case demonstrated, the ACLU puts its agenda before the well-being, and in some cases, the *very lives* of children.*

Whenever parents lose a case against the ACLU in the battle to protect their children from Internet pornography, the ACLU issues a press release calling it a great victory for the First Amendment and families. After a court dismissed a concerned parent's case against the Livermore, California, Public Library, Ann Brick, staff attorney with the northern California ACLU, said, "The library's policy is sensitive both to First Amendment concerns and the concerns of parents. It enables each family to be sure that its children use the Internet in a manner that is consistent with its own values without imposing those values on other families."[62]

Think about that statement for a moment as we paint this scenario.

A fourth-grade boy goes to the local library with his mother to do a research project on the White House. While his mother goes to another section of the library, he goes to a computer terminal—not noticing the signs—or unaware what the terms "filtered" and "unfiltered" mean.† He mistakenly types www.whitehouse.com, instead of www.whitehouse.gov to get the information he needs. He has no idea that www.whitehouse.com (at least until a few months ago) is a hard-core porn site. The boy is immediately exposed to some of the vilest material available on the Internet, and his mother has no idea this happened.

What makes this scenario even more troubling is what Alan found when he served on the Attorney General's Commission on Pornography in the mid-1980s: Regular pornography use can often lead to subsequent anti-social and destructive behaviors, and it often starts with accidental exposure during the childhood years.

With the ACLU's policy on Internet filters at public libraries, parents either have to stand over the shoulder of their child every minute or require the child to do research at home. This alternative affects lower- and middle-class families who often do not have the means or technical know-how to purchase home computers and filtering software and must rely on public libraries for access to the Internet.

---

*In many cases, tax-funded public libraries do not even have "filtered" and "unfiltered" terminal choices. A child can access hard-core pornography from *any* computer.

†In 1999, a Phoenix man attempted to molest a young child at the city library after viewing pornography there.

Even when the ACLU has "compromised" and allowed public libraries to have filtered and unfiltered computer terminals, it has stated that children do not need parental consent before using an unfiltered terminal, allowing them to access hard-core pornography without parental knowledge.[63]

ADF helped win a significant victory against the ACLU and its allies in the Supreme Court case *United States vs. American Library Association;* the Court ruled Congress can require public libraries that receive federal funds to provide Internet filters on computers to protect children. It took three trips to the U.S. Supreme Court to get this favorable ruling for children.[64]

But as always, that does not mean the ACLU has given up. In a memo to its affiliates after this decision, Chris Hansen and Ann Beeson of the ACLU wrote:

> The ACLU remains very interested in this subject. We hope that affiliates monitor their area and find out what is happening. . . . We are contemplating further litigation. Libraries that refuse to unblock or turn off unblocking software (at least for adults) or make unblocking onerous are obvious potential defendants. . . . First and most importantly, libraries should consider turning down the federal funds and refusing [sic] to install blocking software. Obviously, that is our first preference. Libraries should also lobby at the local, state, and federal level to repeal blocking software requirements [and] establish a policy for dealing with minors. We think it is clear that libraries can unblock wrongly blocked sites for anyone.[65]

"Libraries are our nation's storehouses of knowledge," said Ann Brick of the northern California ACLU. "Their mission is to make that knowledge available to young and old alike. Filters are fundamentally antithetical to that mission."[66]

If the ACLU has its way, our public libraries will be more like storehouses for pornography, rather than for useful knowledge. Again, children are used as pawns in the ACLU's clamor for rights beyond anything that the framers of the Constitution and subsequent generations could have ever conceived.

Where can this mind-set lead? When a child gains access to pornographic material—without parental knowledge—it can lead to tragedy. Consider the case of *Herzog vs. Hustler Magazine* (1987) which was litigated during Alan's time in the Reagan administration as executive director of the pornography commission. (Warning: The following information is explicit.)

In its August 1981 issue, *Hustler* magazine featured an article on autoerotic asphyxia or the practice of partially hanging oneself while masturbating to temporarily cut off the blood supply at the moment of orgasm. The article discussed in detail how to perform this dangerous but allegedly exciting and enhancing act.

While *Hustler* did put text on the first page of the article that read, "Hustler emphasizes the often-fatal dangers of the practice of 'auto-erotic asphyxia' and recommends that readers seeking unique forms of sexual release do not attempt this method. The facts are presented here solely for an educational purpose."

One of the major claims used for the defense of hard-core pornography by criminal defense attorneys, the ACLU, and pornographers is "educational value" (do the materials do anything other than teach hate, rape, and disdain for other human beings?).[67] The warning in *Hustler* was like putting an "adults only" sign on a computer terminal that has free and unlimited public access to Internet pornography. It technically may be a warning, but it is hardly even a "slow" sign for a curious child.

A fourteen-year-old boy obtained a copy of the *Hustler* magazine, read the article, and like a lot of teenage boys do, decided to experiment with what he learned to attempt autoerotic asphyxia. The next morning, one of his closest friends, another young boy, found his buddy's nude and lifeless body suspended by his neck in his closet. A copy of *Hustler* magazine, open to the page of instructions, was found near the young boy's feet.

The mother of the dead boy, along with the friend, sued *Hustler*, to recover damages for emotional and psychological harm they had suffered as a result of the boy's death. After an initial ruling in federal district court in favor of the mother and friend, *Hustler* appealed the case to the U.S. Circuit Court of Appeals for the Fifth Circuit, which reversed the ruling. Despite the harsh facts, Supreme

Court precedent was cited as protecting *Hustler* from liability, and several ACLU-supported cases were cited that laid the foundation for this decision.*[68]

Although we may never know all the details about how this young boy acquired a copy of *Hustler* magazine, we do know that cities across America have tried to enact protections for children against pornography, only to be challenged in court by the ACLU and its pornographer allies. Communities have tried to restrict the sale and display of pornographic materials as "harmful to minors" but have faced costly lawsuits brought by the ACLU and its allies to strike down any laws that would shield minors from such materials. The ACLU, which claims parents should be the only limit on pornography, ties the hands of parents when it comes to being able to effectively keep their children from being exposed to such material.

In addition to refusing to protect children from Internet pornography at public libraries, the ACLU believes, as stated in its policy guide and noted earlier, there should be no restrictions on the distribution of child pornography.[69] In both scenarios, children are hopelessly and shamefully exploited.

In *New York vs. Ferber* (see chap. 1), the ACLU submitted a friend-of-the-court brief to the U.S. Supreme Court, arguing that child pornography is protected by the First Amendment. Thankfully, the Supreme Court affirmed that child pornography does not have such protection.[70] When Alan served on the Attorney General's Commission on Pornography, he heard the ACLU's national legislative counsel testify that all such material, once created, is fully protected by the First Amendment. The ACLU added that no government should be allowed to limit the distribution of child pornography between "consenting adults."

Dr. James Dobson, child psychologist, founder of Focus on the Family, and cofounder of ADF, served as a commissioner on the commission with Alan. In the commission's final report, Dobson

---

*Among the ACLU-backed precedents cited were *New York Times vs. Sullivan*, 376 U.S. 254, and *Brandenburg vs. Ohio*, 395 U.S. 444. See *Herceg vs.* Hustler *Magazine*, 814 F.2d 1017, (5th Cir. 1987).

recounted one man's testimony (Warning: The following material is very explicit.):

I will never forget a particular set of photographs shown to us at our first hearing in Washington D.C. It focused on a cute, nine-year-old boy who had fallen into the hands of a molester. In the first picture, the blond lad was fully clothed and smiling at the camera. But in the second, he was nude, dead and had a butcher knife protruding from his chest. I served for 14 years as a member of a medical school faculty and thought I had seen it all. But my knees buckled and tears came to my eyes as these and hundreds of other photographs of children were presented . . . showing pitiful boys and girls with their rectums enlarged to accommodate adult males and their vaginas penetrated with pencils, tooth-brushes and guns. Perhaps the reader can understand my anger and disbelief when a representative for the American Civil Liberties Union testified a few minutes later. He ad-vocated the free exchange of pornography, *all* pornography, in the marketplace. He was promptly asked about material depicting children such as those we had seen. This man said, with a straight face, that it is the ACLU's position that child pornography should not be produced, but once it is in exis-tence, there should be no restriction on its sale and distribu-tion. In other words, the photographic record of a child's molestation and abuse should be a legal source of profit for those who wish to reproduce, sell, print and distribute it for the world to see. And that, he said, was the intent of the First Amendment to the Constitution![71]

The ACLU fights against any form of constitutional protection for children who are sexually violated (and in some cases murdered) by those who take and distribute photos for profit and prurient in-terest of others. In his book *Twilight of Liberty*, William Donohue wrote, "Of the 49 recommendations the [Attorney General's Com-mission on Pornography] made on the subject of child pornography, the ACLU passed no judgment on four of them, found 19 acceptable, found 15 as posing 'substantial threats to civil liberties,' and declared 11 to be an 'inappropriate focus on the fruits of coercion and abuse,' as opposed to coercion itself. A sampling of the ACLU objections reveals a desire to crush the effective enforcement of the child pornography laws."[72]

It is ironic that the ACLU, which fights diligently for the distribution of sexually explicit photographs of young children, has fought hard against security cameras used to help stop or solve crime.[73] In the ACLU's world, sexually explicit photos of young children are allowed, but photos for legitimate law enforcement needs are not.

The Impact on Future Generations

What type of world will our children and grandchildren grow up in if the ACLU is able to achieve its legal agenda? That world would have three characteristics:

1. Organizations that build strong moral character, such as the Boy Scouts and religious organizations, will no longer be able to exist unless they compromise their core values and leadership criteria.
2. There will be *no* legal protections against the sexual exploitation of children, but laws will shield and protect those who seek to sexually exploit children.
3. All innocence will not merely be lost; it will be targeted for exploitation and even profit by adults. Children would be exposed to the vilest images at an early age—with parents legally helpless to stop it.

It could be easy to become depressed after reading how the ACLU's anything-goes agenda in the area of pornography is harming our children. There is a no more crucial area in which we need to stand up to the ACLU and say, "Enough!" That is exactly what ADF is doing.

In a case heard by the U.S. Supreme Court, ADF helped defend the First Amendment right (through the coordination of legal briefs) of the Boy Scouts to determine their leadership standards. ADF provided funding for the defendants in an earlier Supreme Court case that created a favorable precedent for the Boy Scouts to rely on. ADF continues the legal battle to require public libraries to provide common sense protections to shield children from Internet pornography. We are confident of many more victories in the courts that will provide parents the tools to protect their children from hard-core pornography and other exploitation. In addition, we will continue to play a role in defending online protection laws for children and similar laws at the lower court level, so they can return to the Supreme Court and ultimately be recognized as constitutional.

The ACLU's anti-children agenda can be stopped. But it will take years and years of sacrifice and perseverance, as it continues to file lawsuits and appeals to protect the "rights" of those who do not have the best interests of children in mind. ADF and our allies will be there, with God's grace, in each of those battles, so that children's innocence is once again protected and homes are secure.

CHAPTER 5

The ACLU vs. Human Life

*We must change the climate overall from one where abortion
providers are vilified and assaulted to one where they are honored and
upheld as the heroes they are.*[1]
—ACLU press release

*At this point I would rather have a right-wing Christian decide my
fate than an ACLU attorney.*[2]
— Eleanor Smith, a self-described liberal agnostic who is confined to a
wheelchair because of polio

*In all our wars combined 651,000 courageous Americans have died.
But forty-six million Americans, seventy-one times as many, have died
from court approved surgical abortion. That's fourteen million more
Americans than the entire population of Canada.*[3]
— Alan Sears, speaking at the 2005 National Day of Prayer

Warning: This chapter contains graphic material.

On March 21, 1996, Brenda Pratt Shafer, a registered nurse from
Ohio, was called to testify before a subcommittee of the U.S.
House of Representatives. This was not ordinary testimony. Shafer
had come to Capitol Hill that day to testify about a procedure called
partial-birth abortion. She testified to the following:

> In September 1993, [my employer] asked me to accept
> assignment at the Women's Medical Center, which is oper-
> ated by Dr. Martin Haskell. I readily accepted the assign-
> ment because I was at that time very pro-choice. I had even
> told my teenage daughters that if one of them ever got preg-
> nant at a young age, I would make them get an abortion. . . .

So, because of the strong pro-choice views that I held at
that time, I thought this assignment would be no problem
for me.

But I was wrong. I stood at a doctor's side as he performed the partial-birth abortion procedure—and what I
saw is branded forever on my mind. . . .

On the first day, we assisted in some first-trimester abortions, which is all I'd expected to be involved in. . . . On the
second day, I saw Dr. Haskell do a second-trimester procedure that is called a D&E (dilation and evacuation). He
used ultrasound to examine the fetus. Then he used forceps
to pull apart the baby inside the uterus, bringing it out piece
by piece and piece, throwing the pieces in a pan. . . .

On the third day, Dr. Haskell asked me to observe as he
performed several of the procedures that are the subject of
this hearing. Although I was in that clinic on assignment
of the agency, Dr. Haskell was interested in hiring me full
time, and I was being given orientation in the entire range of
procedures provided at that facility. . . .

The mother was six months pregnant. . . . A doctor told
her that the baby had Down's Syndrome and she decided
to have an abortion. . . . Dr. Haskell brought the ultrasound
in and hooked it up so that he could see the baby. On the
ultrasound screen, I could see the heart beating. . . .

Dr. Haskell went in with forceps and grabbed the baby's
legs and pulled them down into the birth canal. Then he
delivered the baby's body and the arms—everything but the
head. The doctor kept the baby's head just inside the uterus.

The baby's little fingers were clasping and unclasping,
and his feet were kicking. Then the doctor stuck the scissors
through the back of his head, and the baby's arms jerked
out in a flinch, a startle reaction, like a baby does when he
thinks he might fall.

The doctor opened up the scissors, stuck a high-powered
suction tube into the opening and sucked the baby's brains
out. Now the baby was completely limp. I was completely

unprepared for what I was seeing. I almost threw up as I watched the doctor do these things. . . .

Dr. Haskell delivered the baby's head. He cut the umbilical cord and delivered the placenta. He threw that baby back in the pan, along with the placenta and the instruments he'd used. I saw the baby move in the pan. I asked another nurse and she said it was just "reflexes." I have been a nurse for a long time and I have seen a lot of death—people maimed in auto accidents, gunshot wounds, you name it. I have seen surgical procedures of every sort. But in all my professional years, I had never witnessed anything like this.

The woman wanted to see her baby, so they cleaned up the baby and put it in a blanket and handed the baby to her. She cried the whole time, and she kept saying, "I'm so sorry, please forgive me!" I was crying too. I couldn't take it. That baby boy had the most perfect angelic face I have ever seen. . . .

Mr. Chairman, these people who say I didn't see what I saw—I wish they were right. I wish I hadn't seen it, and I will never be able to forget it. That baby boy was only inches, seconds away from being entirely born, when he was killed. What I saw done to that little boy, and those other babies, should not be allowed in this country.[4]

Unfortunately, this graphic and cruel procedure continues to happen "legally" on a daily basis in America, mainly because of the legal efforts of the ACLU and its abortion provider allies (which despite its claims of altruism makes tens of millions in profits each year)[5]* that have legally challenged *any* restriction on abortion, regardless of how barbaric or unhealthy the abortion procedure or who it's designed to protect. In addition, the ACLU and its allies have had a cooperative Supreme Court majority, which has agreed to most of their demands to keep all forms of abortion—no matter how cruel—legal. Before President George W. Bush signed legislation[6] barring what Shafer described

---

* Planned Parenthood earned an estimated $104 million from its surgical abortion business alone in 2004. See http://www.discoverthenetworks.org.

above, the ACLU promised to sue to overturn the proposed law, stating: "This bill is nothing more than a political power play by anti-choice lawmakers who are unabashed about endangering women's health in the pursuit of their extreme agenda."[7]

Yet, according to a 2003 Gallup poll, 68 percent of the public supported this "extreme agenda" (as the ACLU called the ban on partial-birth abortion in a press release) because this 68 percent supported a partial-birth abortion ban.[8] But again, the ACLU seldom has regard for the will of the people.

When President Bush finally signed legislation in 2003 that outlawed partial-birth abortion, the ACLU immediately promised to file a lawsuit to challenge the law.[9] And on June 1, 2004,[10] August 26, 2004,[11] and September 8, 2004,[12] they were successful because they found federal court judges in San Francisco,[13] New York,[14] and Nebraska[15] willing to strike down the ban. The final outcome on appeal is pending as this book goes to press.

But this is not surprising. Mary Meehan, who regards herself as a liberal and is head of Democrats for Life, writing in the *Human Life Review*, put it best when she stated, "When it comes to one group of victims, the ACLU fails to live up to this self-image. In its long and relentless campaign against the right to life of unborn children, it has violated its own traditions and principles in a radical way. . . . The defender of free speech helps ensure that millions of human beings will never have a chance to speak."[16]

Former ACLU board member Nat Hentoff, a self-proclaimed atheist who became pro-life after he witnessed firsthand the extremism of the ACLU and its allies on this issue, wrote: "For years, [ACLU] affiliates around the country invited me to speak at their fund-raising Bill of Rights dinners. But once I declared myself a pro-lifer, all such invitations stopped. They know I agree with them on most ACLU policies, but that no longer matters. I am now no better than Jesse Helms [former U.S. senator from North Carolina]. Free speech, after all, has its limits."[17]

The History of the ACLU and Abortion

The ACLU has a long history of advancing unrestricted access to abortion, right up to the moment of live birth. It played an influential role in *Griswold vs. Connecticut* (filing friend-of-the-court briefs and other activities),* *Doe vs. Bolton*, and *Roe vs. Wade*.[18] The ACLU stated in 1980, "Our litigation strategy has been to challenge every statute restricting reproductive freedom. . . . *In states where there are no lawyers willing to undertake these controversial cases, the entire litigation is conducted from the national office.*"[19]

On its Web site, the ACLU trumpets other victories against life. For instance, here is how the ACLU described its "victory" in *U.S. vs. Vuitch*, a key case in its legal battle to legalize abortion: "1971: *U.S. vs. Vuitch:* The Court's first abortion rights case, involving a doctor's appeal of his conviction for performing an illegal abortion. The Court upheld that constitutionality of the statute used to convict, but expanded the 'life and the health of the woman' concept to include psychological well-being, and ruled that the prosecution must prove the abortion was not necessary for a woman's physical or mental health."[20]

Vuitch was a pivotal case because it gave the ACLU and its pro-abortion allies the legal wording that has been used for the past thirty years to either strike down or weaken any law that would stop the most horrific forms of abortion, such as partial-birth abortion. In almost every case challenging partial-birth abortion laws, the ACLU trots out the "health of the mother" argument, which the Court expanded in concept far beyond physical health to the almost undefinable concept of mental health. Therefore, any legal restriction, no matter how reasonable or proper, on abortion is rendered almost meaningless if health-of-the-mother language is inserted. No concern is ever shown for the health of the affected child. This is why the ACLU or its allies file a lawsuit almost immediately when virtually every new law is passed, citing the health of the mother, because they know it will undermine the implementation or impact of the law.

This decision would be strengthened two years later in *Doe vs. Bolton*, another case in which the ACLU participated. The Court ruled, in the ACLU's words, "that whether an abortion is 'necessary'

---

*In an ADF prayer letter, Alan wrote: *"The justice who 'discovered' this 'right to privacy' [used in Griswold] said it existed in the 'emanations' from the 'penumbra' mystically hidden in the 3rd and 4th Amendments to the Constitution and between the 9th and 10th Amendments. Seriously! So what's a penumbra? A cloudy shadow over the moon! The court invoked this phony vibrating moonshadow 'right' in cases leading up to the infamous Roe vs. Wade decision."*

is the attending physician's call, to be made in light of all factors relevant to a woman's well-being."[21]

Among the chief "movers and shakers" behind the ACLU's unwavering support of abortion was Harriet Pilpel, a lawyer who was a devoted proponent of birth control and population control.[22] In a 1964 paper, Pilpel wrote that restrictions on birth control and abortion encouraged "multiplication of births among low income groups."[23] Like many of ACLU founder Roger Baldwin's friends and fellows years earlier, Pilpel demonstrated interest in eugenics, which is an effort to breed a "better human race" by suppressing the birthrate of the handicapped, poor, and minorities.[24]

Testifying on behalf of the New York Civil Liberties Union, Pilpel said that severely restricting abortion would place "an enormous economic burden on the country."[25] In 1969, Pilpel wrote an article titled "The Right of Abortion" in *The Atlantic Monthly*. She decried the lack of sterilization, especially among poor women. She wrote, "Little is done to make sterilization easily available on a voluntary basis, particularly to the poor and underprivileged."[26]

Mary Meehan said with regard to Pilpel's statements and example of ACLU duplicity, "Ironically, at the very time she said this, the ACLU was deeply involved in the civil rights movement, defending the rights of low-income African Americans."[27]

Following in the ACLU's strategy of using misinformation to advance its agenda, Pilpel used allegedly highly inflated numbers of "back alley" abortions and deaths, which helped sway public opinion toward the legalization of abortion. For instance, in a 1965 paper used by the ACLU to determine its abortion policy, Pilpel (and her coauthor William Kopit) said there were between 1 to 1.5 million abortions in the United States and more than 8,000 maternal deaths from those abortions each year.[28] Later research found that the number of abortions ranged from 39,000 in 1950 to 210,000 in 1961.[29] Government figures showed there were actually 197, not 8,000,— meaning she exaggerated by more than 700 percent—possible maternal deaths from illegal abortions in 1965, when Pilpel and Kopit wrote their paper.[30]

Dr. Bernard Nathanson, a former abortionist and advocate, said, "I confess that I knew the figures were totally false, and I suppose the others did too if they stopped to think of it. But in the morality of our revolution, it was a useful figure, widely accepted, so why go out of our way to correct it with honest statistics?"[31]

Apparently, this falsity did not matter to the ACLU's allies and those who advocated legalization of abortion. They continue to use some version of these false numbers to this day to defend practices such as partial-birth abortion.

Let's return to Pilpel. After Alan appeared on William F. Buckley's *Firing Line* in the 1980s, he traveled across Manhattan in a Town Car with Pilpel, who had appeared on the program with him. Over a couple hours' conversation, Alan was amazed at the pride she took in what she had accomplished. She asserted herself as the "godmother" of abortion and told Alan that the facts of the *Griswold vs. Connecticut* case were a setup. She continued to dismiss those who opposed the abortion agenda as "intellectual inferiors."

In 1968, the ACLU adopted its abortion policy, which remains virtually unchanged. Today's policy reads in part: "The ACLU asserts that a woman has a right to have an abortion—that is, a termination of pregnancy prior to the viability of the fetus—and that a licensed physician has a right to perform an abortion, without the threat of criminal sanctions. In pursuit of this right the Union asks that state legislatures abolish all laws imposing criminal penalties for abortions. The effect of this step would be that any woman could ask a doctor to terminate a pregnancy at any time."[32]*

As usual, there is duplicity in this statement. On one hand, the ACLU states abortions should occur only before viability. But on the other hand, it states if criminal penalties for abortions are abolished, a woman is free to get an abortion at anytime. Over the past thirty years, the ACLU has fought numerous attempts to restrict abortion after the time of viability, therefore contradicting the first part of its policy and demonstrating where it really stands: abortion anytime, anywhere, for any reason.

The statement continues: "The discriminatory effect of the prohibition of abortion involves another area of civil liberties interest,

---

*Despite the fact that most fetuses are viable by twenty-eight weeks, the ACLU advocates their death until they fully emerge from the birth canal.

that of equality. The rich can circumvent or violate the law with im-
punity, but the poor are at the law's mercy."[33]

This last statement, which has no more factual basis than many
other ACLU claims, is of interest considering the eugenics past of
Pilpel and others whose efforts contributed to formulating this policy. As we discussed in the first chapter, the ACLU often uses the
poor as pawns to advance its agenda, while demonstrating veiled contempt for them. For instance, in *Doe vs. Bolton*, the ACLU argued
that the Georgia law that restricted abortion resulted in 408 Caucasian women having hospital abortions, compared with 53 African-
American women.[34] Thus, taking the ACLU's argument to its logical conclusion, the problem was that not enough African-American
women were having abortions. In the 1969 article from *The Atlantic
Monthly*, Pilpel bemoaned the fact that only rich, white women could
afford to have abortions.[35]

In addition, the ACLU's math assumed an automatic economic
disparity between Caucasian and African-American women. It did
not take into account faith-based or other reasons why African-
American women would choose not to abort their children.

Mary Meehan wrote, "The eugenicists and population controllers
must have been delighted to see the ACLU put the gloss of rights and
freedom on abortion. It made their effort to suppress the birthrates of
poor people and minorities so much easier. Did ACLU leaders know
or care about that kind of agenda? Aryeh Neier, executive director of
the ACLU from 1970 to 1978, later referred to some African Americans' feeling that there were whites who were eager to eliminate or
limit the number of welfare mother babies out of an anti-black feeling
and that's why they were supporting abortion."[36]

Meehan cited a statement by Neier that backs this up. Neier said
in a 1979 interview, "There's no question that I dealt with some supporters of abortion who are very much in favor of abortion for exactly that reason."[37]

Meehan continued: "Taking chutzpah to new heights, ACLU activists suggested that the ones who were really anti-poor were the defenders of the unborn poor."[38] She referred to an ACLU fund-raising
letter that suggested that financing abortions for the poor was far less
expensive than paying the cost of childbirth and welfare support.[39]

This is basically saying that it's good financial stewardship to allow the government to pay for the killing of unborn children, especially minorities, rather than paying for their upbringing.

Armed with this new policy, the ACLU went to work to push for the legalization of abortion. In a December 1967 memo, ACLU staff member Eleanor Holmes Norton (who has most recently served six terms as representative to Congress from Washington, D.C.) wrote, "I think we should get hot on abortion."[40] The ACLU quickly filed several lawsuits. It first undermined the District of Columbia's abortion law. And while it did not singularly lead the charge for *Roe vs. Wade*, it helped establish the legal climate for it. *Roe* severely limited the ability of states to regulate abortion, even in the final trimester.

In 1985, the ACLU revisited its abortion policy to make it even more radical, conforming to the *Roe vs. Wade* standard.[41] One member of the ACLU committee on "reproductive rights" was worried about late-term abortions, but others stated that a woman had the "right to an abortion right up to the moment of live birth. According to ACLU committee minutes, Dr. Warren Hern, a notorious late-term abortionist, argued that a woman had a right to a "dead fetus."[42] Eventually, the committee recommended that every woman has a "right" to have an abortion at anytime during her pregnancy—by any method—with no viability restrictions.

The ACLU's contempt for human life goes *even further*. In his book *The Politics of the American Civil Liberties Union*, William Donohue wrote:

> There are some officials in the ACLU who not only believe that the unborn lack rights but regard the unborn as "stuff"—the kind of stuff that is sold at an auction. In June 1977 the Louisiana affiliate offered an abortion at its annual fund-raising auction. The price: $30. . . . The state director of the affiliate, Marlene Roeder, said she was surprised by the critical reaction to the abortion auction: "Abortions, after all, are legal, and it's as legitimate, in my perspective, for a woman to get an abortion as it is for someone to get a divorce or to bid on a legal defense for a D.W.I. [driving while intoxicated] or any of the other professional services we offer."[43]

In 1978, the ACLU challenged the policy of American Cyana-
mid, which did some work with toxic chemicals. The policy prohibited women in childbearing years from working in areas that would
expose them to these chemicals. This was a common sense prohibition to protect the health of any female employees' future children.
The ACLU filed a lawsuit against the company, stating that the policy
was discriminatory. William Donohue wrote, "The ACLU read the
policy and saw sexism clear and simple. It did not, or perhaps could
not, see that the policy was designed to protect the future rights of
children. No conflict of rights here, for the ACLU has no sympathy
for such policies and chooses to write them off by employing quota-
tion marks to indicate its position on 'fetal vulnerability.'"[44]

The ACLU's crusade against the unborn child even goes as far
as spying on pro-life elected officials, even to the point of violating
the very civil liberties it swears it fights so hard to protect! Donohue
wrote:

> In its passion for legalized abortions, the ACLU has
> violated the civil liberties of those who do not share its posi-
> tion. A case in point involves the efforts of Representative
> Henry J. Hyde . . . [who] authored a bill to restrict the fed-
> eral financing of abortions. When he began his efforts in the
> late 1970s, the Union was alarmed. One of the Union's main
> contentions was that the law amounted to the enactment
> of Roman Catholic "dogma and doctrine" into law. . . . To
> gather evidence for its case, the ACLU dispatched an agent
> to spy on Hyde's leisure-time activities. What the agent
> found was that Mr. Hyde went to church on Sundays—a
> Catholic church no less—where, as the report noted,
> "pregnant women and children" bore "gifts for life"; the
> same people, including Hyde, were said to have prayed and
> gone to Holy Communion. . . . When Norman C. Miller
> broke this story in December 1978, he accused the ACLU
> of engaging in anti-Catholic bigotry. Ira Glasser, the head of
> the ACLU, responded by defending the Union's policy on
> abortion and labeled the bigotry charge "unsophisticated";
> he never addressed the spy activity.[45]

Hyde said about the ACLU's spying, "I suppose the Nazis did that—observed Jews going to the synagogues in Hitler's Germany— but I had hoped we would have gotten past that kind of fascist tactic."[46] When the ACLU demanded to read Hyde's mail, he complied. According to Donohue, the ACLU wanted to find out if Hyde's opposition to abortion was "religiously based." Hyde reported, "Interestingly enough, I am told the young lady of the ACLU had a big chart, and whenever some citizen would close a letter to me saying 'God Bless You,' the ACLU representative would put a little check by the word 'God,' thus indicating the evil, nefarious religious influence that was molding my approach to this subject."[47]*

And then to top it off, the ACLU (along with its allies) have encouraged Americans to salute the "courage" of those who kill unborn children. In a promotion for "National Day of Appreciation for Abortion Providers," the ACLU wrote:

On this day, stand up with your abortion services providers and say: "Thank you for your heroism, perseverance, courage, and commitment to women." Organize local appreciation day events. Praise clinic staff and doctors with certificates of appreciation. Write your local newspaper and call talk shows to express support. Place ads in local newspapers and newsletters. Ask your local [abortion] provider how you can help. Become a volunteer clinic escort. Use your imagination, creativity, and dedication to help create a climate at clinics where women, doctors, and staff can hold their heads high and receive support instead of harassment. We must change the climate overall from one where abortion providers are vilified and assaulted to one where they are honored and upheld as the heroes they are.[48]

Moving toward Infanticide

But the ACLU's anti-life agenda does not stop at abortion. It has progressively moved toward infanticide. Nat Hentoff realized this when he was involved in the infamous "Baby Doe" cases. One

---

* During the Attorney General's Commission on Pornography, ACLU-affiliated students demanded to read and review Alan's mail on several occasions.

of these cases involved a couple in Bloomington, Indiana, who gave birth to a Down's syndrome infant with a defective digestive system that could have been corrected by routine surgery, but the baby died of starvation on order of the parents.[49]

In fact, these cases, and the ACLU's position concerning them led to Hentoff's splitting from the ACLU. As other similar stories occurred, Hentoff noticed the ACLU repeatedly stood on the side of protecting the "privacy" rights of parents to kill their children. He wrote, "In Baby Doe cases, after the whistle has been blown by a nurse or a right-to-life organization, not once has a ACLU affiliate spoken for the infant's right to due process and equal protection under the law. Indeed, when the ACLU has become involved, it has fought resolutely for the parents' right to privacy. Baby Doe's own awful privacy, as he or she lies dying, is also thereby protected."[50]

Hentoff also shared the following incident: "And then I heard the head of the Reproductive Freedom Rights unit of the ACLU saying . . . at a forum, 'I don't know what all this fuss is about. Dealing with these handicapped infants is really an extension of women's reproductive freedom rights, women's right to control their own bodies.'"[51]

He continued, "That stopped me. It seemed to me we were not talking about *Roe vs. Wade*. These infants were born. And having been born, as persons under the Constitution, they were entitled to at least have the same rights as people on death row—due process, equal protection under the law."[52]

Other ACLU members have been dismayed by the organization's defense of what can only be called infanticide. Hentoff has shared about a letter he received from Barry Nakell, one of the founders of the North Carolina chapter of the ACLU. Nakell told Hentoff he gave a speech at the 1985 annual meeting of the North Carolina chapter. Hentoff recounts:

> He reminded the members that the principle of respect for the dignity of life was the basis for the paramount issue on the North Carolina Civil Liberties Union agenda since its founding. That group was founded because of their opposition to capital punishment. Yet, he said, [in] supporting *Roe vs. Wade*, these civil libertarians were agreeing that the

Constitution protects the right to take life. This situation is a little backward, Nakell told his brothers and sisters. In the classical position, the Constitution would be interpreted to protect the right to life, and pro-abortion advocates would be pressing to relax that constitutional guarantee. In *Roe vs. Wade*, the Supreme Court turned that position upside down and the ACLU went along, taking the decidedly odd civil libertarian position that some lives are less worthy of protection than other lives.[53]

The ACLU has also fought fervently against the Unborn Victims of Violence Act (signed into law by President Bush),[54] which allowed for charges to be brought against an attacker of a pregnant woman if the unborn child she was carrying was injured or killed in the attack. Although the bill clearly stated that nothing in the legislation "shall be construed to permit the prosecution for conduct relating to abortion for which the consent of the pregnant woman . . . has been obtained,"[55] the ACLU staged its usual campaign of misinformation, intimidation, and fear to defeat the legislation.

In a statement, the ACLU said the bill was "a cunning attempt to separate the fetus from the mother in the eyes of the law and in the court of public opinion."[56] To which Hentoff replied, "The ACLU might be surprised to learn that according to a standard medical text, 'The Unborn Patient: The Art and Science of Fetal Development,' . . . the fetus is an individual patient, and to be considered as such 'as much a patient as any other patient.'"[57]

In fact, in the ACLU's viewpoint, abortion is a better alternative than carrying a child to term. In a "reproductive rights" update, the ACLU wrote, "Today, abortion is one of the most commonly performed surgical procedures and is ten times safer than carrying a pregnancy to term."[58] We again challenge the ACLU's medical "data" to prove its claim.

What Free Speech?

Meanwhile, the ACLU, the great defender of free speech, has either been silent, or has actively sought to silence the free speech rights of those who believe in and wish to advocate for the right to life. These actions have even given pause to hard-core ACLU activists like

Robyn Blumner, who is no friend of the pro-life, pro-family cause. She noted that the ACLU has backed Nazis, a college student who posted rape fantasies on the Internet, and Ku Klux Klan members but had decided that pro-lifers are such pariahs that their right to free speech is to be denied. Blumner wrote:

> The ACLU, a group for which I proudly worked as executive director of the Florida and Utah affiliates for more than 10 years, has developed a blind spot when it comes to defending anti-abortion protestors. The organization that once defended the right of a neo-Nazi group to demonstrate in heavily Jewish Skokie, Ill., now cheers a Portland, Ore., jury that charged a group of anti-abortion activists with $107 million in damages for expressing their views. Gushed the ACLU's press release, "We view the jury's verdict as a clarion call to remove violence and the threat of violence from the political debate over abortion. . . ."
>
> None of the anti-abortion group's intimidating writings explicitly threatened violence. Still, the ACLU of Oregon refused to support the defendants' First Amendment claims. . . .[59]

While we want to make it very clear that we decry any form of violence against those who advocate abortion—or anyone we disagree with—this silence toward, or active litigation against, the right of pro-life speech and peaceful advocacy is another example of the duplicity of the ACLU.

In 1997, the ACLU filed a friend-of-the court brief in support of an injunction that required pro-life advocates to stay at least fifteen feet away from the entrances and driveways of abortion clinics. The injunction also provided a fifteen-foot "bubble zone" around each woman who came to the clinic. In effect, this court order created a zone that prohibited free speech directed at pro-life advocates. The ACLU brief stated the injunction creating this zone was consistent with the First Amendment. Three ACLU chapters (including Blumner's) disagreed. An ACLU attorney in Ohio saw through the organization's duplicity, saying, "There are people I consider to be civil libertarians who believe in an abortion exception to the First Amendment. I think that's outrageous."[60]

The ACLU also supported the use of the 1871 Ku Klux Klan Act against peaceful pro-life advocates who blocked access to abortion clinics.[61] In 1994, the ACLU was in favor of legislation titled the Freedom of Access to Clinic Entrances or FACE. FACE bars peaceful pro-life activism such as sit-ins (which the ACLU supports on other issues).[62] When pro-life advocates went to court to defend their First Amendment rights to protest abortion, the ACLU filed a friend-of-the-court brief against them.[63]

In 1970, Congress passed the Racketeer Influenced and Corrupt Organizations statute (RICO) to use as a tool against organized crime.[64] RICO awards triple damages for those who are found to be victims of certain organized criminal activity. It was never intended to be used against peaceful pro-life advocates, or peaceful advocates of any free speech. But that is exactly what happened, when abortion supporters in the mid-1980s started to use these laws to bankrupt pro-life demonstrators.[65] Meanwhile, the great defender of free speech, the ACLU, which opposed the use of RICO by the U.S. Justice Department against distributors of obscenity, stood on the sideline—or in the case of its Reproductive Freedom Project, published a booklet suggesting that abortion clinics could use the RICO statutes against pro-life advocates.[66]

John Leo of *U.S. News and World Report* pointed out this hypocrisy: "The [ACLU] has had a hard time coping with RICO. It came out against the law early, then waffled for years in response to abortion-rights lobbying both outside and inside its structure. Harvey Silverglate, a board member of the Massachusetts ACLU, said sympathy for abortion rights caused the ACLU to drop its guard on a serious violation of political freedom."

Leo recalled a conversation he had with Lynn Paltrow of the ACLU's Reproductive Freedom Project, who said, "It's ACLU policy to oppose application of RICO, but there are those on staff who feel that as long as RICO exists, this kind of behavior [aggressive abortion protests] does sort of fit."[67]

To be fair in our reporting on the ACLU's stance on this issue, we must note that it has flip-flopped regarding application of RICO laws against pro-life advocates. It has either encouraged the use of RICO against pro-life advocates, remained silent when other pro-abortion groups tried to use RICO to bankrupt pro-life groups, or unenthusiastically discouraged the use of RICO against pro-lifers.[68] This waffling is demonstrative of the ACLU's internal conflict between those who claim all speech should be protected even if they privately disagree and those who are so zealous in the promotion of abortion that any First Amendment considerations for pro-life advocates are cast aside.

The ACLU and Euthanasia

Just as the ACLU is dedicated to ending life at its very beginning, so it also seems to be as equally dedicated to hastening death as well.

In 1990, twenty-six-year-old Terri Schiavo went into cardiac arrest for unknown reasons (which one medical professional, along with Terri's relatives claim, may be the result of being beaten and otherwise injured) in her Florida home.[69] Her heart stopped beating and the lack of oxygen to her brain resulted in some serious brain damage.

Although Terri remained bedridden, many of her bodily functions were normal. Her parents and a priest said she could recognize voices and vocalize sounds. She could communicate. This was documented on a video that both authors watched and was verified as an accurate depiction by attorneys funded by ADF. However, she could not feed herself and had food and water provided through a tube. She faced no danger of death.

Eight years after her collapse, Terri's husband, Michael Schiavo, living with another woman,[70] went to court to have her feeding tube removed, which would result in starvation and her eventual death. Terri's father and mother wanted to keep their daughter alive and went to court, with the help of ADF funding, to defend her right to life.

Terri's father, Robert Schindler, wrote to ADF: "One of the miracles God has provided for our family is the funds that have made it possible for ADF to compensate our attorneys over the past few years. The compensation they receive is certainly not as much as they have legitimately earned or deserve, but it has enabled our case to continue in various courtrooms from Pinellas County here in Florida to the halls of the Florida Supreme Court and now even to the United

States Supreme Court. Every day that our case continues is another day that our daughter Terri is able to live and we are able to enjoy each other as a family."[71]

After several legal battles, Terri's feeding tube was removed by court order.[72] Then the Florida legislature stepped in and passed a law (signed by Florida Governor Jeb Bush) that empowered the governor to prevent the withholding of her feeding tube.[73]

There were no extraordinary means or artificial life support. Terri's only assistance was with eating and drinking, which some experts believe she could have learned to do on her own with proper therapy.*

Who jumped into the legal battle against Terri's parents and her right to life? None other than the ACLU, which joined the case as legal counsel.[74] Howard Simon, executive director of the ACLU of Florida, said, "This dangerous abuse of power by the Governor and Florida lawmakers concerns everyone who may face difficult and agonizing decisions involving the medical condition of a family member. Based on the precedent of this case, meddling politicians could set aside court orders they don't agree with."[75]

In another startling case of ACLU duplicity, it stated Governor Bush had set a precedent that would enable public officials to write laws changing any court decision that they wish.[76] However, it was the ACLU—in the legal battle over same-sex "marriage" in San Francisco and elsewhere—that encouraged public officials to take the law into their own hands, defying clearly written state law and ordering same-sex "marriages."[77]

Terri's parents were outraged by the ACLU's actions. Their spokesperson, Pamela Hennessy, said, "I've been contacting the ACLU since the beginning of my involvement in this case to have them speak out against what's going on with Terri. It's going on against her will. She's had her religious freedoms stripped from her. She's had her civil liberties stripped from her. And they're defending the husband?"[78]

---

*Alan has been involved on a personal and professional level with several difficult end of life decision making processes. Despite the media confusion, Terri's case was dissimilar to those that Alan has experienced.

The ACLU's involvement also troubled individuals with disabilities. Joe Ford, an undergraduate student at Harvard University who suffers from severe cerebral palsy, said, "A close examination of the facts of the Schiavo case reveals not a case of difficult decisions but a basic test of this country's decency."[79]

Eleanor Smith, a self-described "liberal, agnostic lesbian," who is confined to a wheelchair because of childhood polio, added, "At this point I would rather have a right-wing Christian decide my fate than an ACLU member."[80]

The ACLU's decision to intervene again caught the attention of Nat Hentoff, who had witnessed the ACLU's promotion of abortion and euthanasia for years. He also questioned the motives of Terri's husband in the case:

So intent is Michael Schiavo on having his wife die of starvation that one of his lawyers, after the governor's order to reconnect the feeding tube, faxed doctors in the county where the life-saving procedure was about to take place, threatening to sue any physician who reinserted a feeding tube. The husband had immediately gone to court [with the help of the ACLU] to get a judge to revoke what the legislature and the governor had done.

The husband claims that he is honoring his marriage vows by carrying out the wishes of his wife that she not be kept alive by "artificial means." As I shall show, this hearsay "evidence" by the husband has been contradicted. The purportedly devoted husband, moreover, has been living with another woman since 1995. They have a child, with another on the way. Was that part of his marital vows?

Ignoring the facts of the case, the American Civil Liberties Union—to my disgust, but not my surprise in view of the long-term distrust of the ACLU by disability rights activists—has marched to support the husband despite his grave conflicts of interests in this life-or-death case. The ACLU claims the governor and the legislature of Florida unconstitutionally overruled the courts, which continued to declare the husband the lawful guardian. On the other hand, the ACLU cheered when Governor George Ryan of Illinois substituted his judgment for that of the courts by removing many prisoners from death row.[81]

Hentoff also stated that neurologists told him that if given proper therapy, which had been denied by her husband, "she could learn to eat by herself and become more responsive."[82]* Terri's brother said that she appeared to laugh and react to her surroundings: "I know she sees and hears us. I see her response. It is not wishful thinking. Terri isn't brain dead. She's disabled."[83]

Nevertheless, the ACLU continued to battle against Terri's right to life.[84] On August 31, 2004, the Florida Supreme Court heard oral arguments in her case, with the ACLU standing firmly on the side of terminating Terri's life.[85] ADF funded a brief for our ally, the Family Research Council, defending Terri's right to life in that case.

On September 23, 2004, the Florida Supreme Court held that the law that reinserted Terri's feeding tube violated the state Constitution. The system, the laws, designed to safeguard the right to life, had been turned against Terri and her family's efforts to keep her alive. In effect, the Florida Supreme Court, with the help of the ACLU, issued a death sentence to Terri.[86]

After the decision was announced, Randall Marshall, legal director of the Florida ACLU chapter, said, "Today's thoughtful and careful opinion will be very important in the history of Florida because it is a strong rebuke to politicians who attempt to negate court decisions . . . simply because they disagree with the outcome."[87] We wonder if the ACLU would have the same message for the mayor of San Francisco? We doubt it.

The legal battle continued on in early 2005, as Terri's relatives sought to find some legal recourse to keep their daughter alive, with the ACLU and activist judges fighting them at every turn. Eventually, the U.S. Congress and President Bush both tried, valiantly but ultimately unsuccessfully, to keep Terri alive, despite the efforts of Michael Schiavo and the ACLU to deny her the right to life.

---

*In another column, Hentoff openly speculated that Terri's husband may have beaten her, which led to her brain damaged condition. According to Hentoff, Dr. Michael Baden, former chief medical examiner of New York City, found that Terri had endured significant head trauma as well as injuries to her ribs, thoracic vertebrae, ankles, and knees. See Nat Hentoff, "Was Terri Schiavo Beaten in 1990?," *Village Voice*, November 14, 2003.

Sadly, on March 31, 2005, thirteen days after her feeding tube was removed, Terri Schiavo died.

Just a few days before her death, Nat Hentoff wrote perhaps the best piece on this latest outrage by the ACLU, as Terri was dying a slow and painful death of dehydration and starvation. Hentoff wrote:

> In dread fact, Terri faces a horrific death from dehydration. In covering previous cases when feeding tubes have been removed, I've found out how terribly painful this way of dying is for someone like Terri who is not in a persistent vegetative state and can feel; by the eighth day, without water, her liver, spleen, kidneys, stomach, esophagus, tongue, and eyeballs will swell and start to crack.
>
> All of her body's organs by her ninth and tenth day will have split and cracked. Not long after this agonizing ordeal, she will die.
>
> Complicent in this egregious denial to Terri of due process and equal protection of the law has been the American Civil Liberties . . . . The ACLU has supported Michael Schiavo's insistence on putting Terri to death. It has not shown any awareness of her husband's blatant conflicts of interest with such results as his withdrawal of therapy and rehabilitation for her. However, the ACLU would insist that a death-row inmate receive vastly more civil liberties than Terri Schiavo has from the Florida courts.[88]

John Leo wrote about the future ramifications of the ACLU's actions in support of Michael Schiavo, writing, "The Schiavo case is a breakthrough for persuading the public to lower the bar on moral constraints. Once we had a bright line between pulling the plug on patients kept alive by life-support systems and killing people like Terri Schiavo who are not on life support but merely being fed through a tube. Requiring clear evidence of consent is no longer required . . . . The killing of [Terri] Schiavo is a scandal successfully redefined as unexceptional and therefore moral."[89]

Nevertheless, the ACLU could not help but crow about its involvement in securing Terri's death. In a statement issued after one of the many failed legal attempts to save Terri's life, ACLU of Florida Executive Director Howard Simon said, "Decisions about whether to continue or discontinue extraordinary or even life-sustaining measures are part of a basic privacy . . . . President [Bush], no doubt, will continue to talk about a 'culture of life,' but what [the] Judge . . . did in his decision was to defend the 'culture of freedom' that each of us has to exercise control over our lives, and the circumstances of our death."[90]

What Mr. Simon fails to point out is that Terri had no control over her life, the decisions made about her future, or the circumstances of her death.

The ACLU has also been at the forefront of pushing euthanasia (or "assisted suicide") in other states as well. In Michigan, the ACLU supported the efforts of "Dr. Death," Dr. Jack Kevorkian, who continually defied the law and euthanized individuals.[91] In another example of duplicity, the ACLU of Michigan, claiming that it was the will of the people to allow physician-assisted suicide,[92] fought for this "right" by asking the state's Supreme Court to set aside the state's ban on assisted suicide, including euthanasia.[93] (But when it comes to same-sex "marriage" and other issues, the ACLU believes the will of the people should be ignored and they should not have the right to vote on the matter.)[94]

Wendy Wagenheim, the legislative affairs director of the Michigan ACLU, said, "Kevorkian has forced the people of Michigan to take a good hard look at this issue, but this issue is far bigger than Kevorkian. The people of Michigan should have the opportunity to vote on this. . . . A competent terminally ill adult should control the circumstances of his or her own death and should have a right to have someone help them."[95]

Howard Simon, former executive director of the Michigan ACLU, in a poor calculation of the public mood, said, "It's now clear that the public has made up its mind. It's not whether people should have the right [to die], it's under what conditions. The way out of the morass is for the medical establishment and Legislature to do what is clear the public wants done, which is to make physician-assisted suicide part of accepted medical practice."[96]

Simon was correct on one thing: The Michigan electorate did make up its mind. It voted 71 percent to 29 percent to reject the ACLU's position and the legalization of assisted suicide in the state.[97]

The ACLU also filed a friend-of-the-court brief in support of legalizing euthanasia in the cases *Vacco vs. Quill* (which challenged New York's ban on assisted suicide) and *Glucksberg vs. Washington* (which challenged the state's ban on assisted suicide).[98] The ACLU and its allies* were hoping that these cases would be the *Roe vs. Wade* of euthanasia and were counting on the support of its former general counsel, Supreme Court Associate Justice Ruth Bader Ginsburg, to discover yet another new constitutional right to be euthanized. ADF awarded a series of substantial grants (the largest in our history at that time) and turned much of the allied organizational focus on these two cases, to help stop the demands of the ACLU and its allies.

ADF and its allies were ecstatic when the Supreme Court ruled, 9–0, including Justice Ginsburg in both cases, that there was no "new right" discovered for assisted suicide.[99]

But as they always do, the ACLU and its allies refused to give up. The assisted suicide forces, defeated at the U.S. Supreme Court level, then engaged in a strategy to undermine this decision. The ACLU and its allies are convinced that even though the Supreme Court ruled against them, they can still find support in the state supreme courts, on independent state constitutional grounds. This is what the pro-abortion forces had done in a few states in the days leading up to and since the *Roe vs. Wade* decision. Therefore, the assisted suicide advocates pursued cases at the state level in Florida[100] and Michigan,[101] which they hoped would lead to a broadening of the "right to die" in individual states, despite their federal constitutional loss. They lost both challenges.

Where does this lead? Nat Hentoff again pointed out the danger of Kevorkian's and the ACLU's pro-euthanasia advocacy, by examining how legalized euthanasia has played out in the Netherlands:

Not all of Dr. Kevorkian's patients were terminally ill, and not all of the people euthanized in the Netherlands in recent years have been terminally ill or in intractable pain. Some have been severely depressed. During the Nazi occupation of the Netherlands, that country's physicians

---

*Other supporters of the effort to convince the Supreme Court to find a "right" to assisted suicide were the Hemlock Society USA and the Euthanasia Research Guidance Organization. See *Vacco vs. Quill*, 521 U.S. 793 (1997).

rebelled against the culture of death by refusing to cooperate with the killing of patients.

But now, their changed attitude reminds me of an Oc[tober] 17, 1933, *New York Times* report from Berlin that the German Ministry of Justice intended to authorize physicians to "end the suffering of incurable patients, upon request, in the interests of true humanity."

Before the gas chambers, before the Holocaust, German doctors euthanized not only the "incurable" but also mentally defective patients on the principle that some lives are unworthy of living. . . . At last, have we learned nothing from the Holocaust?[102]

In its brief in the *Vacco* and *Glucksberg* cases, the ACLU wrote, "In opposition to this right, Washington and New York invoke interests in preserving human life, precluding undue influence or mistake, safeguarding the integrity of the medical profession and a concern over the 'slippery-slope'—i.e., that line-drawing in this area will prove impossible. These interest and concerns, however legitimate, do not justify an absolute ban on physician aid in dying for terminally ill persons and should not outweigh the recognized right of a competent, terminally ill individual to end his or her suffering."[103]

In other words, we should push aside the slippery-slope concern that led to horrors such as the Holocaust, in which more and more justification was found for the taking of innocent human life. Hentoff is right—the ACLU has not learned from history. The ACLU's position on human life, whether at the beginning or end of life, is dangerous to *all* individuals, no matter what stage in life.

For those who believe in the sanctity of human life, the words of Titus Brandsma, who was martyred at the Dachau concentration camp of Adolf Hitler, are important to remember: "He who wants to win the world for Christ must have the courage to come in conflict with it."[104]

It is going to take many legal battles in many courts to turn back the ACLU's anti-life agenda and to protect the right to life for future generations. But there have been victories, and we are confident of more in the future. *Roe vs. Wade* will be overturned. ADF has successfully helped defend parental consent laws and hold back the legal advance of physician-assisted suicide, and we will continue the legal battle to stop the horrific practice of partial-birth abortion. We will continue—through coordination of legal strategy, the training of attorneys, funding, and direct litigation—to fight for the right to life for all Americans.

The cost of not fighting this battle is far too high. We have already seen the premature deaths of more than 46 million unborn children[105] (more than the population of Canada or the state of California and rising), thanks to the work of the ACLU and its allies.

For many who have grown weary, this battle has already gone on too long. It has been more than thirty years since *Roe vs. Wade*. However, we cannot surrender. The tide is turning against the anti-life agenda of the ACLU and its allies and toward the affirmation of the sanctity of human life. More and more Americans are saying they are pro-life[106] as ultrasound technology continues to advance and show, without question, that it is a life, and not a "blob of tissue" as some would call it, developing in the womb.

We can look to the great British statesman William Wilberforce as a source of inspiration. Wilberforce, a Christian, fought tirelessly for twenty years for the abolishment of slavery in Great Britain. He was mocked for years, but his persistence, along with God's grace, eventually moved hearts and minds and led to the British Parliament's voting *287–16* to halt the British slave trade. That victory, in turn, led to the abolishment of slavery in all of the British colonies.[107]

Years later, one of Wilberforce's biographers noted that Abraham Lincoln recalled Wilberforce's name as the person responsible for halting the slave trade but could not remember one man who wanted to keep it alive.[108] We hope that future leaders will remember those who fought hard to preserve the right to life, and the ACLU and its anti-life allies will be forgotten.

CHAPTER 6

The ACLU vs. Religion

When it comes to removing religion from our public life, the Left (commanded by the ACLU, Americans United for the Separation of Church and State, and People for the American Way) marches triumphantly from victory to victory. In the past 10 years, it has banned school prayer (including silent meditation), eliminated graduation invocations, driven crèches and menorahs from public parks, taken carols out of school assemblies, purged Ten Commandments monuments, and now has called into question God in the Pledge of Allegiance.[1]
—Don Feder

Without God, there could be no form of government nor American way of life. Recognition of the Supreme Being is the first—and most basic—expression of Americanism.[2]
—President Dwight D. Eisenhower

It would be unbecoming the representatives of this nation to assemble for the first time in this solemn temple without looking up to the Supreme Ruler of the Universe, and imploring his blessing. . . . Here, and throughout our country, may simple manners, pure morals, and true religion flourish forever![3]
—President John Adams

ACLU Asks Jail for Tangipahoa School Officials[4]
—Associated Press headline about the ACLU's threat to imprison school officials for allowing prayer

I t all began with an e-mail. A paralegal at the ACLU's national office in Washington, D.C., "discovered" there were plaques at the Grand Canyon that quoted selections from the book of Psalms. She quickly fired off an e-mail to the National Park Service, asking why the signs were there.[5]

The plaques the ACLU inquired about had been placed at the Grand Canyon more than three decades earlier by the Evangelical Sisterhood of Mary of Phoenix, Arizona. The plaques were nonsectarian and simply quote selections from Psalms that extol the beauty of God's creation. Mysteriously, the ACLU did not complain about the names given to some of the geological formations and printed on government maps taken from a non-Judeo-Christian religion—in this case, the Hindu faith.

Nevertheless, National Park Service officials apparently were so intimidated by the ACLU's e-mail that they removed the plaques five months later, rather than face more threats, inquiries, or a possible lawsuit from the ACLU.[6] At the request of the Christian sisters, ADF lawyers informed the Park Service the plaques did not violate the U.S. Constitution. The Park Service put the plaques back, but as in any case involving the ACLU, it will likely be heard from again.

The ACLU has used its huge war chest over the years to wage an unrelenting war against any public expression of religious faith but in particular Christianity and Orthodox Judaism. Whether it is the plaques at the Grand Canyon, the posting of the Ten Commandments in a public building, a state Capitol's lawn, or a high school valedictorian who simply wants to give thanks and glory to God, the ACLU and its speech police seemingly are everywhere to attempt to censor and shut down religious speech and expression.

It is not just outspoken Christians who have observed how the ACLU wants to silence religious faith. Conservative Jewish leaders and writers such as Don Feder, Rabbi Daniel Lapin, and Dennis Prager have noticed and commented on this as well. Prager wrote:

> This country is in the midst of its second civil war. It only differs from the first civil war in that it is, thank God, nonviolent. But the passions are as deep, and the stakes are just as high. Among the stakes is whether America will remain a Judeo-Christian country with a secular government or become a secular country with a secular government. Organizations such as the ACLU . . . devote massive funds and effort to changing the nature of this country; and with the help of

like-minded judges, often prevail. That the ACLU would write a letter protesting three little plaques at the Grand Canyon with verses from the book of Psalms provides a clear example of how intent the organization is on destroying the Judeo-Christian moral foundations of this society. This, after all, is the same ACLU that went to court in Florida to protect a Muslim woman's right to be photographed for her drivers' license wearing a veil! If it ain't Judeo-Christian, the ACLU is a big fan of religion. The story also reveals another typical problem: the fear organizations, including governmental ones, have of taking on the ACLU. Given the amount of money and manpower it would take to fight the ACLU, and given the likelihood of facing a judge with ACLU-like values, why bother fighting? So, the National Park Service just lay down and surrendered.[7]

The ACLU proudly promotes itself as a great defender of religious freedom. In reality, nothing could be farther from the truth. It is the number one religious censor in America.

As Prager has detailed, the ACLU stages a continued war of fear, misinformation, and legal intimidation to bully public officials into removing any vestige of America's traditional Judeo-Christian heritage and religious expression from the public square. The ACLU seeks, through legal and political means, not only to eliminate religious expression but also to force many Americans to violate their own core religious beliefs. The following are examples:

- In California, the state Supreme Court—in a case in which the ACLU joined with others against Catholic Charities—ruled that the charity must provide contraception coverage to women as part of any group health care prescription drug program it offers to its employees. This is despite the fact that Catholic faith and its doctrine strictly prohibits the use of contraceptives. The rationale? Because the charity has non-Catholic employees and ministers to non-Catholics. In other words, if the charity did not minister to others, it might be exempt. In other words, "Keep your ministry to yourself." The one dissenting California justice in the case, Janice Rogers Brown, wrote, "This is such a crabbed and constricted view of religion."[8] Yet, we don't see the ACLU's being part of a lawsuit against Planned Parenthood to force it to hand out information on abstinence. But, again, Planned Parenthood agrees with the ACLU's agenda.

• The New York chapter of the ACLU has filed suit against the Salvation Army. The Army's employment policies require that employees divulge their religious affiliation and affirm the Army's Christian mission. The ACLU filed the suit simply because the Salvation Army receives state and city funds to help provide services for children in poverty. Gary McCaleb, ADF senior counsel, said, "If the NYCLU prevails in this case, some of the most effective groups—faith-based groups—[will] either have to surrender their faith-based distinctive—or they will have to unreasonably decline government funds."[9]

• The ACLU backed a lawsuit against Yeshiva University, a conservative Jewish school, because the university would not allow two lesbians to live in married student housing. The school holds the traditional Jewish position that homosexual behavior violates God's law. The school lost, and the ACLU crowed about how it had forced a private faith-based organization to violate its core beliefs. ACLU attorney Matthew Coles of the ACLU's Lesbian and Gay Rights Project said, "It's a fabulous ruling."[10]

• The ACLU policy guide calls for the removal of the words "under God" from the Pledge of Allegiance.[11] The ACLU was strangely quiet, however, in the politically charged Supreme Court challenge brought by Sacramento atheist Michael Newdow to eliminate those words from the pledge. While it did file a friend-of-the-court brief in favor of Newdow,[12] they did not trumpet it in the media. The ACLU knows how to pick its battles, and in the court of public opinion (where polls showed that nine out of ten Americans supported the inclusion of "under God" in the pledge),[13] this one was a loser—this time.[14]

Michael Novak of the American Enterprise Institute summed up the ACLU's goals:

The sweet air of liberty must be replaced with an invisible gas that detects, exterminates, and suffocates any breath that would expel a religious word in public life. Publicly, religion must be totally repressed, so that soon only atheists will find the public atmosphere comfortable. The accommodation this nation long ago reached between believers and non-believers must be abandoned. Religion shall be banned from all public appearances under government auspices, until it is totally squeezed down into private life, underground. There, harmless, it can survive as long as it may. To save the world from intolerance, the ACLU must be rigorously intolerant. Public life in the United States must be made religion-free.[15]

America's Religious Heritage

As hard as it tries, the ACLU cannot deny America's strong religious heritage. That is why it tries to either censor it, or enlist liberal scholars to misinterpret statements made by the Founding Fathers— or in some cases erase or rewrite American history—to advance its agenda. If the ACLU has its way, names like Roger Williams, William Penn, Samuel Adams, Jonathan Edwards, and Patrick Henry would completely disappear.

While many argue that America is not a "Christian" nation, it is hard to deny that America was founded on faith-based principles and that many, if not most, of its founders had a deep and significant faith. Consider the following examples from our nation's history:

- The first act of the Continental Congress in 1774 was a motion to pause for prayer. When the motion was carried, the first prayer was based on Psalm 35.[16]
- General George Washington issued orders to the Continental Army that "the Colonels or commanding officers of each regiment are directed to procure Chaplains accordingly; persons of good characters and exemplary lives."[17] On numerous occasions Washington set aside days of prayer and fasting for his soldiers.[18] The father of our country would have been hauled into court by the ACLU on that one! In fact, the ACLU sued and successfully stopped the practice of the cadets at the Virginia Military Institute to have mealtime prayers.[19] Then it set its sights on the United States Naval Academy.[20]

- The Declaration of Independence recognizes that God is the Creator and source of liberty: "that all Men . . . are endowed by their Creator with certain unalienable Rights." It says that God is the giver of all laws: "Laws of Nature and of Nature's God." God is also described as the ultimate judge: "The Supreme Judge of the World" and the king of all earthly rulers, as the sovereign "divine Providence."[21] Given their typical behavior, if the ACLU had existed back in 1776 it might have filed a lawsuit to stop the publication of the document, citing the yet-to-be-discovered doctrine of "separation of church and state."
- When American troops were being badly beaten, Congress decreed that the states observe a national day of "solemn Fasting and Humiliation" on December 11, 1776. The proclamation read as follows:

  > WHEREAS, the just War into which the United States of America have been forced by Great Britain, is likely to be still continued by the same Violence and Injustice which have hitherto animated the Enemies of American freedom:
  >
  > And, whereas it becomes all public Bodies, as well as private Persons, to reverence the Providence of God, and look up to him as the supreme Disposer of all Events, and the Arbiter of the Fate of Nations:
  >
  > Therefore the CONGRESS hereby resolve:
  > That it be recommended to all the States, as soon as possible to appoint a Day of solemn Fasting and Humiliation, to implore of Almighty God the forgiveness of the many Sins prevailing among all Ranks, and to beg the Countenance and Assistance of his Providence in the Prosecution of this just and necessary War.[22]

- Thomas Paine, the Revolutionary War figure who is often cited by the ACLU and atheist groups as one of their heroes, wrote that he was "not so much of an infidel as to believe that Almighty God could abandon a people committed to the liberty to which he had called them."[23]
- The Revolutionary War officially ended with the Treaty of

Paris in 1783, which recognized the northern and eastern boundaries of the United States. The treaty was negotiated by and signed on behalf of the United States by David Hartley, John Adams (our second president), Benjamin Franklin (called irreligious by the Left), and John Jay (our first chief justice of the Supreme Court). The treaty began with these words: "In the name of the most holy and undivided Trinity . . . ."[24] (and the trinity referenced was not Canada, the United States, and Mexico, as some opponents at the ACLU might suggest).

- When George Washington took the oath of office as the first president of the United States at Federal Hall in New York City, he laid his hand on a Bible opened to Genesis 49 and 50 and added the words repeated by every president since: "So help me God." He then walked over to nearby Saint Paul's Chapel to pray before he attended the inaugural festivities. In his Farewell Address, eight years later, Washington said, "Of all the dispositions and habits which lead to political prosperity, [r]eligion and morality are indispensable supports."[25]

- During the administration of Thomas Jefferson, another ACLU "hero" and the father of the much-abused, much-misunderstood term "separation of church and state,"[26] a church service was held inside the U.S. Capitol. Jefferson not only attended the service, but he saw to it that the Marine Band was there to play music.[27] Today, Jefferson and the Marines would probably find themselves in a courtroom being stared down at by an ACLU attorney.

- When the Northwest Ordinance was enacted by the Confederation of the United States in 1787 to provide government for what would eventually become Ohio, Michigan, and several other states, Article 3 of the ordinance stated: "Religion, morality, and knowledge, being necessary to good government and the happiness of mankind, schools, and the means of education shall forever be encouraged."[28]

- The state constitutions of all fifty states recognize God and pay some sort of homage to His role. For example, the preamble to the Massachusetts Constitution says, "We, therefore, the people of Massachusetts, acknowledging, with grateful hearts, the goodness of the great Legislator of the universe, in affording us, in the course of His providence . . . ."[29] The preamble of the constitution of Pennsylvania reads, "We, the people of the Commonwealth of Pennsylvania, grateful to Almighty God for the blessings of civil and religious liberty, and humbly invoking His guidance, do ordain and establish this Constitution."*

Twisting the First Amendment

There are countless other examples of America's religious heritage. But it is time to examine how the ACLU has used misinformation in their relentless campaign to twist the First Amendment into something its writers would have never imagined.

The ACLU and its allies have based many of their legal attacks on religious expression on the separation of church and state, which they claim is part of the First Amendment of the U.S. Constitution. They have repeated this mantra so many times that most Americans, and many Christians, believe it appears there.

It does not. What the First Amendment says is this: "Congress shall make no law respecting an establishment of religion, or prohibiting the free exercise thereof; or abridging the freedom of speech, or of the press; or the right of the people to peaceably assemble, and to petition the Government for a redress of grievances."[30]

What the framers of the Constitution meant when they wrote the First Amendment was only that the federal government—and only the federal government's Congress—was to be prohibited from establishing a national church, like the Church of England, or requiring that sectarian policy be forced on an individual state or on the federal government. It did not mean that the government could censor public religious expression, deny churches and religious organizations equal access to public facilities, or the church and government could not work together.

Joseph Story was one of the most noted historical commentators on the U.S. Constitution.† What he wrote in his 1833 volume *Commentaries on the U.S. Constitution* proves that the Founding

---

*You can read all fifty state constitutions at http://www.constitution.org/cons/usstcons.htm.

†Joseph Story (1779–1845) was appointed by President James Madison to the U.S. Supreme Court. Madison was a key framer of the First Amendment. Story spent thirty-four years as a Supreme Court justice. During most of that time he was also the Dane Professor of Law atHarvard University, where he was greatly responsible for helping establish the law school's success and reputation. He authored the noted multivolume set of books about the Constitution cited above.

Fathers had a vastly different view of religion and government from what the ACLU wants Americans to believe today. Story wrote, "Probably at the time of the adoption of the constitution, and of the amendment to it . . . sentiment in America was that Christianity ought to receive encouragement from the state, so far as it is not incompatible with the private rights of conscience, and the freedom of religious worship."[31]

He continued: "In fact, every American colony, from its foundation down to the revolution, with the exception of Rhode Island . . . did openly, by the whole course of its laws and institutions, support and sustain, in some form, the Christian religion, and almost invariably gave a peculiar sanction to some of its fundamental doctrines. . . . Indeed, in a republic, there would seem to be a peculiar propriety in viewing the Christian religion, as the great basis on which it must rest for its support and permanence, if it be, what it has ever been deemed by its truest friends to be, the religion of liberty."[32]

Story concluded: "The duty of supporting religion, and especially the Christian religion, is very different from the right to force the consciences of other men, or to punish them for worshipping God in the matter, which, they believe, their accountability to Him requires. . . . The rights of conscience are, indeed, beyond the just reach of human power."[33]

That last sentence is particularly instructive, for the ACLU has gone out of its way in many cases to encroach human and governmental authority, through the courts, on the rights of conscience of sincere religious believers. As mentioned earlier in this chapter, the ACLU has backed lawsuits or submitted briefs against Yeshiva University, Catholic Charities, and the Salvation Army (among others) to force them to violate their rights of conscience. Their antireligious philosophy has persuaded colleges and universities across the land to adopt and enforce policies that discriminate against faith-based organizations. They have succeeded in turning much of the First Amendment's purpose on its head.

The modern term separation of church and state first surfaced in an 1802 letter Thomas Jefferson (who was out of the country as minister to France at time of the debate over the First Amendment) wrote to a group of Baptists in Danbury, Connecticut. As governor of Virginia, Jefferson had helped the Baptists halt state funding of the Anglican Church in Virginia.

The Danbury Baptists, who were a small minority in their home state, had concern about the First Amendment guarantee of the "free exercise of religion." Some believe it was their concern that this guarantee suggested the government might actually try to regulate religious expression. They also were concerned because their home state of Connecticut had established the Congregationalist church as the state's church. Now that Jefferson was president, they wanted to know they could continue to count on his efforts to further their religious expression. Jefferson shared their concerns, and in a personal and private letter, reassured them that the government would never tamper with the free exercise of religion. Jefferson wrote, "Believing with you that religion is a matter which lies solely between Man and his God; that he owes account to none other for his faith or his worship; that the legitimate powers of government reach actions only and not opinions; I contemplate with sovereign reverence that act of the whole American people which declared that their legislature should 'make no law respecting an establishment of religion or prohibiting the free exercise thereof,' thus building a wall of separation between Church and State."[34]

With this letter, Jefferson conveyed his belief that government could not interfere with the free expression of personal religious beliefs. Thus the "wall" he referred to was not meant to limit public religious expression but to limit the federal government's legitimate interference with that expression. And nothing was to be done about the Connecticut state church. Quite a different view from what the ACLU and its allies promote!

In his article "The Wall Jefferson Almost Built," Heritage Foundation fellow Joseph LoConte explains how Jefferson's beliefs would make him a present-day enemy of the state, in the ACLU's view. LoConte wrote:

> One Sunday morning during Thomas Jefferson's presidency, a friend stopped him on his way to Christ Church, then meeting on Capitol Hill. The president had a prayer book tucked under his arm. The man was incredulous. "You do not believe a word in it," he said. Jefferson, pilloried as the village atheist during his first presidential campaign, was

unruffled. "Sir," he replied, "no nation has ever yet existed or been governed without religion. Nor can be." . . . The story is worth recalling as we mark the 200ᵗʰ anniversary of Jefferson's famous statement on religion and politics—that the First Amendment built "a wall of separation between church and state." Many will celebrate the wall metaphor as the defining feature of America's secular republic. But recent scholarship into its background may temper the festivities. The expression is found nowhere in the Constitution, appearing instead in a letter to Connecticut Baptists dated January 1, 1802. . . . Courts now cite the phrase to deny any form of public support for religion, while Liberals quote it as holy writ.[35]

In his book, *Thomas Jefferson and the Myth of Separation,* American University professor Daniel Dreisbach wrote, "It was a political statement, . . . carefully crafted to reassure Jefferson's Baptist constituents in New England of his continuing commitment to their religious rights." Dreisbach concluded that Jefferson's wall "wasn't meant to bar religion from public life but to prevent faith from being either politicized or tread upon by government."[36]

According to Dreisbach, James Hutson, manuscript curator for the Library of Congress, agrees with this conclusion. Hutson said Jefferson placed great value on symbolic support of religion. Two days after writing the letter, as noted above, the president attended church services in the House of Representatives, a practice he would continue for years.[37] LoConte says that Jefferson also opened federal buildings, including the Treasury, the War Office, and the Supreme Court to religious services. "It is no exaggeration to say that, on Sundays in Washington during Thomas Jefferson's presidency, the state became the church," Hutson said. According to him, Jefferson saw no conflict between the First Amendment and the availability of public property, public facilities, and even government personnel to religious bodies.[38]

LoConte also wrote, "The reason went beyond mere politics. When Jefferson remarked that no nation could be governed without religion, he did not have in mind the corrupted variety of government churches. In this, he argued exactly as the most pious Founders did: Religious belief—freely chosen and given wide public space—nurtured morality and thus supported a free society."[39]

Jefferson's words remained substantially dormant for nearly 150 years until the now infamous 1947 *Everson* decision when Supreme Court Justice Hugo Black (himself a former Ku Klux Klansman) resurrected them and gave them new meaning (see chap. 1), when he wrote: "The First Amendment has erected a wall between church and state. That wall must be high and impregnable. We could not approve the slightest breach."[40]

Although several Supreme Court decisions, as well as many constitutional scholars such as Dreisbach have rebutted Black's assertion, the ACLU made this phrase a mantra and has been successful in using it to stifle and eliminate much public religious expression.*

However, this is not the only way that the ACLU and its allies have misrepresented Jefferson, whom they cite as their "hero" in their battle to silence public religious expression and advance the rest of their agenda.

In an article that discussed the recent battles in the U.S. Senate over the confirmation of judges, Lino A. Graglia, professor of law

*You can read a complete article by Daniel Dresibach on this unfortunate metaphor in the appendix located at the back of this book.

at the University of Texas, wrote about how activist judges have expanded their power (with the urging of the ACLU)—something that Jefferson and the other Founding Fathers never intended.

Graglia wrote, "Judge-made constitutional law is the product of judicial review—the power of judges to disallow policy choices (i.e., the will of the people) made by other officials of government, supposedly on the ground that they are prohibited by the Constitution. Thomas Jefferson warned that judges, always eager to expand their jurisdiction, would 'twist and shape' the Constitution 'as an artist shapes a ball of wax.' This is exactly what has happened."[41]

Dr. Robert George, of Princeton University, has commented that like so many other matters the ACLU's invocation of Jefferson is very selective. George states that Jefferson warned after Chief Justice John Marshall instituted judicial review in *Marbury vs. Madison* (1803) that the power judicial review would give to judges to invalidate legislation would lead to a form of despotism (tyranny).[42]

It is this judicial activism—encouraged by the ACLU and its allies time and time again (and as we have seen throughout this book) to overturn the will of the people and silence people of faith—that Jefferson was concerned about, yet the ACLU and its allies now consantly invoke his name to justify something that he abhorred.

The ACLU's War on Religion

In chapter 1, we discussed the "ACLU's Unlucky Thirteen," a sampling of Supreme Court cases the ACLU and its allies have used to limit religious freedom and attack the sanctity of human life and the family.

Most of the ACLU's attacks take place on the local level, often against public officials or small governmental units that do not have the funds or the stamina for a long legal tussle, or by working with officials sympathetic to the ACLU agenda. Merely listing the legal attacks on religious expression by the ACLU would fill an entire book, but here are recent examples of how it has either silenced believers or attempted to eradicate public acknowledgment of religion, in particular, of Christianity.

One of the means the ACLU has long used to force public officials to bow to their demands is the threat of attorneys fees pursuant to federal law.* Congress enacted the current statute after a Supreme Court decision, to provide for those "acting under color of law" who would have to pay fees and costs to successful plaintiffs. Though this law was never meant to be used in "Establishment Clause" claims by the ACLU, it has become a major source of revenue (as we will see later) for them and terror for public officials who fear financial ruin.

The ACLU has filed a lawsuit against the National Park Service demanding that it remove a cross placed in honor of World War I veterans at Sunrise Rock in the Mohave Desert in California. Because in 1994 then-President Bill Clinton declared Sunrise Rock to be a federal reserve, the cross is now fair game for the ACLU to claim that this tribute to the brave individuals who have fought for our nation's freedom is illegal.[43]

In Los Angeles, the ACLU demanded the removal of a tiny cross among many historical symbols on the city's official seal. This demand was in spite of California's religious history that includes Father Junipero Serra, the Franciscan missionary, through whose efforts the El Camino Real, the coastal highway was established. He and his later fellow Franciscans built twenty-one Christian missions from San Diego to San Francisco between 1769 and 1823. In addition, the missions provided the foundation of many California cities—San Diego, Los Angeles, Santa Barbara, San Jose, San Francisco, and San Juan Capistrano.[44]

The Los Angeles threat came after the ACLU was successful in demanding the city of Redlands remove a cross from its seal. Emboldened by that victory, the ACLU's southern California chapter wrote to Los Angeles County, "[The seal] prominently depicts a Latin cross, a sectarian religious symbol that represents the beliefs of one segment of the county's diverse population" and is an "impermissible endorsement of Christianity."[45]

Somehow, the ACLU believes historical reality is irrelevant and missed pointing out that the main figure on the seal was Pomona, the Roman goddess of fruits and trees, which it mysteriously did not demand to be removed. (But she was anyway by the city.)[46] But then again, in the ACLU's eyes, that's probably being inclusive of those who practice paganism. Another symbol on the seal is Pearlette, a

---

*Title 42, U.S.C. § 1988.

prize cow, but the ACLU has (yet) to file a suit on behalf of vegetarians or vegans to have her removed too.

The ACLU letter continued: "Under clearly established law, the seal is unconstitutional" and then threatened to get a court order to get rid of the seal unless it was removed within a "reasonable time frame."[47]

Somehow, this dangerous cross display in the nation's second most populous city had escaped the ACLU's attention for nearly fifty years (the seal was adopted on March 1, 1957). The cross had been placed in the seal to represent the area's undisputable historical settlement by missionaries. In a response to the ACLU's southern California Executive Director Ramona Ripston, Los Angeles County Supervisor Michael Antonovich wrote, "The cross on our county seal reflects these historical facts. It does not mean that we are all Roman Catholics or that everyone who resides in our county is a Christian—it only reflects our historical roots."[48] Antonovich said that the price tag to taxpayers to alter the seal would be in "hundreds of thousands of dollars, if not millions"[49] because the seal is on every piece of printed stationery, city and county vehicle, business cards, public buildings, and so forth.[50] But, as we have seen with the Boy Scouts and other cases, the ACLU has never had a problem forcing taxpayers to pay to advance its agenda and trampling on the taxpayers' religious freedom at the same time.

Nevertheless, fearing an ACLU lawsuit, three supervisors voted to negotiate with the ACLU and replace the cross with depictions of a Spanish mission building and American Indians. Many citizens were outraged, and the supervisors received thousands of e-mails and phone calls, with nearly all of them in favor of fighting the ACLU to keep the cross.[51]

The supervisors caved in even though they were offered free legal support by several organizations, including ADF. Gary McCaleb, ADF senior counsel, said, "Challenging this symbol of the county's cultural and historical roots, solely because it is religious, smacks of anti-religious bias. I think this disrespects the religious community and the history of the county."[52]

Ironically, one of the strongest criticisms about the ACLU's actions came from ACLU member (and self-avowed atheist) Kenneth Kleinberg, a lawyer who represented the family of the artist who drew the seal in 1957. Kleinberg said, "How dare anyone consider tampering with his art. And to challenge the artist's intent without consulting the artist, his family or any art expert, I think, is folly on the part of the ACLU."[53]

Kleinberg's statement exposes the truth about the ACLU. This organization, which prides itself in fighting censorship (and upholds the public funding of even the most profane "art"), has no problem censoring any symbol or any speech, according to its agenda, it deems to be religious.

Dennis Prager compared the ACLU's actions to Soviet-style totalitarianism:

> As a graduate student at Columbia University's Russian Institute, my field of study was totalitarianism. I learned that a major characteristic of Soviet and other totalitarian regimes was their frequent rewriting of history. As a famous Soviet dissident joke put it, "In the Soviet Union, the future is known; it's the past which is always changing."
>
> Given the relationship between changing the past and totalitarianism, there is reason to be amply frightened by the current decision of the Los Angeles County Board of Supervisors to change the seal of Los Angeles County. . . . To some people, this is not an important issue. These people do not understand what is at stake. But the ACLU knows what is at stake—the removal of religion, specifically Christianity, from American history; and the replacing of Judeo-Christian values with leftist ones. . . . The cross represents the Christian history of Los Angeles County. It no more advocates Christianity than the Goddess Pomona advocates Roman paganism or the cow promotes Hinduism. It is therefore a lie to argue Los Angeles County is pushing Christianity on its citizens.
>
> As for the argument put forth by the ACLU's Ramona Ripston that the tiny cross makes non-Christians feel "unwelcome," as a Jew I find the comment equally absurd and paranoid. I have spoken to Los Angeles County rabbis of every denomination, and not one felt the cross should be removed, let alone felt "unwelcome." By the same logic

[as we noted earlier], vegetarians should feel particularly unwelcome in Los Angeles County, given that two panels depict animals as food.

What we have here is an American version of the Taliban. The ACLU and the supervisors are leftist versions of the Taliban—attempting to erase the Christian history of America just as the Muslim Taliban tried to erase the Buddhist history of Afghanistan when they blew up ancient Buddhist sculptures in their country.

Los Angeles County is the largest county in America. If it allows its past to be expunged by a vote of three to two, America's past is sure to follow. If you want to know what happens after that, ask any student of the Soviet Union.[54]

But just five hours north of Los Angeles on the coastal highway lies San Jose, a center of the Internet and computer and software development. In the mid-1990s, a twenty-five-foot-long statue of an Aztec god, Quetzalcoatl, was installed prominently in a city park, despite the loud protests of many.[55] This "god" remains today, and is seemingly immune from ACLU "protective action."[56] We believe it is only a matter of time before the ACLU's purge will include demands that places' names be changed, such as the Mount of the Holy Cross in the Colorado Rockies. When will Corpus Christi (Latin for "body of Christ"), Los Angeles (the City of Angels), San Diego, San Juan Capistrano (a major figure of the Crusades), San Francisco—named for saints—be forced to change their names? Will Maryland, named for a queen known for her religious faith, face ACLU lawsuits as well? How about the literally countless street names, especially in western communities like Phoenix, such as "Palo Christie" (Christ's body), innumerable saints, or even Tierra Buena (a biblical reference to "good earth").

The ACLU has also been successful in getting religious symbols removed from the seals of Stow, Ohio; Redlands, California (mentioned earlier); Duluth, Minnesota; Plattsmouth, Nebraska; and Republic, Missouri.[57] ADF and its allies have been successful in stopping the efforts of the ACLU and its allies in numerous other cases involving the removal of public displays of religious faith, including a Ten Commandments monument at a downtown Phoenix park.[58] ADF has provided funding for cases such as *Mercier vs. City of LaCrosse,*

Wisconsin (Seventh Circuit Court of Appeals), *ACLU of Nebraska vs. City of Plattsmouth, Nebraska* (Eighth Circuit Court of Appeals), and *Summum vs. City of Duchesne, Utah* (U.S. District Court–Utah), which are currently winding their way through our nation's judicial system. An important pair of Ten Commandments cases are before the U.S. Supreme Court as this book goes to press.

In Chester County, Pennsylvania, the ACLU and the Freethought Society of Philadelphia sued to have an eighty-five-year-old plaque of the Ten Commandments removed at the county courthouse. A lower court ruled in favor of the ACLU and its allies and ordered the plaque covered with a shroud so it would not *offend* someone.

With ADF funding for a friend-of-the-court brief and other assistance, county officials appealed the case to the U.S. Court of Appeals for the Third Circuit. In 2003, a three-judge panel issued a unanimous decision that overturned the lower court ruling and allowed the plaque to be displayed again.

Colin Hanna, a Chester County commissioner, said, "This is a great day for Chester County, for America, for the Constitution, and for the original intent of the framers of the Constitution."[59]

Pastor Mark Roberts, a Presbyterian pastor in Irvine, California, pointed out the lunacy of the ACLU's position. He asked if a public school history book did an article on D-Day and included a photograph of the American cemetery in Normandy with more than nine thousand crosses on the graves of our soldiers, would the ACLU argue the textbook was promoting Christianity?[60] Since tens of thousands of Christian crosses and Jewish Stars of David appear in government maintained veteran's cemeteries, how long will it be before the ACLU demands their removal as well or seeks to ban faith-based commitment on graveside memorials? Will they ultimately try to ban use of active duty servicemen and women in funerals and memorial services as well?

But are the ACLU's actions driven solely by its belief that the separation of church and state requires every vestige of public religious expression be eliminated? Or is there another motive?

Veteran pro-family activist Phyllis Schlafly, who fought valiantly to block the passage of the Equal Rights Amendment in the 1970s and 1980s, expressed her opinion that many ACLU threats (and lawsuits) are driven not only by its hostility to religious—and in particular, Christian—expression but also by its desire to fill its coffers with taxpayer money. She wrote:

A little known 1976 federal law called the Civil Rights' Attorney's Fees Awards Act enables the ACLU to collect attorneys' fees for its suits against crosses, the Pledge of Allegiance, and the Ten Commandments. This law was designed to help plaintiffs in civil rights cases. But the ACLU is using it for First Amendment cases, asserting that it is a civil right to NOT to see a cross or the Ten Commandments.

The financial lure created by this law is the engine that drives dozens of similar cases nationwide. Every state, county, city, public park or school that has a cross, a Ten Commandments monument, or recites the Pledge of Allegiance, has become a target for ACLU fundraising. . . . In Utah, the ACLU even announced a scavenger hunt with a prize for anyone who could find another Ten Commandments monument that the ACLU could find an activist judge to remove.[61]*

When the ACLU and its allies filed their lawsuit to force former Alabama Chief Justice Roy Moore to remove the Ten Commandments monument from the Supreme Judicial Building in Montgomery, they were awarded $540,000 in attorneys' fees and expenses from Alabamans.[62] (The judge who ruled against Moore spoke at an ACLU conference on international law only a few days later. We discuss the ACLU's assault on American sovereignty through the advocacy of international law in a later chapter.)

Kentucky taxpayers footed a $121,500 bill when they had to pay the ACLU for its legal action against a Ten Commandments display outside the state capitol. A Tennessee county was told to pay $50,000 to the ACLU for the same pleasure of being sued.[63]

But besides the potential financial awards for the ACLU, the core issue comes back to the duplicity of the ACLU. While it tries to ensure no one pushes religious views on others, it makes sure everyone

---

*The authors believe Congress should clarify that it never meant for this to be used in so-called Establishment Clause claims against public officials who acknowledge, or allow others, especially those from past generations, God on public property.

conforms to its agenda and beliefs. The ACLU does not care how much it costs taxpayers or anyone else to conform to its revision of America's history, heritage, and faith.

As we stated in the introduction of the book, prominent Christians are not the ones trying to force non-Christians to accept their beliefs or else. Ann Coulter illustrated how the ACLU tries to force its beliefs on Americans, while claiming others engage in this action:

It's never Jerry Falwell flying to Manhattan to review high-school graduation speeches, or James Dobson making sure New York City schools give as much time to God as to Mother Earth, or Pat Robertson demanding a crèche next to the schools' Kwanzaa displays. . . .

The ACLU got word of a Ten Commandments monument in a public park in Plattsmouth, Nebraska (pop. 7,000) and immediately swooped in to demand that the offensive symbol be removed. . . . Soon cranes were in the park ripping out a monument that had sat there, not bothering anyone, for 40 years.

ACLU busybodies sued Johnson County, Iowa, demanding that it remove a Ten Commandments monument that had been in a public courtyard since 1964. Within a year, the 2,500-pound granite monument was gone.[64]

Coulter then correctly pointed out how the ACLU has used its disinformation (perpetuated by activist judges) about what the First Amendment requires to wage its war on the religious freedom of millions of Americans:

The alleged legal basis for removing all of these Ten Commandments monuments is the establishment clause of the First Amendment. That clause provides: "Congress shall make no law respecting an establishment of religion." The vigilant observer will note instantly that none of the monuments cases involves Congress, a law, or an establishment of religion.

Monuments are not "laws," the Plattsmouth, Nebraska, public park is not "Congress," and the Ten Commandments are not a religion. To the contrary, all three major world religions believe in Moses and the Ten Commandments. Liberals might as well say the establishment clause prohibits

Republicans from breathing, as that it prohibits a Ten Commandments display.[65]

Some people, including many Christians and Orthodox Jews, sometimes wonder what the issue is with the removal of public symbols of faith such as the Ten Commandments. To that argument, we quote President Harry S. Truman: "The fundamental basis of this nation's laws was given to Moses on the Mount. The fundamental basis of our Bill of Rights comes from the teachings. . . . If we don't have the proper fundamental moral background, we will finally wind up with a totalitarian government which does not believe in rights for anybody except the state."[66]

When the ACLU and its allies file their seemingly endless and costly lawsuits to remove the Ten Commandments, and other public vestiges of faith, they are systematically stripping our nation of its legal heritage and history. If we forget our moral foundation, then all other aspects of a free and democratic society will come tumbling down. In addition, once we remove the moral basis for our laws, the respect for all law weakens, resulting in social anarchy and a far more dangerous place to live. With the moral basis for laws gone, the ACLU can reach its goal: a society in which virtually anything goes morally, if the ACLU approves of it, at anytime.

The systematic removal of the moral basis of our law led to the mayor of San Francisco's open defiance of state law to issue marriage licenses to same-sex couples. It has led to the increased rejection of the moral authority of the church in society. It has led to the weakening of parents's rights to direct their children's upbringing. It has led to exalting self over sacrifice and rights over responsibilities.

It Doesn't Stop There

The ACLU's legal assault on religious expression doesn't stop at public displays of the Ten Commandments or religious symbols on city seals. These so-called "free speech" advocates have become the number-one religious censor in America in many ways.

Franklin County Children's Services of Columbus, Ohio, wanted to stage a gospel concert at a local church to help raise awareness of adoption and the need for foster parents and mentors among the religious community. In the previous year, the agency received more

than five hundred inquiries about adoption and foster parenthood from those who attended. But the religious censors at the ACLU caught a whiff of it and threatened legal action.

The ACLU sent a letter to Children's Services threatening a lawsuit if the concert wasn't immediately canceled. The agency's director could not believe the unreasonableness of the ACLU's position. He said, "Our efforts do not constitute a subsidy of any religious group, nor do we require any child to observe any particular religious denomination." The director noted that the *majority* of adoptive or foster parents had been part of the religious community.[67]

In Manatee County, Florida, the ACLU was involved in a lawsuit against a school district for allowing a small Baptist church to rent vacant classrooms to hold Sunday services and to store its hymnals during the week. The ACLU apparently was afraid that impressionable schoolchildren might see a Bible or hymnbook and be irreparably harmed. An ADF-funded lawyer argued the case and the ACLU lost.[68] This was exactly the type of case that the ACLU would have probably won by default in years past. If the ACLU had won, it would have set another dangerous legal precedent to use against other counties and states to deny churches their constitutional right to rent school facilities for services and meetings during non-school hours as other groups are allowed to do.

In Oklahoma for more than thirty years, school teacher George Warrington, as a volunteer, had been teaching Bible lessons to his students during non-school time. The curriculum was written by Bible Fellowships, and the students voluntarily participated. Then the

ACLU religious censors caught a sniff of the alleged "violation" of the separation of church and state and went to work.

They filed a lawsuit on behalf of two parents against George and Bible Fellowships claiming that they were "co-conspirators to establish religion." The case went to a jury, who found against George and Bible Fellowships but only awarded the parents $251—an indication of how they really felt about the ACLU lawsuit.

But the story does not end there. ACLU-backed attorneys turned around and sought more than *eighty thousand dollars* from George for their legal fees and costs. When they didn't get enough, they filed a costly appeal to a higher court.

George was unable to defend himself against the ACLU's form of legalized extortion. ADF stepped in, free of charge, in order to provide him with an adequate defense. When the case was finally decided by the federal court of appeals, the ACLU-backed attorneys only got a fraction of their original demand. In fact, the court noted, "When a plaintiff only recovers nominal damages [in a federal lawsuit] . . . the only reasonable [attorneys] fee is no fee at all."[69]

In Louisiana, the ACLU asked a federal judge to punish public school officials in Tangipahoa Parish because an adult prayed over the PA system before a high school baseball game. ACLU of Louisiana Executive Director Joe Cook called the school's actions "un-American and immoral" to allow the prayer.[70]

The ACLU then asked the federal court judge to sentence the school administrators and teachers to jail because a prayer had been offered at an awards banquet that included the words "In Jesus' name we pray." The ACLU also claimed that one teacher was holding prayers in her classroom, and that Bible study classes were being held in the school cafeteria.

Joe Cook said about this latest "outrage": "The federal court must rein in religious extremists who have taken over the Tangipahoa Parish school system by hijacking Christianity and using it to carry out their agenda of indoctrinating and proselytizing captive students under their control."[71] ADF is providing legal assistance to the school district in this case.

This is the same ACLU that has filed lawsuits to force mandatory "tolerance" training for school children to indoctrinate them in homosexual behavior. It is also another example of the ACLU's use of government coercion to force its agenda on America.

Also in Louisiana, the ACLU filed a lawsuit challenging a voluntary prayer group of Christian teachers who met on their own time during recess, not during instructional time.[72] While the ACLU was attacking private, voluntary prayer during recess, it sued the city of Nashville, Tennessee, to stop it from prohibiting fortune-telling there.[73] If religion in general keeps the ACLU up at night, why hasn't it demanded that names for some Grand Canyon landmarks that reflect Eastern religions—Brahma Temple, Vishnu Temple, Siva Temple—be changed? Those must be OK to the ACLU, but a nonsectarian plaque that gives glory to God (gasp!) might be an insidious form of religious indoctrination. What about Quetzalcoatl in San Jose? It is obvious that the ACLU's battles are selective; Christianity and Orthodox Judaism with their moral absolutes must be rooted out of our society in the view of the ACLU and its allies.

The Current Climate for Religious Freedom

The result of the ACLU's legal assault on religious freedom (through its misapplication of the First Amendment) can be seen in communities across America on an almost daily basis.

Drawing from statements in the ACLU policy guide, Michael Novak and John Templeton wrote about in which direction the ACLU would like to take America:

In 2007, the American Civil Liberties Union was finally successful in getting Ten Commandments plaques removed from public buildings in all fifty states. In addition:

1. They forced the Ten Commandments to be expunged from the Supreme Court building;
2. They obliged the U.S. Senate and House of Representatives to fire their chaplains;
3. They won a ban on official chaplains in the military;
4. They removed "In God We Trust" from all currency and public documents;
5. They removed "Under God" from the Pledge of Allegiance;

6. They removed all crosses, Stars of David, and crescents from the gravestones of American soldiers in military cemeteries around the world;

7. Finally, as a coup de grace, they succeeded in getting major revisions or deletions in the public use of American historical documents, including:

- The removal from the Declaration of Independence of the words: "Nature's God," "Creator," "Supreme Judge," and "Divine Providence."

- Deletion from the public use of letters and speeches by America's founders of any reference to God, Providence, the Ten Commandments, or religion in general, including numerous such references made by George Washington, John Adams, Thomas Jefferson, James Madison, and Abraham Lincoln.

- Deletion—when sung in public—of the last God-laden stanzas of "My Country 'Tis of Thee" and "The Star Spangled Banner."

With the completion of this public-spirited contribution, the ACLU began criminal prosecution against any minister or priest who argued from the Bible in public forums to suggest that any given act might be judged morally wrong— contending that such judgment is discriminatory against anyone engaging in such an act, and serves to diminish his or her dignity and/or self-esteem.

A brochure published by the ACLU in mid-2005* argued that it is morally permissible to hate traditional religions for their discriminatory teachings. It is no violation of hate speech codes, the ACLU pamphlet argues, to express hatred of those who uphold the narrow teachings of Christianity and Judaism.

God bless the ACLU for cleansing the public life of the United States, at last, of discriminatory religious speech.[74]

---

*Note: the authors are talking about a hypothetical brochure. We are not aware of any plans of the ACLU to publish such a document in the near future; they still have a lot more of what's left of the Constitution to rewrite first.

Sound far-fetched? Consider these real-life examples that ADF
and its legal allies have been involved in, thanks to the legal climate
promoted by the ACLU:

- In some states, government officials have refused to rent public schools or town halls to churches for Sunday worship, at
  any price, but open their doors to secular groups.[75] In other
  instances, they have tried to charge churches multiple times
  the rent charged to secular groups.

- Senior citizens had their transportation to get prescription
  drugs and attend funeral services for friends and even their
  food service threatened to be cut off—simply because they
  wanted to worship God in a public senior center, where no
  objection was made to secular activities.[76]*

- A public school told an eight-year-old girl she couldn't distribute her handmade valentines at school because they said "Jesus
  Loves You" and "Freely Rely on God," but dozens of other
  secular messages of love and philosophy were allowed.[77]

- A couple endured a nearly two-year legal battle to win the
  right to choose a religious message in a tile fund-raising
  program for an elementary school wall to honor their children. The objectionable tiles read, "God Bless Haley" and
  "God Bless Quinn."[78] Another school in Manhattan Beach,
  California, demolished an entire wall of tiles, spurning the
  voluntary fundraising efforts, because the officials were so
  adamant not to allow a set of tiles in the shape of a cross.[79]
  However, scores of other personal expressions and comments were accepted.

- School officials are told they cannot sponsor, or even permit,
  baccalaureate services or select clergymen to give nonsectarian prayers.[80] In addition, school districts have been told
  that they cannot allow student-led, student-initiated prayer
  before football games (the confusing result of another U.S.
  Supreme Court decision from an ACLU-involved lawsuit)[81]
  and at graduation ceremonies (which students may do, ac-

---

*Kelly Shackelford of ADF ally Liberty Legal Institute provided many of these details.

cording to the U.S. Supreme Court, but it is almost always legally challenged by the ACLU).[82]

Concerning public acknowledgment of faith at graduation ceremonies, ADF has taken the battle directly to the ACLU. We sent a memorandum (included in the appendix) to all state boards of education and state education associations advising them that the U.S. Constitution does "not require the banning of baccalaureate services or student-initiated, student-led prayers at graduation." The memo instructed school administrators on how they can develop constitutionally sound policies to allow baccalaureate services and student-initiated graduation prayer.

As a result of these efforts to give school officials and students the truth about religious expression at graduation ceremonies, victories are already happening.

In Norfolk, Nebraska, seniors had voted to have two nonsectarian prayers—an invocation and a benediction—during their graduation ceremony. After one student complained and went with his mother to the ACLU, the ACLU informed the school superintendent it would take "immediate" legal action if the prayers were allowed.

At the beginning of the commencement ceremony, the school board president told those assembled, "With deepest regret from the Board and Administration, and with our most sincere apologies to the Senior Class of 2003, we will need to remove the Invocation and Benediction from today's graduation ceremonies. . . . we are saddened that it has come to this."[83]

Another school board member had had enough of the ACLU's bullying tactics. When he got up to speak, he recited the Lord's Prayer, without asking people to bow their heads or stand, in protest of this unconstitutional censoring of religious speech. The result was the ACLU and the family filed a lawsuit against two members of the school board.

Normally, the ACLU would have had the heads of the two officials served to them on a platter. But this time, ADF-allied attorney Jeff Downing came to the defense of the two school board members. On August 20, 2003, the U.S. Circuit Court of Appeals for the Eighth Circuit held that the school board member was privately opposing the school board's decision to omit the prayers when he recited the

Lord's Prayer, and therefore he was engaging in constitutionally protected speech. The claims against the other board member had been previously dropped.[84]

In Iowa, Mathew Reynolds had achieved the highest grade-point average in his senior class and thus was selected to be valedictorian. When he wanted to give credit to Jesus Christ for his achievements, school officials informed him his speech must be secular and not mention his religious faith, even if Mathew made it clear at the beginning of the speech that his opinions were personal and did not represent those of the school.

Mathew and his parents contacted ADF staff counsel Kevin Theriot, who quickly fired a letter to the school informing officials of Mathew's constitutional right to talk about his faith during his speech. The school relented, and Mathew was able to share the following thoughts:

> In preparing for my speech today, my original intention was to focus upon our achievements and successes and to celebrate all that lies ahead of us; however, as this day approached I found myself being pressured by a number of people not to talk about God. I was told to keep my speech secular, and that previous speeches that had acknowledged Jesus Christ had been offensive and inappropriate. Some people even suggested that it was unconstitutional to acknowledge Jesus Christ in a commencement address. I must admit, I was troubled by these remarks. They challenged me to be true to the foundation of my life, and to examine the foundational principles upon which our nation was built. For too many years now, the voices of those speaking out against God and his place in our public life, has been louder than those speaking for God. Christians in America have been humble and meek, which are things that God would have us to be, but Jesus set an example for Christians to also be bold. When the temple was out of order he turned over the tables and set things right. Today, it is our society that is out of order, and it is the foundation of our country that is being threatened. . . . I am not here

today to be accepted. I am here to be true to the foundation of my life and of my country.[85]

We could not have said it better. The ACLU and its allies, through their relentless attack on religion and religious expression, are going after the very foundation on which our nation rests. Whether someone believes in Christ or not, he can see that the continued erosion of moral authority gone unchecked, and enabled by the continued legal assaults of the ACLU, will cause more damage to our society than any external enemy could ever do.

For an example of how the ACLU uses a legal precedent to directly challenge the religious freedom of churches, we can look at the ACLU-assisted case of *Bob Jones University vs. United States*, which the ACLU describes on its Web site: "1983: *Bob Jones University vs. United States:* The Court rejected two fundamentalist Christian schools' claim, supported by the Reagan Justice Department, that the First Amendment guarantee of religious liberty forbade the denial of income tax exemptions to educational and religious institutions that practice racial discrimination. Instead, the Court held that the IRS is empowered to set rules enforcing a 'settled public policy' against racial discrimination in education."[86]

Of course, we reject categorically any form of racial discrimination and as Christians believe from the creation account of Genesis that we humans are descendents of the same parents. However, this decision, and its multiple outgrowths, are being used to force private religious organizations such as Catholic Charities in California to violate their core religious tenets by ordering them to offer contraceptive coverage in their health insurance plans.[87] The California Supreme Court, using the ACLU's argument, concluded that the requirement that a charity conform to "settled public policy" in order to qualify for tax-exempt status trumped religious doctrine. The U.S. Supreme Court refused to hear the case.[88] If same-sex "marriage" were to become "settled" public policy, would churches and religious organizations that would not employ active homosexual marriage advocates, perform the ceremonies, or allow the use of their facilities for these "weddings" be charged with discrimination and lose their tax-exempt status, as Bob Jones University did?

Raising concerns about how this ruling could later be used by homosexual advocates to file discrimination claims against the church and threaten its nonprofit status, Alan wrote long before the *Lawrence vs. Texas* (sodomy) decision:

> If the Supreme Court, or a plethora of courts of appeal, adopts a new test—a new standard for Constitutional review—for all claims of sex/gender discrimination under the same rules and policies that racial discrimination is now viewed (i.e., "strict scrutiny"), or decides that the Constitution, public policy, or law of the United States protects or provides special privileges for sodomy and other homosexual behavior, it is only a matter of time, application of legal "logic," and litigation before it is claimed that sex/gender and sexual orientation/behavior "discrimination" is akin to racial discrimination and thus in all instances contrary to public policy and therefore those who engage in such actions are not "entitled" to the public "benefit" of tax exemption. . . . The Supreme Court, analyzing the government's grant of tax exemptions or allowance of deductions, stated: "History buttresses logic to make it clear that, to warrant exemption under 501 (c)(3), (the IRS code for non-profit organizations), an institution must . . . be in harmony with the public interest. The institution's purpose must not be so at odds with the common community conscience as to undermine any public interest that might otherwise be conferred."[89]

In fact, in Canada, a homosexual couple has filed a complaint with a Human Rights Tribunal against the Knights of Columbus (a Catholic organization) for refusing to rent their meeting hall to them for their "wedding reception."[90] A complaint has also been filed against the Catholic Bishop of the Diocese of Sault Ste Marie for his exercise of free speech.[91]

Richard Land of the Southern Baptist Convention's Ethics and Religious Liberty Commission put it succinctly: "If political correctness wins the struggle for hearts and minds, then you may see tremendous pressure to take away the tax-exempt status of churches and denominations and organizations that refuse to fully firmly affirm and accept the homosexual lifestyle."[92]

Raymond Flynn, former U.S. ambassador to the Vatican and former mayor of Boston, concurred: "The issue of legalizing same-sex marriages in Massachusetts and California raises the question: Does this mean there will be a case brought against the Catholic Church for discrimination? I think it is the next step."[93] (See appendix 2 for information on how churches can take moral stands and speak out on the issues of the day without jeopardizing their tax-exempt, nonprofit status under current decisions.)

We share these examples because this is exactly where the ACLU and its allies want to go in America if churches do not bow to their agenda.

The ACLU has also tried to poke its nose into internal church issues. In the early nineties, a small Oregon church had dismissed their youth pastor—who subsequently filed a lawsuit against the church to force it to pay into the state unemployment compensation fund. The case was heard by the state Employment Appeals Board (EAB), which sided with the discharged employee. This case set a dangerous precedent of permitting a state employment board to be involved in the process of determining "legitimate reasons" for a church to dismiss a pastoral employee—thus disqualifying him or her from the benefits. Such a precedent could have led to the state telling churches who and why they can hire or fire ministers or priests and is the exact entanglement of religion that the First Amendment forbids.[94]*

Who provided key legal support to get the government entangled with the private, internal religious dispute? You guessed it: the Oregon chapter of the ACLU![95]

If the ACLU is allowed to win this battle, here's what our children will face:

- The ability to live and proclaim the faith will be greatly compromised and increasingly restricted legally, especially when it comes to public display or expression.
- They will grow up with little or no knowledge of America's religious heritage and history and potentially with the perception that traditional religion is a negative force in society.

---

*While we are sympathetic to the potential need for a dismissed pastor to have some type of unemployment benefits, the greater issue here is the ACLU's and government's insert into private employment matters of a church.

- The religious freedom that Americans have enjoyed will not
  be available to them and their children; it is likely that they
  will face persecution for their faith as well.
- As the influence of religion declines in society, the emptiness
  will be filled with dangerous and destructive behaviors, leading to a less-civilized society.

Scholar Michael Novak summed up the ACLU's brave new
world of a secular society when he wrote, "And what will happen to
our own civilization, when the full atheistic agenda of the ACLU has
finally and completely been accomplished? When there is no one who
can speak publicly, under government auspices, about the ground of
our rights? When no public symbols or ceremonies remind the young
of these sacred sources, from whose depths alone spring their special
nobility and unique calling? When the United States has thoroughly
abandoned in public the faith of our forbearers, and only the desolate
winds of atheism blow across our monuments? When our rights are
reduced to those of a barnyard?"[96]

He concluded the result will be a time of bloody revolution as the
secular replaces the sacred and *all* respect for faith, life, and the family
is replaced by the exaltation of self.

We will lose our liberties if we don't fight the ACLU, its agenda,
and its many allies. We'll lose them when we give in to the ACLU's
demands. We'll lose when we quit singing "God Bless America" or
when we allow the ACLU to take "In God We Trust" off our currency. We'll lose when students can no longer express their faith at a
graduation ceremony. We'll lose when we return to the morally and
legally repugnant practice of issuing governmental licenses to clergymen, as the British did in colonial America and as totalitarian regimes
still do today.

And the America that our Founding Fathers—and millions of
others in succeeding wars—risked and sacrificed their lives to protect
will cease to exist. That is why ADF is engaged in this battle and will
continue to be as long as it takes to preserve God's gift of religious
freedom for America.

CHAPTER 7

The ACLU vs. Christmas

'Twas the night before Christmas, when all through the house
Not a creature was stirring, not even a mouse.
The stockings were hung by the chimney with care.
In hope that St. Nicholas soon would be there.
When out on a lawn there arose such a clatter,
I sprang from my bed to see what was the matter.
There was Santa again, on his annual journeys,
Ensnared in a group of eight tiny attorneys.
They looked pretty grim and they threatened to sue,
So we knew in a flash—"It's the ACLU!"
They paid us no heed, but went straight to their work,
Handcuffing poor Santa, then said with a smirk:
　　"This is secular airspace, we can't have a saint
　　Flying our flightpaths—we need some restraint.
　　A sleigh full of toys is OK, we suppose,
　　But faith-based incursions we've got to oppose."
Litigation on Christmas is something we dread,
So we nestled our children all under their beds,
The grinch doesn't scare them, and Scrooge they see through,
But what kids are prepared for the ACLU?
The reindeer were shackled as a further incitement,
Then the lawyers unpackaged a 12-count indictment.
"Merry Christmas to all!" they just had to foreclose
(Though they had no complaint about all the "Ho Hos").
One lawyer objected to Santa's red clothing.
"It's religiously tainted," he said with some loathing.
"Poinsettias (the red ones) everybody must note, are
A church-state offense in St. Paul, Minnesota!"
Santa's climb up each chimney (one lawyer made mention)
Is a symbolic reference to Jesus' ascension.

And the reindeer, of course, recall the Apostles,
And those who deny it are nothing but fossils.
These lawyers had labored at neighborhood schools,
Making Christmas extinct there as part of the rules.
Praise Kwanzaa or Ramadan—they think it's quite splendid,
But say "Merry Christmas" and you might get suspended.
Our children, God bless them, don't get or recall
Why "inclusiveness" doesn't include them at all.
Why diversity theory (as the lawyers insist) must
Require the annual quashing of Christmas.
In Canada, home of post-everything living,
Now the "12 Days of Christmas" are "The 12 Days of Giving."
Christmas trees aren't party to the season at all,
They buy "multicultural trees" at the mall.
At a hospital (Catholic), the staff is ashamed
To use the word Christmas, so their tree is misnamed,
As a "care tree," though some would prefer "tree of life."
(Why not "tall lit-up flora" to avoid any strife?)
Australians are told they should have no compunctions
Calling parties at Christmastime "end of the year functions."
The idea is to make Christmas somehow unmentionable,
A tactic I think of as wholly contemptionable.
Instead of "White Christmas" they will probably sing,
"I'm dreaming of a snow day sometime in pre-Spring."
Here's my suggestion, a harsh one I fear,
Why not call Christmas "Christmas?" (It's just an idea.)[1]*
—John Leo

The poem above, by John Leo of *U.S. News and World Report*,[2] was written with tongue in cheek but with a great element of truth. Many of the scenarios he mentions are actual cases that have been part of a relentless legal assault against the public expression of Christmas. While not all of the cases were filed by the ACLU, they are the products of the legal environment fomented by the ACLU to censor any public mention of Christmas, despite a 2000 Gallup poll that found *96 percent* of Americans—Americans of all faith— celebrate Christmas.[3]

*The authors want to thank John Leo for graciously allowing us to reprint this column in its entirety.

For instance, red poinsettias were banned from the Ramsey County Courthouse–St. Paul, Minnesota, City Hall because someone deemed them a "Christian symbol."[4] The city of Pittsburgh renamed the Christmas season "Sparkle Days," lest anyone be offended by the dreaded C-word.[5] ADF and its allies had to sue the Plano, Texas, Independent School District because it barred the wearing of red and green clothing at school "winter break" parties because the colors allegedly symbolized Christmas. Officials there also told students they could not write "Merry Christmas" in letters they sent to members of our armed forces in Iraq.[6] In Rochester, Minnesota, two thirteen-year-old girls were *suspended* for wearing red and green scarves and saying "Merry Christmas" in a school video presentation.[7] In Connecticut, a library refused to display paintings of Jesus' nativity and resurrection as part of a rotating display of local art. In Queens, New York, a school district that allowed a menorah and an Islamic star and crescent in its holiday display would not allow a young child to include a Nativity scene. The Indiana University School of Law removed a Christmas tree and replaced it with a generic depiction of winter.[8]

A student in Indianolo, Iowa, was told by his school that he could not say "Merry Christmas" because it might offend someone. After an ADF-allied attorney got involved, the school changed its position and allowed the "offending" words to be uttered.

In Hanover Township, New Jersey, the school district threatened to outlaw Christmas carols at school concerts.[9] In a story featured on ABC World News Tonight with Peter Jennings, a school in Maplewood, New Jersey, even ordered purely instrumental Christmas music to be banned.[10] Central Michigan University warned Christians that Christmas "may be offensive to others within a place of employment."[11] (No warnings were issued for observers of the non-Christian holidays.)

Then there's the case of Sergeant Wayne Bird. Before he left for Afghanistan after the terrible events of September 11, 2001, he wanted to place an ornament that simply said "God Bless America" on the Wisconsin State "holiday" (what was once called Christmas) tree at the state capitol. He was quickly told by the Municipal Clerks Association that "no ornaments of religious nature" could be displayed on the tree. What was really prohibited were ornaments that referred to religions recognizing the holiday. With the assistance of an ADF-allied attorney, Sergeant Bird (after the case was featured on Fox News' *Hannity and Colmes* show) won back his constitutional right to put the ornament on the tree.[12] Although the ACLU was not directly involved in these cases, they illustrate the legal climate the ACLU has sought to create as demonstrated in the following ACLU legal actions against the public expression of Christmas.

In Baldwin City, Kansas, a local public school had a standing tradition of inviting a member of the community to dress as Santa Claus and visit elementary school children. That was until the ACLU got involved.

The school allowed an associate pastor from a local church to be Santa. When he asked why we celebrate Christmas, a little girl said, "Because it's Jesus' birthday."

That brought out the ACLU censors, who sent a letter to the school district demanding that this long-standing tradition be brought to an immediate halt. Why? Because the name "Jesus" had been said in a public school!

The ACLU was banking on its usual strategy of legal intimidation, misinformation, and fear to force the school officials to meekly defer to its demands. But that wasn't going to happen this time. An ADF staff attorney got involved and equipped the school district with the information needed to successfully confront the ACLU and protect the school's traditional Christmas tradition. Instead of the school district caving in to the ACLU's demands, it was the ACLU that quietly slunk away.

In Benton, Louisiana, the ACLU filed a lawsuit against Bossier Parish Schools because the school displayed a Nativity scene on school property. The U.S. Supreme Court has ruled that religious symbols on public property—like Nativity scenes—are constitutional if placed for the legitimate secular purpose of celebrating a holiday or depicting its origins. ADF attorney Mike Johnson got involved, and the outraged citizens staged a huge rally in support of the school district and against the ACLU.[13]

In Tipton, Iowa, the ACLU threatened to sue the Cedar County Board of Supervisors if they allowed a Nativity scene to be displayed on the county lawn. The Tipton Chamber of Commerce had permission to put the Nativity scene on courthouse grounds for several years, with never a hint of protest. Other private groups had the right to put up secular displays, but none had asked to do so. The ACLU Christmas police caught a whiff of this nefarious act and sent a demand letter off to the county threatening a lawsuit. It read in part: "We [the ACLU] have received numerous complaints concerning the display over the years and are now writing to ask the County to discontinue the practice of displaying the crèche on public grounds beginning with this holiday season. We would be happy to assist Cedar County in choosing a constitutionally appropriate method of celebrating the solstice holidays."[14]

It would have been interesting to see what the ACLU would have come up with if the county had accepted the offer of assistance for celebrating the "solstice holidays." But the county did not. Instead, the county contacted ADF for help. ADF-allied attorney Doug Napier sent a response to the ACLU, advising that the law allowed the Nativity display, and the ACLU backed down.

The ACLU sued the city of Cranston, Rhode Island, which had opened the front lawn of its city hall on an equal basis for "seasonal and holiday displays." Citizens were allowed to provide displays, which could be either religious or secular. The city also posted a disclaimer: "The public holiday displays are strictly from private citizens or groups. They do not represent an official view of the City of Cranston, nor are they endorsed by the city."

That wasn't good enough for the ACLU. It said, asserting that the privately funded religious displays—in this instance a Nativity scene—although surrounded by secular displays, was a violation of the "separation of church and state."

(As we will see later in the chapter, the ACLU publicly argues that religious displays can be constitutional if surrounded by secular images, such as snowmen and reindeer. Yet, its public statements are often very different from its actions, such as in this case).

An ADF-allied attorney came to the defense of the city, and a U.S. district court judge dismissed the ACLU's lawsuit. He noted that nothing in the city's public statements or in its implementation of its policy for Christmas displays "reveals or even remotely supports an inference that a religious purpose was behind the creation of the limited public forum."

After the loss, the ACLU warned it might file another lawsuit: "We'll have to look and see if the city has sufficiently *degraded* the religious nature of the crèche by surrounding it with snowmen and the like, so that it can pass constitutional muster."[15]

In Norwood, Massachusetts, the ACLU filed a lawsuit against a local school district because of its tradition of allowing a crèche on a school lawn. The school lawn was designated a "public forum," and other groups were allowed to put up displays as well, but none have chosen to do so. An ADF-allied attorney drafted a legal memo for the school, advising it of its rights. As a result, the school committee refused not to back down.[16]

In Kaneohe, Hawaii, the ACLU tried to get residents to change the name of the annual Christmas parade to "holiday parade." The parade organizers did not know how to respond because they were fearful of an ACLU lawsuit. An ADF-allied attorney sent the parade organizers a legal memo advising them that they could continue to call it a Christmas parade.

In Elizabeth, Colorado, the ACLU tried to censor the Christmas program of a local charter school. When the ACLU and one of its allies found out that the school was planning to include traditional Christmas carols as part of the program, they sent a letter, demanding that the school "must take immediate steps to comply with the constitutional separation of church and state."[17] If the ACLU had its way, the students could not even sing the purely secular song "Jingle Bells"![18] They then proceeded to make the usual threat of a lawsuit unless the school gave in to their demands. An ADF-allied attorney, Barry Arrington, quickly assisted the school, and the Christmas celebration was preserved.

This case appeared on the radar screen of Fox News talk-show host Bill O'Reilly, who invited Alan to discuss this ACLU legal assault on Christmas. During the interview, Alan helped expose the ACLU's campaign of misinformation and explained that the charter school had followed the law by including an "opt-out" provision for those students who might object to any music that mentioned the name of Christ. Alan informed O'Reilly and the viewing audience, that the Tenth Circuit Court of Appeals had ruled several years earlier that school programs featuring traditional Christmas carols are constitutional, as long as there was an opt-out provision. Of course, the ACLU neglected to mention this case, in the same federal circuit as the school, in its letter to the principal.[19]

Barry Arrington, the attorney in the case, said, "The school is faced with a decision at this point to fight for its rights and the rights of the students and the parents and the teachers, or just make the whole thing go away by caving in. Usually, the cheapest thing to do is cave-in. That's always been the ACLU's big ace-in-the-hole. Even if they're wrong, and they're wrong in this case, in order to vindicate that right, they must take someone to court, and money has to be spent on attorneys."[20]

Arrington added, "The truth is that no court has ever ruled that public schools must ban the singing of religious Christmas carols, and no court has ever held that celebrating Thanksgiving and Christmas as religious holidays requires recognition of all other religious holidays. The ACLU has a different vision for America and a different vision for Colorado than our founding fathers."[21]

In addition, ADF's legal engagement of the ACLU came to the attention of John Leo of U.S. News and World Report, who echoed Arrington's comments: "In the old days, when an American Civil Liberties Union lawyer would show up to hammer some tiny school board into submission, the legal costs of resisting were so high that the boards usually caved in. Now the anti-Grinches have some legal muscle of their own.... The Arizona-based Alliance Defense Fund ... claims to have 700 lawyers ready to fight anti-Christmas assaults around the country."[22]

As Leo stated, these are the type of cases the ACLU and its allies routinely won when no one called their bluff. That is why ADF launched the Christmas Project, to take the battle to the ACLU to stop its use of legal intimidation, misinformation, and fear to silence the public expression of Christmas.

But much legal and cultural damage has already been done. Many Americans now are afraid of saying, "Merry Christmas." In some areas of the country, like the San Francisco Bay area, local television stations routinely wish viewers "Happy Kwanzaa" or "Happy Ramadan" but never dare utter the C-word, in fear of offending someone.*

---

*Craig has noticed this when he visits family in northern California at Christmas.

At a local high school not far from the ADF offices in Arizona, you can see this cultural transformation on the school's marquee. Ten years ago, the school proudly announced "Christmas Break." Then one year, it suddenly became "Holiday Break." A few more years went by, and "Holiday Break" morphed into "Winter Vacation." What's next? "Secular Release Days"? Or "Sparkle Season"?

Of course, the ACLU denies it is attacking the public expression of Christmas. In one of its newsletters, it sounded like the patron saint of Christmas defense. ACLU President Nadine Strossen wrote:

> As president of the ACLU, I am proud of our steadfast assistance to the many citizens, all over the country, who complain about state-sponsored sectarian symbols—many of whom are deeply religious and celebrate Christmas and Hanukkah in their homes, churches and synagogues. . . . Maintaining government neutrality toward religions is at least as essential for the holiness of the religion sphere as it is for the pluralism of the secular state. . . . In short, those who celebrate Christmas and Hanukkah as religious holidays—holy days—should understand that the ACLU is their ally in seeking to stop the government from converting these occasions into commercial carnivals.[23]*

This statement reminds us of the old "we have to destroy this village in order to save it" logic. That is, we have to banish Christmas from the public square in order to preserve its private sacredness. We have to make sure no one hears the story of Christmas in public to avoid its misuse.

However, is allowing children to sing traditional Christmas carols as part of a secular school program turning Christmas into a "commercial carnival," as Strossen wants us to believe? How about a small child who innocently says that the meaning of Christmas is the birth of Jesus or mentions that "Christ" is in the name? Is that crass commercialism? The ACLU's words about being a great friend of those who celebrate Christmas do not match its actions for the past generation.

---

*The Supreme Court justices the ACLU cites as great defenders of religious freedom and principles are Harry Blackmun, the author of *Roe vs. Wade*, and William Brennan, who led the charge against the public expression of religious faith in almost every significant Supreme Court case for more than thirty years.

A few years after this ACLU newsletter was written, Alan debated Nadine Strossen on CNN's *Lou Dobbs Tonight* over the issue of the public celebration of Christmas. Even the usually low-key Dobbs could not believe the ACLU's extremism in removing any mention of Christmas from public discourse.

Dobbs asked Strossen about any ACLU objections to inviting Santa Claus to a classroom. Strossen said, "I don't think a reasonable observer looking at Santa Claus would say that's an endorsement of religion."

When asked about Nativity scenes on public property, Strossen continued to repeat that the ACLU supported the U.S. Supreme Court's "three reindeer rule" (we will discuss this later), which states that Nativity scenes on public property are constitutional as long as secular symbols are there too.

When Dobbs told Strossen he was troubled by the ACLU's legal intimidation of public schools, regarding children singing Christmas carols, Strossen replied, "Have you heard me object to that? I have not objected to that nor have our clients. If you're talking about a nativity scene that's very different from singing 'Jingle Bells' or Christmas carols."

Alan countered by pointing out that the ACLU had sent a letter (noted earlier) to a charter school in Elizabeth, Colorado, demanding that all Christmas carols be removed from the school's holiday program. Strossen replied, "I read that letter. It was not complaining about Christmas carols."[24]

But the truth is that, the ACLU said in a letter that "Jingle Bells" could not be sung (in the Colorado case),[25] they sent another demand to stop a school from having Santa Claus visit,[26] and they filed the lawsuit against placing a crèche on the lawn of a school in Massachusetts.[27] Despite Strossen's carefully crafted denial, it was the ACLU that filed a lawsuit against the city of Cranston, Rhode Island, even though the city allowed secular symbols to be included around the Nativity scene.[28]

It is mind-boggling that the ACLU finds "Jingle Bells" offensive. What could have possibly upset the ACLU about "Jingle Bells"? The dreaded C-word (Christ) is never mentioned. Could it be animal cruelty? Insensitivity to accident victims? Or perhaps ageism? Who knows? Or is it simply the reminder that, at least once each year, most of our nation pauses to remember the Creator? And that Creator, who gave us "inalienable rights," gave another gift to the world: Jesus Christ? Is that just too much for them?

All the documentation for these cases is on file at the offices of ADF or its legal allies. Yet, while the ACLU's president carefully seems to deny its pattern of threats exists, the ACLU and its allies terrorize local communities on an almost daily basis with letters, e-mails, and telephone calls to silence Christmas and other religious activity.

What is even more incredible are comments by the former national legislative counsel for the ACLU that show how the ACLU says one thing and does another. He charged that, "This mixing of secular and religious symbols ought to be seen as a bad thing, not a good thing, for Christian believers. Unfortunately, some of the Christian pressure groups seem to have it backwards." He added, "I think it's fair to say it's a mistaken notion that they have a mandate to put more nativity scenes up because George Bush was elected."[29] It seems the ACLU's allied lawyers, like the one quoted, who has now moved to Americans United for the Separation of Church and State, actually are beginning to claim that the rash of legal actions and adverse court decisions against the public expression of an uncluttered Christmas have come about because of the Religious Right. It seems the ACLU either cannot remember who started the fight to "cleanse" the public square or it actually doesn't know the results of the myriad of lawsuits it has filed or supported over the past decades!

The Truth about Religious Expression at Christmas

So, after years of legal intimidation, misinformation, and fear from the ACLU, many Americans are understandably confused about what they can and cannot do to publicly celebrate Christmas. Even after the years of assault and many confusing rulings:

- *It's still OK to sing Christmas carols.* Carols sung in public schools do not violate the Constitution. Religious carols may be sung by individual students or by a group of students such as a choir during school activities, Christmas programs, and other events. Public schools have been successful in defending this freedom against legal challenges brought by the ACLU and others who seek to silence Christmas.[30]

- *It's OK for schools to call Christmas "Christmas."* School officials can refer to the school break in December as a "Christmas
  Holiday" without offending the Constitution. The Supreme
  Court has acknowledged that government has long recognized
  holidays with religious significance such as Christmas.[31]
- *School districts cannot ban individuals—teachers or students—from saying "Merry Christmas."* The Supreme Court
  has stated that teachers and students do not "shed their constitutional rights to freedom of speech or expression at the
  schoolhouse gate."[32] In order to violate the Establishment
  Clause of the First Amendment, teachers would have to use
  their authority to promote religion to their students.[33]
- *Schools may teach about the religious origins of Christmas.*
  The religious and cultural origins and history of Christmas
  can be studied in the classroom without offending the Constitution. Even when limiting public displays, the Supreme
  Court has said that "the Bible may constitutionally be used
  in an appropriate study of history, civilization, ethics, comparative religion, or the like."[34]
- *Schools may display religious symbols, such as Nativity scenes.*
  The Supreme Court has held that a Nativity scene is constitutional if it is displayed for legitimate secular purposes, such
  as to celebrate a holiday or depict the origins of a holiday,
  such as Christmas.[35]
- *Cities may sponsor Nativity scenes and other religious displays in public parks and on public land* without offending the Constitution. To determine the constitutionality
  of municipal religious displays, lower courts evaluate
  whether the religious display passes the Supreme Court's
  three-prong *Lemon* test.[36] Under the *Lemon* test (which
  ADF and most of our legal allies believe is not consistent
  with the original intent of the Constitution and the First
  Amendment but the way the High Court interprets them
  for now and have filed a number of briefs with the U.S.
  Supreme Court that say so), courts will inquire "whether
  the challenged law or conduct has a secular purpose,
  whether its principal or primary effect is to advance or

inhibit religion, and whether it creates an excessive entanglement of government with religion."[37]

In addition to the loose language of the *Lemon* test, which has become more known for inconsistency than anything else, some courts often look to the endorsement test, what is called the "three reindeer rule," which asks whether a reasonable observer would believe a municipal display constitutes an endorsement of religion by the government.[38] Such a rule requires a municipality to place a sufficient number of secular objects in close enough proximity to the Nativity scene to render an overall display to be "sufficiently secular"[39]—hence, the Rhode Island ACLU's promise that it would review a Nativity scene to make sure it had been "significantly degraded."[40] We can imagine George Washington's (the presiding officer of the 1787 constitutional convention and president when the First Amendment took effect) reaction to this interpretation? Would he have degraded his promise at the First Inaugural from, "So help me God," to "So help me various vibrations from the universe?"

That's the truth about the public celebration of Christmas that the ACLU doesn't want most Americans to know. Despite decades of efforts by the ACLU religious censors, it's OK to say Merry Christmas.

Even with these legal restrictions, but nonetheless guidelines, the ACLU remains undeterred in their demand for even more lawsuits. It claims the law is confused, chaotic, and hard for public officials to follow. Of course, the ACLU fails to say its cases created the confusion in the first place. It continues to write threatening letters or e-mails or call school districts or local governments whenever a dreaded Christmas carol or a religious display shows on its radar screen. It continues to intimidate public officials to force them to remove Christmas displays from public property. The bottom line is that the ACLU wants as little public religious expression of Christmas as possible. The court test that would please them would be one that completely drove Christmas to disappear into the private, nonpublic sphere.

Noted author, commentator, and one-time presidential counselor and lawyer Charles Colson commented on the ACLU's continued disregard for settled law when it comes to Christmas:

Christmas is coming, and for towns and municipalities across the nation 'tis the season to be worried—worried about lawsuits, that is.

Local officials in Vienna, Virginia . . . were so worried that they banned religious carols at their annual Christmas Celebration. "Frosty the Snowman" and "Jingle Bells" were permissible, but not "The First Noel" or "Joy to the World." What made officials so skittish is that in 1991, Vienna was the target of a lawsuit by the ACLU for allowing a local group to set up a nativity scene in front of a community center.

The town had been careful to add secular displays alongside the Nativity scene: plastic reindeer, Santas, and snowmen. This was in accord with the 1984 Supreme Court ruling known as the reindeer rule, which requires any religious display on public property to be balanced by secular displays in order to avoid any hint that the state is endorsing religion.

However, in Vienna, the careful balancing was all for naught. The ACLU charged that, in spite of the Santas and the reindeer, the crèche was still the primary focus of the display and hence violated the separation of church and state.[41]

It is important to note that this 1984 Supreme Court decision is the same one glowingly promoted by Nadine Strossen in the 2003 CNN debate. The reindeer test is the one Strossen said was "reasonable and fair."[42] The city of Vienna complied with the Supreme Court decision and still faced a 1991 lawsuit from the ACLU. As always, the ACLU seeks to prohibit what the Constitution doesn't prohibit, simply to advance its agenda.

Colson continued:

In 1992 the controversy was about Christmas carols. At the advice of nervous lawyers, Vienna officials banned all religious songs at the annual town celebration. In protest, the Vienna Choral Society withdrew from the program. On the day of the festivities, 200 people massed in the parking lot across the street to hold a counter-celebration. They erected a crèche and lifted their voices to sing "Away in a Manger," "Silent Night," and all the well-loved carols.

A few protestors brought banners. One banner read: "A baby in a manger or a fat guy in a red suit? The choice is yours." Another banner took aim at the ACLU. "The ACLU is jealous of manger scenes," it read, "because it doesn't have three wise men or a virgin in its organization."

It was a well-aimed jab. But all humor aside, who can forget the pathos of the image on the news that evening? The protestors were huddled behind barricades—carefully keeping their feet off the public property—praying and singing their carols. Instead of Christmas joy, the atmosphere was one of confrontation and protest.

Have we really come to this? Here in the shadow of the nation's capitol, the beacon of religious freedom for the whole world, Christians are having to fight for the right to sing traditional religious carols. The image recalled scenes from Eastern Europe before the fall of communism.

It ought to be a sober lesson for all Christians, and indeed all citizens. If we don't speak out against the secularization of society—if we stand by quietly while the ACLU takes away our rights, one by one—then Americans will lose what our forefathers called the first liberty: the freedom of religion.[43]

The bottom line is, that many people, in fact most people, from other faith backgrounds—the people the ACLU feels it must protect from the C-word—*are not offended* by the public celebration of Christmas. Consider the words of Rabbi Daniel Lapin, president of the interfaith Jewish organization Toward Tradition:

Well, 2004 has arrived which means that dreaded "C" word is behind us. Put politely, "the holiday season" has passed. Having shopped in New York, Los Angeles, and Seattle lately and having listened to talk radio in each city, I couldn't help noticing a startling double standard. Overwhelmingly, store assistants and talk radio hosts bid farewell to Jewish guests with a cheerful "Happy Chanukah" while others, including those identified as Christians, received the generic "Happy Holidays." With each passing year, secular fundamentalism more successfully injects into

American culture the notion that the word "Christmas" is deeply offensive. . . .

The storm troopers of secularism who so diligently guard the rest of us from inadvertent exposure to the Christmas virus can rest for another year. Their work is done for now, but right after Thanksgiving, they'll be back, you'll see. Hey! I have a great idea—this year, let's be ready for 'em.[44]

Alan's family has friends who are Vietnamese refugees who escaped Communism and created a new life in America. Even though they are Buddhists, they joyfully celebrate Christmas each year. Their shop in a Phoenix strip mall has the largest Christmas tree and the brightest lights. They don't understand what Christmas is all about, but they know that its acknowledgment is something American.

Alan and his family pray that the Lord will use them to help this family come to fully understand the true meaning of the reason for the season because Christmas has been a wonderful witness of God's love to them.

This story is exactly *why* the ACLU and its allies want to drive out all public celebration of Christmas. They know Christmas offers a religious message that God sent His Son, Jesus Christ, on a mission to die for the sins of the world. They know that the spirit of liberty created by Christianity protects the freedom of people of all faiths and heritages. That is the wonder of Christmas.

Columnist Don Feder, an Orthodox Jew, wrote, "This isn't a war over Jingle Bells and holly wreaths, but a war on Christianity, which in turn is a war on the Judeo-Christian ethic."[45]

Christmas also reminds people of the unique historical role of Christianity and its impact in America, which the ACLU and its allies are trying to eradicate on a daily basis.

Despite the protests of Nadine Strossen, the ACLU, and its loud allies, it is their years of lawsuits and threats that have created the climate of fear and launched the politically correct "holiday" season in our country.* And this has censored and suppressed the rights

---

*Over the years the ACLU has filed lawsuits against various forms of public religious expression of Christmas in many communities including: Wall Township, New Jersey; Birmingham, Alabama; St. Charles, Illinois; Florrisant, Missouri; and Frankfort, Kentucky.

of 96 percent of Americans to freely, publicly celebrate Christmas. For too many public officials, the letters "ACLU" generate as much genuine fear today as the initials of police agencies in some totalitarian countries. And if the ACLU has its way, it won't end there.

Ramifications for Future Generations

For many Americans, some of the fondest memories of childhood are from the Christmas season. School Christmas programs and parties, hearing the Christmas story, and the sound of religious carols such as "Silent Night" and "The First Noel" floating through the air.

For others, it is the voices of young children softly singing these traditional hymns and carols of Christmas. For a brief moment in time, the world seems to take a deep breath as we listen to these soothing reminders of the true meaning of Christmas.

Unfortunately, if the ACLU has its way, future generations won't have such memories to enjoy. Their recollections will be of cold and impersonal, secular "winter breaks" or Alan's favorite: "sparkle season."[46] School Christmas parties will be a thing of the past (ADF has already been involved in several situations where schools have decided to cancel these events because of fear of the ACLU). The ability to say or communicate "Merry Christmas" on public property or for public employees may soon no longer exist.

Because of these attacks on the right to publicly celebrate Christmas, ADF has gone on the offensive to protect this right, for our children, grandchildren, and all those who follow. With God's grace, we will not allow the ACLU to rob future generations of the joy of celebrating Christ's birth.

In 2003, ADF launched a nationwide campaign called the Christmas Project. ADF's legal team prepared informational letters for school officials, parents, and students, as well as published a booklet about the public expression of Christmas. Letters and booklets were sent to school districts representing 12,213 schools. Twelve states were covered along with every state Board of Education and state chapter of the National Education Association. In 2004, representatives of more than forty-eight thousand schools received this information from ADF. (ADF makes available legal information at no charge on our Web site: www.telladf.org.)

Nearly eight hundred ADF-allied attorneys were equipped with information and resources to take on the ACLU and win. The result included the victories cited earlier in this chapter, many of those in cases which the ACLU quietly backed down after ADF-allied attorneys countered ACLU arguments.

The good news is that this year—and in years to come, with God's grace, ADF and its allies will be ready for the ACLU. We will continue to protect the rights of Americans to celebrate Christmas. The God-given victories we have experienced thus far are only the beginning of the effort to reclaim the joy of Christmas from the secular clutches of the ACLU and its allies. We are delighted that more and more in the media are recognizing and covering the two sides of this story.

We pray thousands will join this effort and that future generations will always be able to say "Merry Christmas," sing "Silent Night" on the public property they own or help pay to maintain, and enjoy the beauty and majesty of the Christmas story. As Christians, we call on all Americans to stand up to the ACLU and prevent it from taking away the joy that comes from the celebration of Christ's birth—in public as well as in private.

CHAPTER 8

The ACLU vs. American Sovereignty

They [who drew and ratified the Due Process clauses of the Constitution] knew times can blind us to certain truths and later generations can see that laws once thought necessary and proper in fact serve only to oppress.[1]
— Supreme Court Associate Justice Anthony M. Kennedy

[T]he world is now flat, and the U.S. is beginning to be involved in international law.[2]
— Associate Justice Anthony M. Kennedy

The internationalization of law, particularly constitutional law, is further along than you may think.[3]
— Robert Bork

George had been wheelchair-bound for several years.* Many of his infirmities were because of advancing age that eventually robs us of our strength and vitality. But there was more to George's story than aging.

George was a veteran of World War II, one of the "greatest generation" as dubbed by Tom Brokaw.[4] George was one of the last known survivors of the infamous Bataan "death march."

In April 1942, after the Japanese captured the Philippines, more than 78,000 U.S. and Philippine soldiers were forced to march in the

---

*To protect the privacy of George's family, we have withheld his last name. He was a sergeant in the U.S. Army Air Corps (later known as the U.S. Air Force) and a personal friend of Craig's late father.

searing sun for more than a week with little or no water, little or no food (the food they received was contaminated rice), and hardly any sleep. If a soldier tried to drink, he was executed. One survivor remembered, "One of our stops was at a bridge. . . . The water you couldn't even see because there was a green scum covering it. Some of the guys jumped in . . . and started to fill their canteens. I did not, as there was a dead soldier, perhaps several, that had been in the water a couple of days, and in the 100-degree sunshine you could imagine the smell. . . . It became a game for the [captors]. They would lower their bayonets and run for anyone trying to drink. Either you were bayoneted or shot."[5]

Those who collapsed fell on the bodies of their dead colleagues.[6] According to George and other survivors of the march, some soldiers were buried alive. Approximately fifteen thousand soldiers did not survive.[7]

Once they reached their destination, the survivors were put through horrifying experiences in POW camps that ignored any form of humane treatment of prisoners. Twenty-six thousand additional Allied soldiers would die in these camps over the next three years.[8] Afterward George talked about the public beheadings—for little or no reason other than man's inhumanity toward his fellow man—he witnessed firsthand at the camps.

But the imprisonment would go on for longer than the war itself. George told of the emotional and physical trauma he suffered for years afterward. His bones were brittle from the years of starvation and brutal treatment by enemy soldiers. An accident that would result in a slight bruise for most people was a broken bone to George. By the early 1990s, his ravaged body finally started to decline.

Yet, despite the incredible toll that the march and prison camp experience had taken on his body and mind, George was always upbeat, even when he was confined to a wheelchair. When asked if the pain and suffering were worth it, he quietly replied, "The pain was a small price to pay to preserve freedom."

George is no longer with us; his body finally gave out several years ago. But when Americans hear the accounts of courageous individuals like George who endured horrific experiences to preserve our country's freedom, they cannot help but express their gratitude for

what these soldiers did to preserve America's sovereignty and freedoms for future generations.

Sadly, the ACLU, working with its allies, is now trying to undermine that sovereignty and freedom, the very things that George and
his fellow soldiers sacrificed and died to preserve. The ACLU and
its allies, frustrated by their inability to advance their radical agenda
more swiftly under the U.S. Constitution, now intend to convince
the American judiciary to look to international law as a means to
their ends.

The ACLU and International Law

The ACLU sponsored a conference at the Carter Center in Atlanta, Georgia, October 9–11, 2003, to promote the use of international law in U.S. courts. The conference was titled "Human Rights
at Home: International Law in U.S. Courts." Publicity for the event
stated, "The emphasis throughout the conference will be on using
international law and human rights norms to advance justice in U.S.
courts or on behalf of U.S. clients." Some of the alleged human rights
"injustices" cited were in the areas of "environmental justice," "gay,
lesbian, bisexual and transgender rights," and "children's rights."[9]

ACLU publicity included comments from ACLU Executive
Director Anthony Romero and conference organizer Ann Beeson.
Romero said, "Our goal is no less than to forge a new era of social justice where the principles of the United Nations Universal Declaration
of Human Rights are recognized and enforced in the United States."[10]

Beeson added, "From the grassroots level all the way to the Supreme Court, international human rights law is beginning to emerge
as a tool for the victims of discrimination here at home." (The ACLU
believes such "victims" include those who advocate and practice homosexual behavior.)[11]

Some of the other conference topics included:

- "Using International Law to Advance Public Policy." This
  was a discussion on how to implement international human
  rights "standards" at the local government level and in federal legislation.
- "Using Non-U.S. Court and Regional Fora." According
  to the conference agenda, "This session will discuss the ju-

risprudence and venues other than U.S. courts, such as the Inter-American Commission on Human Rights, the UN Human Rights Committee, and the European Court of Human Rights."

- "Rap Session with Judges." According to the agenda: "Judges will discuss reasons for resistance within the bench to international law and share their perspective on the prospects for change." One of the invited speakers was U.S. Supreme Court Justice Stephen Breyer.[12] Another invited speaker was Judge Myron Thompson, the federal judge who ordered former Alabama Supreme Court Justice Roy Moore to remove a Ten Commandments monument he had placed in the rotunda of the State Supreme Court building.[13]

The ACLU's efforts to use international law to advance its agenda and to further rewrite, undermine, and bypass the U.S. Constitution have already gone beyond academic discussion and posturing at conferences such as this. In several recent court decisions the ACLU or its allies have participated in at the state and federal level, justices are weaving international law into their decisions.

In the June 2003 *Lawrence vs. Texas* decision[14] (in which the ACLU filed a brief on behalf of the homosexual petitioners), Justice Anthony Kennedy, writing for the majority of the U.S. Supreme Court, looked to international law in his decision, which discovered for the first time in two hundred years what had been theretofore unknown, that the Constitution protected adult, consensual same-sex sodomy.[15] This case overturned previous decisions and hundreds of years of precedent, legal history, and culture that allowed states to have laws that prohibited this behavior. Justice Kennedy wrote:

The sweeping references by Chief Justice Burger [in the 1986 *Bowers vs. Hardwick* decision that upheld Georgia's sodomy statute][16] to the history of Western civilization and to Judeo-Christian moral and ethical standards did not take account of other authorities pointing in an opposite direction. A committee advising the British Parliament recommended in 1957 the repeal of laws punishing homosexual conduct. . . . Of even more importance, almost five years before *Bowers* was decided, the European Court of Human

Rights considered a case with parallels to *Bowers* and to
today's case. . . . The court held that the laws proscribing
the conduct [of sodomy] were invalid under the European
Convention on Human Rights.[17]*

To the extent *Bowers* relied on values we shared with a
wider civilization, it should be noted that the reasoning and
holding in *Bowers* has been rejected elsewhere. The European Court of Human Rights has followed not *Bowers* but
its own decision in *Dudgeon vs. United Kingdom*. . . . Other
nations too have taken action consistent with an affirmation of the protected right of homosexual adults to engage
in intimate, consensual conduct. . . . The right the petitioners seek in this case has been accepted as an integral part of
human freedom in many other countries. There has been no
showing that in this country the governmental interest in
circumscribing personal choice is somehow more legitimate
or urgent.[18]

The six-justice majority looked to a ruling by the European Court
of Human Rights as precedent for discovering, and thus creating, yet
another new "right" in the Constitution, the "right" to engage in
same-sex sodomy, something we seriously doubt was debated at the
constitutional convention in 1787. (The delegates came from thirteen
states that all strongly proscribed sodomy, and continued to do so
after the new Constitution was adopted.) Participants in America's
constitutional convention wanted to create a framework for freedom
distinctly different from anything that had previously existed in Europe. In the weeks following their *Lawrence* decision, several justices
commented on how they planned to look to international law to help
interpret, to, in effect, rewrite, the U.S. Constitution, including Justice Ruth Bader Ginsburg, the former general counsel of the ACLU.

Speaking in Moscow, Idaho, on August 2, 2003, Ginsburg said,
"Our island or lone ranger mentality is beginning to change. [Jus-
tices] are becoming more open to comparative and international law
perspectives."[19]

---

*We cannot help but note the irony of comparing thousands of years of Jewish, Christian, and
world history to the European Convention on Human Rights, which was written in 1950. See
http://en.wikipedia.com/wiki/European_Convention_on_Human_Rights.

Justice Sandra Day O'Connor, just a few months later, added:
There is talk today about the "internationalization of legal relations." We are already seeing this in American courts, and should see it increasingly in the future. This does not mean, of course, that our courts can or should abandon their character as domestic institutions. But conclusions reached by other countries and by the international community, although not formally binding upon our decisions, should at times constitute persuasive authority in American courts. . . . I suspect that with time, we will rely increasingly on international and foreign law in resolving what now appear to be domestic issues, as we both appreciate more fully the ways in which domestic issues have international dimension, and recognize the rich resources available to us in the decisions of foreign courts.[20]

In fact, in 2002, O'Connor had already predicted the international law trend in a speech to the American Society of International Law:

One of the topics discussed at this annual meeting is the internationalization of legal relations. We are already seeing this in American courts, and should see it increasingly in the future. . . . Although international law and the law of other nations are rarely binding upon our decisions in U.S. courts, conclusions reached by other countries and by the international community should at times constitute persuasive authority in American courts. . . . I have not even scratched the surface of the issues and areas of application of foreign and international law in U.S. courts. The fact is that international and foreign laws are being raised in our courts more often and in more areas than our courts have the knowledge and experience to deal with. There is a great need for expanded knowledge in the field, and the need is now.[21]

Fortunately, a few justices still are not willing to go along with the ACLU's drumbeat of international law. They do not believe international law should have "pervasive authority in American courts," as O'Connor noted.

In 2002, the U.S. Supreme Court held in *Atkins vs. Virginia* that
execution of certain classes of convicted murderers violated the Constitution. The Court noted that "within the world community, the
imposition of the death penalty for crimes committed by mentally
retarded offenders is overwhelmingly disapproved."[22] In his stinging
minority opinion (joined by Chief Justice Rehnquist and Associate
Justice Thomas), Justice Antonin Scalia wrote,

> But the Prize for the Court's Most Feeble Effort to
> fabricate "national consensus" must go to its appeal (deserv-
> edly relegated to a footnote) to the views of assorted profes-
> sional and religious organizations, members of the so-called
> "world community," and respondents to opinion polls. . . .
> I agree with the Chief Justice . . . that the views of profes-
> sional and religious organizations and the results of opinion
> polls are irrelevant.
>
> Equally irrelevant are the practices of the "world com-
> munity," whose notions of justice are (thankfully) not
> always those of our people. We must never forget that it is
> a Constitution for the United States of America that we are
> expounding. . . . [W]here there is not first a settled con-
> sensus among our own people, the views of other nations,
> however enlightened the Justices of this Court might think
> them to be, cannot be imposed upon Americans through the
> Constitution.[23]

In 2003, Justice Stephen Breyer outlined some of his views on the
subject.[24] And shortly after the *Lawrence* decision, he told a national
television audience, "[How] our Constitution . . . fits into the governing documents of other nations I think will be a challenge for the
next generation."[25]

Why have the ACLU and its allies turned from the most inge-
nious form of government ever designed by man to international
law? Probably because they know that even with their broad theories
and legal demands, the U.S. Constitution can be stretched only so
far, so fast, to advance their radical agenda. They can find only so
many "emanations from penumbras" to invent new "rights" that the
Founding Fathers never authored, intended, or even conceived of.
And with a former ACLU general counsel on the Supreme Court,

other justices are now going along for the ride, as Ginsburg put it, the American "lone ranger" mentality "is fading."[26]

Former Yale law professor and federal court of appeals judge Robert Bork put the motives of the ACLU and its allies this way: "International law is not law but politics. For that reason, it is dangerous to give the name 'law,' which summons up respect, to political struggles that are essentially lawless. [The result is that] international law becomes one more weapon in the domestic culture war."[27]

The ACLU's and its allies' advocacy of international law took another step in the November 2003, 4–3 decision of the Supreme Judicial Court of Massachusetts in *Goodridge vs. Department of Health*. This case opened the door to same-sex "marriage" in Massachusetts. The ACLU filed a friend-of-the-court brief in support of creating this new right.[28]

In her decision inventing same-sex "marriage," Chief Justice Margaret H. Marshall wrote:

We face a problem similar to one that recently confronted the Court of Appeal for Ontario, the highest court of that Canadian province, when it considered the constitutionality of the same-sex marriage ban under Canada's Federal Constitution, the [Canadian] Charter of Rights and Freedoms. . . . Canada, like the United States, adopted the common law of England that civil marriage is the "voluntary union for life of one man and one woman, to the exclusion of all others." . . . In holding that the limitation of civil marriage to opposite-sex couples violated the Charter, the Court of Appeal refined the common-law meaning of marriage. We concur with this remedy.[29] [The Court of Appeal in Ontario had recently ordered same-sex "marriage."]

By referring to a previous decision by the Court of Appeal for Ontario to find a basis for same-sex "marriage," the Supreme Judicial Court of Massachusetts turned four hundred years of American and colonial jurisprudence on its head and opened the door for those advocating new and special legal privileges, such as the ACLU. This is in the Commonwealth of Massachusetts whose constitution says, "It is the right as well as the duty of all men in society, publicly, and at stated seasons to worship the Supreme Being, the great Creator and Preserver of the universe."[30]

Besides the issue of same-sex "marriage" and the promotion of other new rights through the application of international law, the ACLU is also turning to international sources to undermine our nation's national security. For instance, the ACLU filed a formal complaint with the United Nations Working Group on Arbitrary Detention against the United States, stating that the United Nations violated international law when it detained 765 Arab Americans and Muslims for security reasons after the September 11, 2001, terrorist attack on our nation. Eventually, 478 were deported. ACLU Executive Director Anthony Romero said, "With today's action, we are sending a strong message of solidarity to advocates in other countries who have decried the impact of U.S. policies on the human rights of their citizens. We are filing this complaint before the United Nations to ensure that U.S. policies and practices reflect not just domestic constitutional standards, but *accepted international human rights principles regarding liberty and its deprivations.*"[31]*

Romero makes the United States sound like a rogue nation with little or no regard for human rights, not the beacon of liberty to which millions have fled to escape tyranny and oppression.

But that is pretty much how the ACLU and its founders historically viewed the United States. The ACLU's 2003 International Civil Liberties Report illustrates its contempt for America and desire to remake America, using international law as one of its means:

This year saw serious ongoing human rights abuses by the United States here and abroad, along with unexpected progress as courts began to reference global human rights norms in domestic cases. . . . [T]here was cause for hope this year among advocates seeking to implement global human rights principles in the United States. . . . Anticipating a new

---

*It should be noted that when the United States ratified the UN Convention against Torture and Other Cruel, Inhuman, or Degrading Treatment or Punishment, it lodged a reservation to Article 16, saying America had agreed to be bound by the prohibition on cruel, inhuman, or degrading treatment only to the extent that this term matched the constitutional ban on "cruel and unusual" punishments. In laymen's terms, this means the United States is not technically bound to "obligations" under the convention that would violate our own Constitution. It is a stretch by the ACLU to equate cruel and unusual punishment with the deportation of potentially dangerous individuals.

era in which courts recognize the relevance of global human rights here in the United States, the ACLU moved to further expand its use of human rights principles in addition to constitutional ones. . . .

It is clear that we can no longer count on the Constitution alone to protect fundamental freedoms in the United States. . . . We must emphasize the positive face of globalism. . . . We must use human rights documentation to hold our government accountable for its actions here and abroad. We must raise human rights arguments more frequently in our domestic litigation, and provide the courts with more opportunities to—at least—reference international human rights.[32]

Why should there be a concern about the ACLU filing a formal complaint with the United Nations? To ordinary Americans, this does not seem to affect their everyday lives. But it will, eventually.

In spring 2003, a group from the United Nations Human Rights Commission (UNHRC), of which former ACLU officials Paul Hoffman and John Shattuck are a part,[33] met and discussed a resolution to add "sexual orientation" to the UNHRC's discrimination list. Homosexual activists at the meeting called for a "showdown with religion," clearly intending to use international law to silence religious speech that does not affirm homosexual behavior.[34]

At the forum, panel members stated that Roman Catholics and evangelical Protestants were the main opponents in the attempt to implement this agenda. One panel member openly questioned whether or not religion should be "limited" because it posed a "challenge" to the homosexual legal agenda.[35] The panel also discussed ways to successfully implement a proposed UNHRC resolution that would expand the UN's definition of discrimination to include sexual orientation.[36]

Harold Hongju Koh, a professor of international law at Yale University, said, "In the U.S., we're ahead on some issues, but behind on others, such as the death penalty, gay rights. . . ."[37]

The ACLU dedicates a section of its Web site to advocacy of international law. On the Web page, the ACLU mentions it is using "international law principles" to oppose censorship of online communication, and, with the ACLU's track record, this likely means hard-core or even child pornography on the Internet.[38]

However, the main threat of the ACLU's advocacy of international law is to the freedom of speech, religious exercise, and conscience of Americans. In some other countries, laws are being pushed, and in some cases, enacted that essentially criminalize many forms of religious speech and activity that does not affirm homosexual behavior.

In April 2004, the Canadian Parliament passed Bill C-250, which could classify as "hate speech" portions of the Bible that address homosexual behavior. The Canadian Bible Society put out repeated warnings that the bill could have a chilling effect on religious freedom and evangelism in Canada. Janet Epp of the Buckingham Evangelical Fellowship of Canada said, "Pastors are afraid. They're afraid to preach on this subject. Nobody wants to have the police come to their door."[39] The bill, which added "sexual orientation" to Canada's hate-propaganda law, has now become law. No one knows how it will be enforced. The bill reads: "Every one, who by communicating statements, other than in private conversation, willfully promotes hatred against an identifiable group, is guilty of an indictable offense and is liable to imprisonment for a term not exceeding two years."[40]

In the Canadian province of Saskatchewan, the Human Rights Commission ruled that a newspaper ad with biblical references denouncing homosexual activity exposed homosexual men to "hatred." The advertisement featured an icon of two stick figures holding hands. The figures were covered with a circle and a slash, and were accompanied by four references from the Bible, without even quoting the words. The commission said, "The slashed figures alone were not enough to communicate the hatred. . . . But the addition of the Biblical references are more dangerous."[41] The newspaper that carried the item and the man who placed the advertisement were forced to pay monetary fines to each of the three complainants. Attorney Valerie Watson, who represented the homosexual advocates, said, "It is obvious that certain of the Biblical quotations suggest more dire consequences and there can be no question that the advertisement can be objectively seen as exposing homosexuals to hatred or ridicule."[42] This ruling was upheld by a Canadian court in Saskatchewan.[43]

These types of laws go beyond Canada. In Sweden, the parliament approved an amendment that forbids speech and the distribution of materials opposing homosexual behavior and other alternative sexual activity. Violators could spend up to two years in jail. According to Annalie Enochson, a Christian member of parliament, Christians could be arrested for speaking about homosexual behavior in churches. "That means people coming from [the homosexual] lobby group could sit in our churches having on the tape recorder and listen to somebody and say, 'What you're saying now is against our constitution.'"[44] In June 2004, a Swedish court sentenced Ake Green, a Pentecostal pastor to a month in prison, under this law, for "offending" homosexuals in a sermon.[45] The decision was later overturned, but the government is attempting to appeal. [46]

The French government approved a bill outlawing "homophobia." The bill made "incitement to discrimination, hatred or violence against a person on the basis of gender or sexual orientation" punishable by a year in prison and a 45,000-euro ($54,000) fine.[47]

All these laws have been passed (and the subsequent punishments administered) under the umbrella of "human rights"—rights for everyone except those with traditional Evangelical Protestant, Roman Catholic, and Orthodox Jewish beliefs. There have been reports of members of the ACLU and other groups, such as the Mainstream Coalition and Americans United for Separation of Church and State, attending services at conservative, evangelical churches in Missouri and Kansas to "monitor" sermons that talk about moral issues, such as homosexual behavior.[48]

Thus, when the ACLU says, "We must raise human rights arguments more frequently in our domestic litigation, and provide the courts with more opportunities to—at least—reference international human rights laws,"[49] the great defender of free speech is referring to the use of international law in its usual tactics of legal intimidation and fear to silence or change the behavior of those expressing any viewpoint that does not adhere to its beliefs. ACLU Executive Director Anthony Romero said the ACLU's goal is to "forge a new era of social justice where the principles of the United Nations Universal Declaration of Human Rights are recognized and enforced in the United States."[50]

As we mentioned in a previous chapter, homosexual activists actively planned at their 1999 international conference on same-sex "marriage" to use international law and litigation to undermine the democratic process of nations and force same-sex "marriage" worldwide.[51] If the Supreme Judicial Court of Massachusetts can cite marriage law from Ontario to create same-sex "marriage," and the U.S. Supreme Court can look to the European Court of Human Rights to tell state legislatures what topics (sodomy) they can or cannot address in their state's criminal code, the ACLU and its allies, armed with sympathetic judges, could expand the use of international law (as they intend to do) to systematically force America to conform to their image or face drastic legal consequences.

But we also must note, even on the general topics of homosexual behavior and marriage, the selectivity of the ACLU's viewpoints and advocacy. On one hand, the ACLU wants American lawyers and courts to follow international law, but only the laws of foreign nations and other international entities that agree with or further its agenda. On the other hand, the ACLU chooses to ignore the many other nations—most notably those in the Muslim world and Africa and Central and South America—that strongly and clearly oppose the demands of the homosexual legal agenda.

This arbitrary and selective approach to international law is already being used in U.S. courts—picking the nation or court which appears to best fit the desired outcome. Favorable references have been made by American judges to opinions in such courts as those of Jamaica and Zimbabwe.[52] While only two nations out of 193 in the world have voluntarily redefined marriage to include same-sex partners,* the courts gallop ahead to impose international customs to the contrary.

In March 2005, the United States Supreme Court cited international law *again* in *Roper vs. Simmons,* a case dealing with the administration of the death penalty to juveniles. An ACLU press release proudly stated, "Finally, it is worth noting that six members of the United States Supreme Court (the five-person majority plus Justice O'Connor) expressly upheld the relevance of international law and practice in determining which punishments are cruel and unusual under our own Constitution."[53]

---

*The only two nations that have passed laws legalizing same-sex "marriage" are the Netherlands and Belgium. Numerous nations in Europe legally recognized "civil union" type arrangements for homosexual couples. At the time of this writing, a bill was being introduced to legalize same-sex "marriage" in Canada.

Whether you oppose or favor the death penalty for anyone, we should all be most alarmed with the selective way the High Court is edging out the Constitution's role as the authority for U.S. law—with the ACLU standing right beside cheering them on.

Supreme Court Justice Anthony Kennedy wrote in the majority opinion, "It is proper that we acknowledge the overwhelming weight of international opinion."[54]

In his vigorous dissent, Justice Antonin Scalia said, "[This] court thus proclaims itself sole arbiter of our nation's moral standards—and in the course of discharging that awesome responsibility purports to take guidance from the views of foreign courts and legislatures.[55]

Justice Sandra Day O'Connor, who dissented, also advocated the use of international law, writing, "I disagree with Justice Scalia's contention . . . that foreign and international law have no place in our . . . jurisprudence . . . . [T]he Court has consistently referred to foreign and international law as relevant in its assessment of evolving standards of decency."[56]

The Wall Street Journal, in its March 2, 2005, edition, warned: "Perhaps the most troubling feature of *Roper* is that it extends the High Court's recent habit of invoking foreign law in order to overrule American laws . . . . We thought the Constitution was the final arbiter of U.S. law, but apparently that's passé."[57]

Justice Scalia isn't amused by the advance of the ACLU's international law agenda. In a televised debate with Justice Stephen Breyer (an international law advocate), Scalia said, "After having read the foreign law, I'm afraid that societies don't always mature. Sometimes they rot."[58]

This march to internationalism is all despite the different legal traditions of the United States—with its English common law tradition and belief in a higher law and inalienable rights endowed by the Creator—and the much different sources for much foreign law. Other legal traditions are based on ancient Roman law and secular and other legal traditions of much of Europe and the non-Western world; these share a belief that rights come from man or government. The world's other legal systems differ in many ways and are often incompatible. They cannot be used interchangeably; otherwise legal chaos would result.

The Consequences for America

More than 225 years ago, our nation's forefathers gathered in Philadelphia to debate and draft a unique document. A single page announced the independence of a new country—one that would no longer find itself in the clutches of a foreign state. The document, signed on July 4, 1776, is known worldwide as the Declaration of Independence.

Eleven years later, many of the same men gathered again in Philadelphia to lay the written groundwork for how this nation would be governed. The result was the Constitution, creating a system of government like no other, "by the people, of the people, and for the people."

For the past two centuries, hundreds of thousands of courageous men and women have given their lives to protect America's sovereignty and freedom. Countless others, like George, sacrificed and lived through tremendous hardship to protect this precious liberty.

If we are going to turn the interpretation of our laws to international jurisprudence—to the decisions of foreign courts, judges, and legislatures—why did we fight a war of independence? Why was such a price paid?

In his Farewell Address to the nation, George Washington asked why Americans would surrender America's great legal, social, and political advantages to European influence. Having fought a war of independence from Great Britain, he issued a warning about future entanglements with other countries. He asked, "Why forego the advantages of so peculiar a situation? Why quit our own to stand upon foreign ground? Why, by interweaving our destiny with that of any part of Europe, entangle our peace and prosperity in the toils of European ambition, rivalship, interest, humour, or caprice?"[59] Yet, more than two hundred years later, our nation's courts, with the assistance of the ACLU, are doing exactly what Washington warned against.

It is as if many of our courts (with the demands of the ACLU) have forgotten that one reason for the massive immigration to this country was for the protection its laws, courts, and Constitution afforded—for all people of all faiths and backgrounds—like no others'. Will our country return to what our ancestors fled from? They often risked their lives to sacrifice for their children and grandchildren to grow up in freedom. Did men like George, his colleagues, and others who died or suffered tremendously to defend America's sovereignty, die or suffer in vain?

If the ACLU successfully advances its international law agenda, the Declaration of Independence and the U.S. Constitution will become increasingly irrelevant documents. As we have seen in numerous high-profile cases in recent years, the handwritten parchment copies are considered nice to be displayed as historic art on the walls of public buildings, but if anyone wants to teach or explain the sources and reasons behind the words penned, he may be stopped.* More and more of America's freedoms will be sacrificed on the ACLU altar of international law.

And the America we pass down to our children will cease to be the America our forefathers envisioned and the America we know and love. Left unchecked, the ACLU's war to reshape America in its own image will almost be complete. Our precious freedoms—of speech, at least public religious speech, of association, of worship, of living our faith—will have all but vanished. The ACLU's vision of freedom—the public sale and prime-time display of hard-core pornography; the legalization of child pornography, public profanity and blasphemy; the redefinition, and perhaps abolition, of marriage; the silencing of the church and ministries on moral issues such as homosexual behavior; and legalized, unlimited abortion and euthanasia—will be manifest. For those who believe in the morals and values that made America great, the stakes are high and we cannot stand idly by.

ADF and its allies are committed to legal battles to defend these freedoms and to protect American sovereignty. The ACLU may be trying to change the rules in the middle of the game, but it will not be successful. ADF will do all it can, with God's grace, to stop the ACLU's efforts.

ADF staff and allied attorneys are developing strategies to discredit and defeat the ACLU's advocacy of international law. We will forcefully remind judges and other public officials that they have sworn an oath to uphold the U.S. Constitution, not international

---

*This includes instruction about the connections between Orthodox Jewish and Christian religious beliefs, biblical text, and teachings, Christian pilgrims, Spanish missionaries, and immigrants.

law or UN policies, for their decisions and that the ACLU's way is not the best way for America.

As with all legal battles against the ACLU, this will take persistence, focus, and most of all, prayer. As the ACLU has from its beginning, it will continue to look for ways to circumvent our nation's democratic process, our federal Constitution, and our national sovereignty when these interfere with the ACLU's dreams for tomorrow.

Nevertheless, we are commanded to pray for those who oppose us (Matt. 5:44). Our prayer is that the very truth the ACLU has tried so hard to silence will touch the hearts and minds of their lawyers and followers as they are confronted with God's love through His people. That, perhaps more than any other reason, is why we need to stand up to the ACLU and its agenda, so that ACLU followers, too, will ask the reason for our hope and come to know the all-encompassing love and grace of God and His Son Jesus Christ.

CHAPTER 9

Taking America Back from the ACLU

In his 1953 inaugural address, President Dwight D. Eisenhower said, "We are called as a people to give testimony in the sight of the world to our faith that our future shall belong to the free."[1]

More than fifty years later, those words still ring true. Regardless of the ACLU's actions to transform America into a religion-free, secular fiefdom, millions of Americans still hold fast to the traditions and values of faith, family, and life that have made America the "shining city upon a hill" the late President Ronald Reagan, whose administration Alan was honored to serve, spoke about so eloquently in his farewell to the nation in January 1989.[2]

Despite the ACLU's decades-long war on the public expression of Christianity, millions of Americans still proudly proclaim the name of Jesus Christ. Despite the ACLU's war on parental authority, millions of parents still do all they can to raise their children to honor and embrace the faith, morals, and values that made our nation strong. Despite the ACLU's efforts to promote abortion, every year more and more Americans are professing to be pro-life.[3] Despite the ACLU's war on marriage and its attempted legal roadblocks to deny the will of the people, American voters are going to the polls and voting to affirm marriage as between one man and one woman.*

---

*Marriage has been strongly supported and same-sex "marriage" has been overwhelmingly defeated in every state in which it has been put to a public vote. Go to www.domawatch.org for a state-by-state list of votes and laws. In fact, forty states have enacted Defense of Marriage Acts (DOMA's), and eighteen states have amended their Constitution since the ACLU joined the recent national attack on marriage in the mid-1990s.

While there is little doubt the ACLU's war on America and its values have taken a toll on several segments of our society, it has yet to break the spirit, faith, and the will of the American people. This *spirit, faith,* and *will* of millions of Americans enable the ADF team of lawyers and dedicated professionals to keep up the good fight against the ACLU and its allies. When ADF-allied attorneys walk into a courtroom or work late into the night, on a brief, they know their work will help shape a future that protects and affirms our first liberty—religious freedom.

These attorneys know that at stake is the future of millions of children blessed to grow up in a family, with a mom and a dad. They know that the lives of those yet to be born, and those whose lives are winding down, are at peril. They know that unless we vigorously engage and win the legal battles of today with the ACLU, our children and grandchildren will not experience the freedoms for which our forefathers sacrificed, fought, and in many cases, died.

But we will need to continue to pay a price if we are to be successful in stopping the ACLU and its attempt to secularize America. As President Eisenhower knew from his World War II experiences, a war that cost more than 400,000 American casualties,[4] the price of preserving freedom is high, but it is a cost *we must pay* for the generations yet to come. That is why we cannot stand idly by and allow the ACLU to run roughshod over our nation's legal system.

At ADF, we know the ACLU's legal attacks are far from over. But we also know that through strategic planning, coordination, training, funding, and litigation, the tide is being turned. Through ADF's National Litigation Academy program, hundreds of allied attorneys have been trained; each has made a faith promise to donate his or her time and talent to defend the right to speak and hear the truth—the truth of the gospel of Jesus Christ. Through ADF's Blackstone Fellowship program, hundreds of America's brightest law students have been given the opportunity to receive the highest level training in Christian worldview and constitutional law to help break the stranglehold the ACLU and its allies have on our nation's law schools and judicial system. And the great news is, with God's grace, *we have won much, we are winning more, and we will continue to win if people of faith stand and do what needs to be done.*

In only a decade, the ACLU has gone from being virtually unopposed in our nation's courts to having to play defense more often as ADF and its like-minded lawyers have shown up, challenged the ACLU, and have seen the ACLU either back down, or lose, time and time again. With a growing number of victories at the U.S. Supreme Court and in nearly three out of every four cases at lower-court levels, ADF and its allies are gaining in the legal battle against the ACLU.

Eisenhower also started that 1953 inaugural address with a public prayer on public property. He prayed:

Almighty God, as we stand here at this moment my future associates in the executive branch of government join me in beseeching that Thou will make full and complete our dedication to the service of the people in this throng, and their fellow citizens elsewhere.

Give us, we pray, the power to discern clearly right from wrong, and allow all our words and actions to be governed thereby, and by the laws of this land. Especially we pray that our concern shall be for all the people regardless of station, race, or calling.

May cooperation be permitted and be the mutual aim of those who, under the concepts of our Constitution, hold to differing political faiths; so that all may work for the good of our beloved country and Thy glory. Amen.[5]

As Eisenhower noted in his prayer, only God can grant us the power to discern right from wrong and help us put aside our differences for the common good of the people. As we watch and read the numerous stories about how our country is "divided," we cannot help but reflect that the continued ACLU-led and ACLU-inspired attacks on religious freedom have caused us to turn on each other as we, as a nation, have turned away from God.

Eisenhower concluded his address:

At such a time in history, we who are free must proclaim anew our faith. This faith is the abiding creed of our fathers.

It is our faith in the deathless dignity of man, governed by eternal moral and natural laws.

This faith defines our full view of life. It establishes, beyond debate, those gifts of the Creator that are man's inalienable rights, and that make all men equal in His sight.

This faith rules our whole way of life. . . . The enemies of this faith know no god but force, no devotion but its use. They tutor men in treason. They feed upon the hunger of others. Whatever defies them, they torture, especially the truth. . . .

Freedom is pitted against slavery; lightness against the dark. . . .

We must be willing, individually and as a Nation, to accept whatever sacrifices may be required of us. A people that values its privileges above its principles soon loses both.[6]

These words are a poignant reminder that we must remain engaged in the legal battle to defend our first liberty. We cannot rest, we cannot grow weary, in defense of this most precious of freedoms. The peril we face, and the price we will pay, is too high if we forget that it is our faith that made us free, and it is only our faith that will sustain that freedom for generations to come.

General, Supreme Allied Commander, and President Eisenhower knew this well. He played a pivotal role in saving the free world from those who sought to promote tyranny and reject freedom. We must remember his words whenever the ACLU shows up in our communities with its campaign of fear, legal intimidation, and misinformation. If we the people of these great United States follow the ACLU's road of special privilege above the road of principles, we will soon lose both. We must continue to stand up to the ACLU, in town after town and court after court, so the future will indeed belong to the free.

How can we stand up to the ACLU? Students of history know that the winner of the battle is often the one that has the best quartermaster and supplies needed for victory. The ACLU has an almost unlimited war chest at its disposal to advance its agenda. ADF and its allies need financial and manpower supplies to not only confront the ACLU and its allies in the courtroom, but to eventually surpass them to return our legal system to what our Founding Fathers, and not the ACLU, intended.

Besides praying for and financially supporting organizations such as ADF, we can raise awareness of the ACLU's threat to our nation's Constitution and legal system among like-minded friends. If we know of other attorneys who are disturbed by the actions of the ACLU and its allies, we can tell them about the work of ADF and refer them as possible candidates for the National Litigation Academy attorney training program. We can help educate the public about the ACLU's true agenda—that it was never a "good organization" that took a wrong turn somewhere along the line. We can help educate our pastors, along with school and public officials, on the legal misinformation spread by the ACLU and provide them with solid legal resources (available from ADF) to stand up to the ACLU's intimidation tactics.

Our friends in Congress can make a difference as well. They can confirm only judges committed to applying the original text of the Constitution as its authors intended. They can stand firmly against inappropriate encroachment of the judiciary into legislative and executive roles. They can oppose the abuse of international law and foreign law by American courts. They can enact a federal marriage amendment and present it to the states for ratification. Finally, they can eliminate millions of dollars from the ACLU and its allies' coffers by clarifying that the Federal Fee Statute, 42 U.S.C. § 1988, does not provide for attorney fee awards for Establishment Clause claims.

It will take sacrifice, perseverance, and a concerted effort by millions of Americans to defeat the ACLU, its many allies, and their agenda. But with God's grace, we are confident it can and will be done. Once again, America's governing documents can serve as a shield for people of faith, instead of a sword of wrath against them. America's law can once again affirm religious freedom, the sanctity of human life, and the traditional family.

Epilogue

The ACLU's attempt to silence religious expression over the years has shown no rational bounds. The climate of fear and intimidation that has been created through its systematic attacks on people of faith has grown to such an extent that many public officials have developed a knee-jerk response to anything "religious." So deep and effective are its efforts, that even a small town in the buckle of the Bible Belt was not left untouched.

The Senior Center in Balch Springs has, for years, been *the* place for seniors to gather and socialize in this small Texas town. If you were to ask them to tell you their personal stories, you would quickly be awash in tales that would fill your heart and enrich your soul. There's Barney, a former Navy man and welder, who served in World War II. He's still proud of his service to the country but reticent to recount the memories of his fellow soldiers, many of whom didn't return home. There's Marcelline, or "Marcy" as her friends call her. She's a ninety-one-year-old articulate powerhouse who raised four handsome boys and committed herself to caring for the "elderly" after her husband's death. There's Betty, who was raised picking cotton and caring for the livestock on a remote, Texas farm. She went on to work for the United States Post Office until she retired in 1999. And there are many others, including Barbara, whose story we'll save for the end.

What you have gathered in that Center is, simply, a snapshot of America.

For twenty years, these senior citizens have used the Center for programs and recreational events. A group of those seniors, who were Christians, also gathered there to sing gospel songs and hear a retired pastor teach from the Bible. As was their tradition, they would also say a quiet, thankful word of prayer before receiving their meals. All prayers and participation were voluntary—no one was coerced into attending or praying, and the government never interfered.

But in August of 2003, the city of Balch Springs decided to enact a new policy that demanded that all mealtime prayers, gospel music, and "religious messages" cease *immediately*. *No other* group suffered this same censorship—only these Christians.

Think for a moment about what these guileless seniors were suddenly facing. Imagine them being told they could no longer pray over a meal after years of faithfully and humbly doing so. Imagine them having a key source of fellowship and hope being stripped away. Imagine what it must have been like being placed in this very vulnerable position simply because of your faith, your age, and your lack of financial resources.

Now imagine these brave citizens saying "enough is enough" and taking an unwavering, uncompromising stand. That's exactly what they did.

They organized. They appealed to the city, but the city ignored them. They pressed on. They decided to let the community know of their plight. So they *picketed*. Marcy took it upon herself to make the placards. With a wry smile on her face, she carried one that read, "Don't mess with Grandma—she's *mad!*"

This fearless act apparently enraged city officials. They promptly fired the Center's events planner and bus driver, cutting off the seniors' access to such things as educational outings, entertainment options, and even transportation to the drugstore to fill their prescriptions. The city even went so far as to refuse transportation to the funerals of these seniors' friends.

But this strong-arm tactic didn't weaken the resolve of these determined citizens.

Kelly Shackelford, an Alliance Defense Fund allied attorney and chief counsel of the Liberty Legal Institute, learned of their plight and gladly offered assistance at *no charge*. He immediately sent a demand letter to the city. The city once again ignored the entreaty. This forced the seniors to file a lawsuit against the city. And what was the city's response? *They threatened to stop meal service unless the seniors withdrew their suit!*

The seniors refused to be intimidated.

Finally, at the request of Mr. Shackelford, the United States Department of Justice got involved and opened an investigation into the city's policies. Ultimately, the city relented, the senior's religious liberties were secured, and the city was even forced to pay damages to these unshakable people of faith and action.

If the senseless discrimination and harassment in this case boggles your mind and engenders a sense of personal outrage, take heart. These senior citizens worked tirelessly to reclaim the liberties *guaranteed* them under our Constitution. Their courage lifts our spirits and gives us hope and inspiration.

And speaking of inspiration . . . remember Barbara, the one whose story we waited to tell? Well, she went on to do something she never dreamed of: she entered the following year's election, challenging those on the city council who treated the seniors so disrespectfully. Barbara won in a *landslide!*

• • •

This is only one of *many* such encouraging and motivating stories. The *complete* story of these wonderful and inspiring people along with many others is contained in a *free* booklet entitled "America Responds!"

In addition to individual stories of inspiration and hope, the booklet contains *practical steps* that YOU can take when faced with religious discrimination. These stories, along with this step-by-step guide, will provide you with the encouragement and strength to stand tall against those who try to silence people of faith.

Request your FREE copy online at www.acluvsamerica.com.

Information for Churches
Who Find Themselves under Legal Attack from the ACLU for Exercising Their Constitutional Right to Speak on Moral Issues

June 4, 2004
Dear Pastors:

A great battle rages within our nation; a battle to determine whether the very foundation of our society—one man and one woman, joined in marriage—will survive. Advocates of same-sex "marriage" fight fiercely for new "rights," focusing on individuals' emotions and government benefits. But marriage is more than feelings and money; it's about providing a mom *and* a dad for every child; about building a strong society through certain time-tested methods rather than radical social experiments. Indeed, the very reason that governments choose to benefit and regulate marriage is because it *is* the proven basis for Western civilization. Proponents of same-sex "marriage" cannot show otherwise.

I assure you that the Alliance Defense Fund will spare no effort to ensure that America's Christians will not be silenced in the battle for marriage.

In the past decade, radical advocates of same-sex "marriage" have sought to establish new rights in Alaska, Hawaii, Vermont, Massachusetts, Arizona, and elsewhere. All but one of these battles resulted in their defeat—and pro-homosexual forces may yet be defeated in Massachusetts, where court actions and constitutional amendments to defend traditional marriage remain very much alive.

Across America, citizens are fighting to save marriage by advancing pro-marriage legislation at the state and federal level. Homosexual activists know that their arguments will fail if they are put directly to our nation's citizens, and they do all that they can to prevent the issue from ever coming to a vote. Thus, pro-homosexual groups are threatening churches across the nation with the loss of tax-exempt status, or they allege that various state political campaign laws were violated, when churches simply preach about marriage or allow petitions on their property. It is a simple scare tactic, designed to silence Christians.

Such tactics are not new. They have been tried time and again *and have consistently failed.* For example, in 1996, 1998, and 2000, pro-homosexual activists targeted churches that supported a proposition in California that defined marriage between one man and one woman. In one mailing, activists sent out some eighty thousand threat letters. (See Erik J. Ablin, *The Price of Not Rendering to Caesar: Restrictions on Church Participation in Political Campaigns,* 13 Notre Dame J. L. Ethics & Pub. Pol'y 541, 557, 1999.) These would-be censors failed to suppress Christian speech, the California measure ultimately passed, and no church had its tax-exempt status revoked. These tactics of hate and intolerance must fail again in 2004.

By this letter, we assure you that churches have broad constitutional rights to express their views on marriage, as explained below. Furthermore, other activities such as allowing parishioners to sign petitions for legislative action to protect marriage are almost undoubtedly permissible under federal tax law. In the same way, the First Amendment to the U.S. Constitution most likely prevents states from demanding that churches register as a "political committee" or report "contributions" when the churches merely preach about marriage or allow petitions to be signed at their facilities.

If you are contacted by any government official or private activist group on such issues, please call us immediately. The Alliance Defense Fund's attorneys will promptly review your situation and make every effort to defend your church's legal rights to speak freely in support of marriage. Ahead we briefly discuss the relevant law.

Legal Analysis: Federal Tax Law

There are two broad areas of concern regarding the effect of political activity by churches that hold tax-exempt status under Internal Revenue Code (IRC) sec. 501(c)(3). First, the IRC prohibits churches from participating or intervening in the political campaign of a *candidate* for public office. However, the IRC is much more accommodating in regard to churches that work to influence *legislation*, allowing such activity so long as a "substantial part" of church efforts is not devoted to such activities. This legislative issue is what we are concerned about here.

Fortunately, the courts understand that advocating morality, both in church and in civil life, is properly at the heart of religious faith. Religion includes a way of life as well as beliefs upon the nature of the world and the admonitions to be "doers of the word and not hearers only" (James 1:22) and to "Go, therefore, and make disciples of all nations" (Matt. 28:19). These are as old as the Christian church. The believer's step from accepting the gospel to seeking to influence others is a natural one and is found in many religious groups.

Girard Trust Co. vs. Comm'r, 122 F.2d 108, 110 (3d Cir. 1941) (emphasis added; omission in original). The Supreme Court said, "Adherents of particular faiths and individual churches frequently take strong positions on public issues including . . . vigorous advocacy of legal or constitutional positions. Of course, churches as much as secular bodies, and private citizens have that [constitutional] right." *Walz vs. Tax Comm'n,* 397 U.S. 664, 670 (1969).

Whether a church devotes a substantial part of its resources to influencing legislation is a question of facts and circumstances, *Kentucky Bar Foundation, Inc. vs. Commissioner,* 78 T.C. 971 (1982), and courts have taken different approaches to the matter. For example, in *Seasongood vs. Commissioner,* 227 F.2d 907 (6th Cir. 1955), the court established a 5 percent safe harbor rule based on total expenditures applied to legislative activities. *Id.* at 912. More recently, the decision in *World Family Corporation vs. Commissioner,* 81 T.C. 958 (1983) raised that bar when the tax court ruled that an exempt organization's lobbying activities that used between 5 and 10 percent of the group's resources were "insubstantial."

It should be noted that one court relied on a balancing test, rather than a percentage of expenditures, in determining that a tax-exempt religious organization had devoted a substantial part of its resources to influencing legislation. See *Christian Echoes Nat'l Ministry, Inc. vs. U.S.*, 470 F.2d 849 (10th Cir. 1972). This court observed that the percentage test obscured the "complexity of balancing the organization's activities in relation to its objectives and circumstances." *Id.* at 855.

The *Christian Echoes* court stated that "the political [activities of a charity] must be balanced in the context of the objectives and circumstances of the organization to determine whether a substantial part of its objectives [not just expenditures] was to influence or attempt to influence legislation." *Id.* However, the lobbying undertaken by the Christian Echoes ministry went far beyond simply preaching about a moral issue or circulating petitions for proposed legislation. Rather, the group "attempted to mold public opinion in civil rights legislation, Medicare, the Postage Revision Act of 1967, the Honest Election Law of 1967, the Nuclear Test Ban Treaty, the Panama Canal Treaty, firearms control legislation, and the Outer Space Treaty." *Id.* It urged supporters to take no less than twenty-two different actions to influence American and international politics, including urging congressional representatives to support or oppose specific bills, abolish the federal income tax, withdraw from the United Nations, and so on. *Id.* Under these unusual facts—*including support of candidates* as well as legislation—the court found that the defendant organization had devoted a substantial part of its resources to lobbying and affirmed the revocation of its tax-exempt status. *Id.* at 858.

Unless a church has an extensive history of lobbying efforts (as exemplified by the *Christian Echoes* case), it is unlikely that simple efforts to defend marriage—such as preaching about marriage or making petitions available to be signed—would be seen as a substantial portion of church resources. Such activities should be entirely permissible under federal tax law. Certainly, a church that devotes less than 5 percent of its resources to influencing legislation should be on very safe ground in this respect.

State Political Campaign Law

State governments have an interest in informing the public about campaign financing. The theory is that such information helps voters evaluate which interests are supporting particular legislation. See, for example *Buckley vs. Valeo*, 424 U.S. 1 (1976) (upholding federal campaign disclosure requirements). Yet however strong that interest may be, it does not justify imposing campaign law willy-nilly on churches that incidentally support legislation.

It is not possible to consider the political campaign laws of each state in this brief letter. Nonetheless, any requirement that a church register as a political action committee or report expenditures supporting legislation, simply because the church preached about marriage or allowed parishioners to sign petitions, raises serious questions under the Free Speech Clause and Free Exercise Clause of the First Amendment to the Constitution.

Indeed, the courts have recognized that applying broadly worded campaign reporting statutes to groups that do not engage in *substantial* advocacy would violate the First Amendment. For example, in *New Jersey State Chamber of Commerce vs. New Jersey Election Law Enforcement Commission*, 411 A.2d 168 (N.J. 1980), various secular groups challenged a campaign reporting law as being unconstitutionally overbroad because it was triggered by virtually any communication between a private person and a legislator that sought to "influence" legislation. The court held that the law was constitutional, but *only* if it was narrowly construed so that it applied "only to persons whose direct, express, and intentional communication with legislators for the purpose of affecting the outcome of legislation are undertaken *on a substantial basis.*" *Id.* at 179, accord *Bemis Pentecostal Church vs. Tennessee*, 731 S.W.2d 897 (Tenn. 1987) (holding a church responsible to report expenditures for purchasing media advertisements that opposed specific liquor legislation, *but* also held that broadcasting the church's religious services and distributing church newsletters, even if advocating a particular election result, were not subject to campaign law). In other words, campaign law is not *carte blanche* for the government to limit private church speech or religious exercise.

Other issues are implicated by unlimited application of state political campaign laws to churches. For example, demanding that churches register as political committees would operate as a prior restraint on speech, which is strongly disfavored under the U. S. Supreme Court's First Amendment jurisprudence. Similarly, it would chill the speech of other churches that would rightfully fear investigation and possible punishment by state election officials. Both situations offer solid bases to invalidate a state campaign law if that law were applied to churches in this context.

Homosexual activists' outrageous, intolerant effort to stop churches from expressing their faith will succeed only if pastors succumb to fear and stand mute when marriage is attacked. But nothing in the law supports these activists' demands, and no pastor should yield to fear. Rather, pastors can (and should) speak clearly regarding moral truth and freely participate in the political processes within the limits set forth by our laws.

This material is a brief overview of a complex area of the law and should not be construed as legal advice relevant to a particular church's situation. If you have any questions or believe your church's rights were violated, please feel free to contact us at the Alliance Defense Fund.

Sincerely,
Gary S. McCaleb
Senior Counsel

Legal Guidance for School Officials

Memorandum

TO: Parents, School Boards, Superintendents, Principals, Educators, and Administrators

FROM: Alliance Defense Fund Law Center

RE: Constitutionality of Prayer at High School Graduation/Baccalaureate.

The Alliance Defense Fund Law Center is America's largest public interest Christian legal alliance. As part of our mission, we seek to educate public officials about the constitutional rights of citizens, in this case, students.

After the Supreme Court decisions in *Lee vs. Weisman* and *Santa Fe Independent School District vs. Doe,* it is quite understandable that there would be widespread confusion on the issue of prayer at official school events. However, it is crucial to note *the Supreme Court has never said students are forbidden to pray at graduation or to hold baccalaureate ceremonies.*

We are providing legal analysis in advance of this year's graduation season in order to assist parents, school boards, superintendents, principals, educators, and administrators in making constitutionally correct decisions about student prayer. Too often, school officials feel trapped between a "rock and a hard place" when dealing with the First Amendment. However, if you are challenged by radical groups, such as the ACLU, for allowing student-initiated, student-led prayer at graduation, please contact us that we may review your situation and possibly assist you. It is our hope that this memo will provide clarity to school officials in this important area of the law. A broad overview of First Amendment law in the school context is presented first, followed by an analysis of specific criteria needed for a constitutional policy.

First Amendment Principles in the School Setting

A. Religious Speech Is Protected under the First Amendment

It is a fundamental principle of constitutional law that a government body may not suppress or exclude the speech of private parties just because the speech is religious or contains a religious perspective. *Good News Club vs. Milford Central School Dist.*, 533 U.S. 98 (2001); *Lamb's Chapel vs. Ctr. Moriches Union Free Sch. Dist.*, 508 U.S. 384 (1993); *Widmar vs. Vincent*, 454 U.S. 263 (1981). This principle cannot be denied without eviscerating the essential First Amendment guarantees of free speech and religious freedom.

It is equally axiomatic that religious speech is protected by the First Amendment and may not be singled out for discrimination. *Good News Club vs. Milford Central School Dist.*, 533 U.S. 98, 108–10 (2001); *Widmar vs. Vincent*, 454 U.S. 263, 269 (1981) (citing *Heffron vs. Int'l Soc'y for Krishna Consciousness, Inc.*, 452 U.S. 640 (1981); *Neimotko vs. Maryland*, 340 U.S. 268 (1951); *Saia vs. New York*, 334 U.S. 558 (1948); *see also, Rosenberger vs. Rector and Visitors of the Univs. of Virginia*, 515 U.S. 819 (1995); *Capitol Square Review and Advisory Bd. vs. Pinette*, 515 U.S. 753 (1995); *Board of Educ. of the Westside Cmty. Sch. vs. Mergens*, 496 U.S. 226 (1990). The Supreme Court has stated: "Our precedent establishes that private religious speech, far from being a First Amendment orphan, is as fully protected under the Free Speech Clause as secular private expression. . . . Indeed, in Anglo-American history, at least, government suppression of speech has so commonly been directed *precisely* at religious speech that a free-speech clause without religion would be *Hamlet* without the prince." *Pinette*, 515 U.S. at 760 (emphasis in original).

B. Students Do Not Abandon Their Constitutional Rights of Free Speech When They Attend Public School

"It can hardly be argued that either students or teachers shed their constitutional rights to freedom of speech or expression at the schoolhouse gate." *Tinker vs. Des Moines Indep. Cmty. Sch. Dist.*, 393 U.S. 503, 506 (1968). The Supreme Court has squarely stated that a student's free speech rights apply "when [they are] in the cafeteria, or on the playing field, or on the campus during the authorized hours. . . ." Id. at 506. This includes prayer: "Nothing in the Constitution as interpreted by this Court prohibits any public school student from voluntarily praying at any time before, during, or after the school day." *Santa Fe Indep. Sch. Dist. vs. Doe*, 530 U.S. 290, 313 (2000) (emphasis added).

> [I]n our system, state-operated schools may not be enclaves for totalitarianism. School officials do not possess absolute authority over their students. Students in school as well as out of school are persons under our Constitution. They are possessed of fundamental rights which the state must respect, just as they themselves must respect their obligations to the state. In our system, students may not be regarded as closed-circuit recipients of only that which the state chooses to communicate. They may not be confined to the expressions of those sentiments that are officially approved. *Tinker*, 393 U.S. at 511.

C. The So-Called Separation of Church and State Does Not Require the Banning of Student-Initiated, Student-Led Baccalaureates or Graduation Prayers

Schools and school officials often mistakenly believe that allowing students to engage in religious speech at school would violate the separation of church and state—a doctrine often cited in connection with the Establishment Clause of the First Amendment. This very argument has been reviewed and *rejected* by the United States Supreme Court. In *Board of Educ. of the Westside Cmty. Sch. vs. Mergens*, 496 U.S. 226 (1990), the Supreme Court stated as a general proposition that the activities of students in a public school do not present any Establishment Clause problem: "Petitioners' principal contention is that the [Equal Access] Act has the primary effect of advancing religion. Specifically, petitioners urge that, because the student religious meetings are held under school aegis, and because the state's compulsory attendance laws bring the students together (and thereby provide a ready-made audience for student evangelists), an objective observer in the position of a secondary school student will perceive official school support for such religious meetings. . . ." [*We disagree.*] *Mergens*, 496 U.S. at 249–250.

The Establishment Clause of the First Amendment merely "requires the state to be a neutral in its relations with . . . religious believers and nonbelievers; it does not require the state to be their adversary." *Everson vs. Bd. of Educ.*, 330 U.S. 1, 18 (1947). Likewise, "[s]tate power is no more to be used to handicap religions, than it is to favor them." *Everson*, 330 U.S. at 18. Therefore, the Establishment Clause has *no* applicability to student-initiated, student-led prayers or baccalaureate ceremonies in the graduation context. Restricting or banning such events because they involve religious prayer or worship violates the constitutional requirement of neutrality. See for example, *Hedges vs. Wauconda Cmty. Sch. Dist.*, 9 F.3d 1295, 1299 (7th Cir. 1993).

While it is true that school-sponsored graduation prayers have been declared unconstitutional, "there is a crucial difference between *government* speech endorsing religion, which the Establishment Clause forbids, and *private* speech endorsing religion, which the Free Speech and Free Exercise Clauses protect." *Mergens*, 496 U.S. at 250 (emphasis in original). Private student speech can never violate the Establishment Clause. *Id.;* see also *Pinette*, 515 U.S. at 764. Student-initiated, student-led baccalaureates and graduation prayers *are* private student speech.

Any possible misperceptions that the school is "endorsing religion" are cured by the school's ability to insert disclaimers. *Pinette*, 515 U.S. at 769 ("If Ohio is concerned about misperceptions, nothing prevents it from requiring all private displays in the Square to be identified as such."); and see *Id.* at 776 ("the presence of a sign disclaiming government sponsorship or endorsement on the . . . cross, would make the State's role clear to the community.") (O'Connor, J., concurring); *Id.* at 784 (disclaimer cures confusion over misperceptions of endorsement) (Souter, J., concurring in part and concurring in judgment). Even the liberal Ninth Circuit has adopted this position in the school context: "It is far better to teach students about the first amendment, about the difference between private and public action, about why we tolerate divergent views. *The school's proper response is to educate the audience rather than squelch the speaker. Schools may explain that they do not endorse speech by permitting it.*" *Hills vs. Scottsdale Unified Sch. Dist.*, 329 F.3d 1044, 1055 (9th Cir. 2003) (quoting *Hedges*, 9 F.3d at 1299–1300) (internal quotations and brackets omitted).

Specific Legal Criteria for Constitutional Graduation and Baccalaureate Policies

A school may certainly permit a baccalaureate ceremony with religious content on its property when the event is sponsored and or ganized by private parties. A private event that happens to be graduation related simply does not pose a constitutional problem, as long as it is clearly private. As the Supreme Court held in *Santa Fe,* a key question in deciding the constitutionality of prayer at a school event is whether an objective observer would view the policy or the prayer as a "state endorsement of prayer in public schools." 530 U.S. at 308. The same holds true for baccalaureate ceremonies.

Graduation ceremonies have slightly different rules because a private speaker (the student) is speaking at a government-sponsored event. In the graduation context, we believe that the following policy elements will prevent any appearance of "state endorsement":

1. Students in the graduating class choose whether to include an invocation/benediction or "message" as part of graduation.
2. A majority of the graduating class must approve the inclusion and select the student who will give the message.
3. There can be no involvement or prior review of the speaker's message by the school or school staff.
4. Any message with religious content should be nonsectarian and nonproselytizing.

Under this policy, the Supreme Court's "objective observer" can easily conclude that the inclusion of such invocations/benedictions is by *student* choice, not by the endorsement or coercion of the school. If there is concern that an objective observer might still be confused, an additional solution is for the school to include a disclaimer in the graduation program that informs the audience the students, not the school, decided to include an invocation/benediction. This comports with the principle described in the *Hills* and *Hedges* cases as "educat[ing] the audience rather than squelch[ing] the speaker."

The fourth element above is constitutional as long as it serves only as a guideline. If the students are required to submit their invocation/benediction for review to determine whether it is nonsectarian and nonproselytizing, this would inject a degree of school involvement that likely would not be permissible. Therefore, the school may not review student speech to ensure it is nonsectarian and nonproselytizing. Simply put, the school should not place itself in the position of controlling student speech in this context.

At least one circuit court has held that a complete ban on prayer in the public context is unconstitutional. *Chandler vs. Siegelman,* 230 F.3d 1313 (11th Cir. 2000). In *Chandler* the court noted that "the Establishment Clause does not require the elimination of private speech endorsing religion in public places. The Free Exercise Clause does not permit the State to confine religious speech to whispers or banish it to broom closets." *Id.* at 1316. While no one can legally force a school to allow student-initiated, student-led baccalaureate ceremonies or prayer at graduation, it would be unfortunate to eliminate long-standing traditions or a general community desire for such events when it is quite unnecessary to do so. As this memo demonstrates, any school may adopt a policy that will comply with the First Amendment. In fact, it would likely be unconstitutional to completely ban private religious expression at graduations. What message would it send to our nation's students if schools would rather censor all religious expression instead of taking reasonable steps to ensure compliance with the law?

We understand the fear associated with a lawsuit by the ACLU or other like-minded groups. However, courts across the nation have examined policies containing some or all of the elements listed above and have concluded that student-initiated, student-led graduation prayer and private baccalaureate ceremonies are constitutional. See *Adler vs. Duval County Sch. Bd.,* 250 F.3d 1330 (11th Cir. 2001); *Chandler,* 230 F.3d 1313 (11th Cir. 2000); *Jones vs. Clear Creek Indep. Sch. Dist.,* 977 F.2d 963 (5th Cir. 1992) *cert. denied* 508 U.S. 967 (1993). Even the Ninth Circuit's negative decision on graduation prayer can be distinguished because the school in that case (1) preauthorized the invocation (instead of letting the graduates decide), and (2) retained editorial control over the content of the prayer. *Cole vs. Oroville Union High Sch. Dist.*, 228 F.3d 1092, 1102-03 (9th Cir. 2000). A school in the Ninth Circuit may be able to take the simple steps outlined above and avoid the constitutional entanglement that troubled the court in *Cole*.

Of course, each situation is different, but as we stated at the outset of this memo, if someone threatens legal action against the school for allowing constitutionally permitted student prayer and student baccalaureate ceremonies, please contact us immediately, and we may be able to assist the school in resisting such bullying tactics.

We hope the information provided has been useful and will assist you in discussions of this important issue.

View

How Thomas Jefferson's "Wall of Separation" Redefined Church-State Law and Policy*

No metaphor in American letters has had a greater influence on law and policy than Thomas Jefferson's "wall of separation between Church and State." Many Americans accept it as a pithy description of the constitutionally prescribed Church-State arrangement, and it has become the locus classicus of the notion that the First Amendment separated religion and the civil state, thereby mandating a strictly secular polity.

More important, the judiciary has embraced this figurative phrase as a virtual rule of constitutional law and as the organizing theme of Church-State jurisprudence, even though the metaphor is not found in the Constitution. Writing for the U.S. Supreme Court in 1948, Justice Hugo L. Black asserted that the justices had "agreed that the First Amendment's language, properly interpreted, had erected a wall of separation between Church and State." Our democracy is threatened, Justice John Paul Stevens warned last term, "[w]henever we remove a brick from the wall that was designed to separate religion and government."

What is the source of this figure of speech, and how has this symbol of strict separation between religion and public life come to dominate Church-State law and policy? I address these questions in

*Daniel L. Dreisbach is a professor of justice, law, and society at American University. This essay is adapted from Daniel L. Dreisbach, *Thomas Jefferson and the Wall of Separation between Church and State* (New York University Press, 2002) and reprinted with permission from the May 2003 issue of *Chronicles: A Magazine of American Culture.*

my new book, *Thomas Jefferson and the Wall of Separation Between Church and State* (2002).

On New Year's Day, 1802, President Jefferson penned a missive to the Baptist Association of Danbury, Connecticut. The Baptists had written the new president a fan letter in October 1801, congratulating him on his election to the "chief Magistracy in the United States." They celebrated his zealous advocacy for religious liberty and chastised those who had criticized him "as an enemy of religion[,] Law & good order."

In 1800, Jefferson's Federalist Party opponents, led by John Adams, dominated New England politics, and the Congregationalist Church was still legally established in Connecticut. The Danbury Baptists were outsiders—a beleaguered religious and political minority in a state where a Congregationalist-Federalist establishment dominated public life. They were drawn to Jefferson's political cause because of his unflagging commitment to religious liberty.

In a carefully crafted reply endorsing the persecuted Baptists' aspirations for religious liberty, the President wrote:

Believing with you that religion is a matter which lies solely between Man & his God, that he owes account to none other for his faith or his worship, that the legitimate powers of government reach actions only, & not opinions, I contemplate with sovereign reverence that act of the whole American people which declared that their legislature should "make no law respecting an establishment of religion, or prohibiting the free exercise thereof," thus building a wall of separation between Church & State.

The missive was written in the wake of the bitter presidential contest of 1800. Candidate Jefferson's religion, or the alleged lack thereof, was a critical issue in the campaign. His Federalist foes vilified him as an "infidel" and "atheist." The campaign rhetoric was so vitriolic that, when news of Jefferson's election swept across the country, housewives in New England were seen burying family Bibles in their gardens or hiding them in wells because they fully expected the Holy Scriptures to be confiscated and burned by the new administration in Washington. (These fears resonated with Americans who had received alarming reports of the French Revolution, which Jefferson was said to support, and the widespread desecration of religious sanctuaries and symbols in France.) The Danbury letter was written to reassure pious Baptist constituents of Jefferson's continuing commitment to their rights of conscience and to strike back at the Federalist-Congregationalist establishment in Connecticut for shamelessly vilifying him in the recent campaign.

Jefferson's wall, according to conventional wisdom, represents a universal principle on the prudential and constitutional relationship between religion and the civil state. To the contrary, this wall had less to do with the separation between religion and all civil government than with the separation between federal and state governments on matters pertaining to religion (such as official proclamations of days of prayer, fasting, and thanksgiving). The "wall of separation" was a metaphoric construction of the First Amendment, which Jefferson time and again said imposed its restrictions on the federal government only (see, for example, Jefferson's 1798 draft of the Kentucky Resolutions). In other words, the wall separated the federal regime on one side from state governments and religious authorities on the other.

How did this wall, limited in its jurisdictional application, come to exert such enormous influence on American jurisprudence? The political principle of separation between religion and politics began to gain currency among Jeffersonian partisans in the campaign of 1800, not to promote liberty but to silence the Federalist clergy who had denounced candidate Jefferson as an infidel and atheist. In the Danbury letter, Jefferson deftly transformed the political principle into the constitutional principle of separation between Church and State by equating the language of separation with the text of the First Amendment. The constitutional principle was eventually elevated to constitutional law by the Supreme Court in the mid-twentieth century, effectively recreating First Amendment doctrine.

By late January 1802, printed copies of Jefferson's reply to the Danbury Baptists began appearing in New England newspapers. The letter, however, was not accessible to a wide audience until it was reprinted in the first major collection of Jefferson's papers, published in the mid-nineteenth century.

The phrase "wall of separation" entered the lexicon of American constitutional law in the U.S. Supreme Court's ruling in *Reynolds* vs. *United States* (1879). Opining that the missive "may be accepted almost as an authoritative declaration of the scope and effect of the [First A]mendment thus secured," the Court reprinted a flawed transcription of the Danbury letter. Most scholars agree that the wall metaphor played no role in the Court's decision. Chief Justice Morrison R. Waite, who authored the opinion, was drawn to another clause in Jefferson's text, but he could not edit the letter artfully to leave out the figurative phrase. The Chief Justice relied on Jefferson's statement that the powers of civil government could reach men's actions only, not their opinions. The Reynolds Court was focused on the legislative powers of Congress to criminalize the Mormon practice of polygamy and was apparently drawn to this passage because of the mistranscription of "legitimate powers" as "legislative powers." But for this erroneous transcription, the Court might have had little or no interest in the Danbury letter, and the wall metaphor might not have entered the American legal lexicon.

Nearly seven decades later, in the landmark case of *Everson vs. Board of Education* (1947), the Supreme Court "rediscovered" the metaphor and elevated it to constitutional doctrine. Citing no source or authority other than Reynolds, Justice Hugo L. Black, writing for the majority, invoked the Danbury letter's "wall of separation" passage in support of his strict separationist construction of the First Amendment prohibition on laws "respecting an establishment of religion." "In the words of Jefferson," the Court famously declared, the First Amendment has erected "'a wall of separation between church and State'. . . . That wall must be kept high and impregnable. We could not approve the slightest breach." Like *Reynolds,* the *Everson* ruling was replete with references to history, especially the roles played by Jefferson and Madison in the Virginia disestablishment struggles. Jefferson was depicted as a leading architect of the First Amendment, despite the fact that he was in France when the measure was drafted by the First Federal Congress in 1789.

Black and his judicial brethren also encountered the metaphor in briefs filed in *Everson.* In a lengthy discussion of history supporting the proposition that "separation of church and state is a fundamental American principle," an amicus brief filed by the American Civil Liberties Union quoted the clause in the Danbury letter containing the "wall of separation." The ACLU ominously concluded that the challenged state statute, which provided state reimbursements for the transportation of students to and from parochial schools, "constitutes a definite crack in the wall of separation between church and state. Such cracks have a tendency to widen beyond repair unless promptly sealed up."

The trope's current fame and pervasive influence in popular, political, and legal discourse date from its rediscovery by the Everson Court. Shortly after the ruling was handed down, the metaphor began to proliferate in books and articles. In a 1949 best-selling anti-Catholic polemic, *American Freedom and Catholic Power,* Paul Blanshard advocated an uncompromising political and legal platform favoring "a wall of separation between church and state." Protestants and Other Americans United for the Separation of Church and State (today known by the more politically correct name "Americans United for Separation of Church and State"), a leading strict-separationist advocacy organization, wrote the phrase into its 1948 founding manifesto. Among the "immediate objectives" of the new organization was "[t]o resist every attempt by law or the administration of law further to widen the breach in the wall of separation of church and state."

The Danbury letter continued to be cited frequently and favorably by the Supreme Court. In *McCollum vs. Board of Education* (1948), the following term, and in subsequent cases, the Court essentially constitutionalized Jefferson's phrase, subtly and blithely substituting his figurative language for the literal text of the First Amendment. In the last half of the twentieth century, the metaphor emerged as the defining motif for Church-State jurisprudence.

Metaphors are a valuable literary device. They enrich language by making it dramatic and colorful, rendering abstract concepts concrete, condensing complex concepts into a few words, and unleashing creative and analogical insights. But their uncritical use can lead to confusion and distortion. At its heart, *metaphor* compares two or more things that are not, in fact, identical. A metaphor's literal meaning is used nonliterally in a comparison with its subject. While the comparison may yield useful insights, the dissimilarities between the metaphor and its subject, if not acknowledged, can distort or pollute our understanding of the subject. Metaphors inevitably graft onto their subjects connotations, emotional intensity, and/or cultural associations that transform the former understanding of the subject. If attributes of the metaphor are erroneously or misleadingly assigned to the subject and the distortion goes unchallenged, the metaphor may reconceptualize or otherwise alter the understanding of the underlying subject. The more appealing and powerful a metaphor, the more it tends to supplant or overshadow the original subject, and the more we are unable to contemplate the subject apart from its metaphoric formulation. Thus, distortions perpetuated by the metaphor are sustained and magnified.

The judiciary's reliance on an extraconstitutional metaphor as a substitute for the text of the First Amendment almost inevitably distorts constitutional principles governing Church-State relations. Although the "wall of separation" may felicitously express some aspects of First Amendment law, it seriously misrepresents or obscures others. In *Thomas Jefferson and the Wall of Separation between Church and State*, I contend that the wall metaphor mischievously misrepresents constitutional principles in at least two important ways.

First, Jefferson's trope emphasizes separation between Church and State—unlike the First Amendment, which speaks in terms of the nonestablishment and free exercise of religion. Jefferson's Baptist correspondents, who agitated for disestablishment but not for separation, were apparently discomfited by the figurative phrase. They, like many Americans, feared that the erection of such a wall would separate religious influences from public life and policy. Few evangelical dissenters (including the Baptists) challenged the widespread assumption of the age that republican government and civic virtue were dependent on a moral people and that morals could be nurtured only by the Christian religion.

Second, a wall is a bilateral barrier that inhibits the activities of both the civil government and religion—unlike the First Amendment, which imposes restrictions on civil government only. In short, a wall not only prevents the civil state from intruding on the religious domain but also prohibits religion from influencing the conduct of civil government. The various First Amendment guarantees, however, were entirely a check or restraint on civil government, specifically on Congress. The free-press guarantee, for example, was not written to protect the civil state from the press but to protect a free and independent press from control by the national government. Similarly, the religion provisions were added to the Constitution to protect religion and religious institutions from interference by the national government, not to protect the civil state from the influence of, or overreaching by, religion. As a bilateral barrier, however, the wall unavoidably restricts religion's ability to influence public life, and, thus, it necessarily exceeds the limitations imposed by the Constitution.

Herein lies the danger of this metaphor. The "high and impregnable" wall constructed by the modern Court has been used to inhibit religion's ability to inform the public ethic, deprive religious citizens of the civil liberty to participate in politics armed with ideas informed by their spiritual beliefs, and infringe the right of religious communities and institutions to extend their ministries into the public square. The wall has been used to silence the religious voice in the public marketplace of ideas and to segregate faith communities behind a restrictive barrier.

If, as I have argued, the wall is a profoundly flawed metaphor for First Amendment doctrine, then should we search for a better, alternative metaphor, such as James Madison's "line of separation"? I think not. Although other tropes may yield interesting insights, we are best served by returning to the First Amendment itself.

Jefferson's figurative language has not produced the practical solutions to real-world controversies that its apparent clarity and directness led its proponents to expect. Indeed, this wall has done what walls frequently do: It has obstructed the view. It has obfuscated our understanding of constitutional principles governing Church-State relationships.

The repetitious, uncritical use of felicitous phrases, Justice Felix Frankfurter observed, bedevils the law: "A phrase begins life as a literary expression; its felicity leads to its lazy repetition; and repetition soon establishes it as a legal formula, undiscriminatingly used to express different and sometimes contradictory ideas." Figures of speech designed to simplify and liberate thought end often by trivializing or enslaving it. Therefore, as Judge Benjamin N. Cardozo counseled, "[m]etaphors in law are to be narrowly watched." This is advice that courts would do well to heed.

Notes

Introduction

[1]"1992 Policy Guide of the ACLU," policy 4d, p. 7, and policy 4g, p. 9.

[2]Ibid., policy 4e, p. 8.

[3]"ACLU Defends Library against Parent Seeking Internet Censorship," ACLU of Northern California press release, January/February 2000; http://www.aclunc.org/aclunews/news12000/library.html, and "ACLU Defends California Library against Parent Seeking to Compel Internet Censorship," ACLU press release, June 10, 1998.

[4]"1992 Policy Guide of the ACLU," policy 2a, p. 3.

[5]Ibid., policy 39a, p. 82.

[6]"Ban on Gays in the Military Goes on Trial: 'Don't Ask, Don't Tell,' Faces Challenge in Brooklyn," ACLU press release, March 12, 1995; http://archive.aclu.org/news/n031295c.html.

[7]"1992 Policy Guide of the ACLU," policy 62a, p. 120, and policy 86, p. 168.

[8]Ibid., policy 81, p. 161.

[9]Ibid., policy 88, p. 171, and policy 89, p. 172.

[10]Ibid., policy 91a, p. 175.

[11]Adrian Brune, "ACLU Takes Center Stage in Gay Marriage Debate," *Washington Blade*, April 16, 2004.

[12]See *Griswold vs. Connecticut* 381 U.S. 479 (1965), in which the U.S. Supreme Court found, "The Connecticut statute forbidding use of contraceptives violates the right of marital privacy which is within the *penumbra* of specific guarantees of the Bill of Rights." This decision would provide the basis for *Roe vs. Wade*, which legalized abortion, several years later.

[13]http://www.nrlc.org/abortion/facts/abortionstats.html

[14]"Freedom Is Why We're Here," ACLU position paper; http://www.aclu.org.

[15]Robyn E. Blumner, "ACLU National Director Retires for Much More Freedom," *St. Petersburg Times*, September 3, 2000, 1D.

[16]American Civil Liberties Union Foundation; http://www.guidestar.org/Fin Documents/2004/136/213/2004-136213516-1-9.pdf (password needed for access).

[17]"$8 Million Gift Will Boost ACLU Campaign to Fight Bush Administration's Assault on Civil Liberties," ACLU press release, January 15, 2003; http://www.aclu.org/about/about.cfm? ID=11607%26c=190.

[18]"Ford Foundation Gives $7 Million to ACLU Endowment Campaign," ACLU press release, June 28, 1999; http://www.aclu.org/news/1999/n062899a. html.

Chapter 1

[1]Peggy Lamson, *Roger Baldwin: Founder of the American Civil Liberties Union: A Portrait* (Boston: Houghton-Mifflin, 1976), p. 192.

[2]William Donohue, *The Politics of the American Civil Liberties Union*, (New Brunswick, NJ: Transaction Publishers, 1985), p. 45.

[3]George Grant, *Trial and Error: The American Civil Liberties Union and Its Impact on Your Family* (Brentwood, TN: Wolgemuth and Hyatt, 1989), 38–39.

[4]Robert C. Contrell, "Roger Baldwin: Founder, American Civil Liberties Union, 1884–1991"; http://www.harvardsquarelibruary.org/unitarians/bald win_r.html.

[5]Grant, 52.

[6]Lamson, 9.

[7]Grant, 52–53.

[8]Lamson, 2.

[9]Ibid., 5.

[10]Ibid., 5.

[11]Grant, 53.

[12]Lamson, 2.

[13]"Civil Liberties at Risk through Ballot Initiatives," ACLU press release, November 4, 1998; http://archive.aclu.org/news/n110498c.html.

[14]Diane Garey, *Defending Everybody: A History of the American Civil Liberties Union* (New York: TV Books, 1998), 133–35.

[15]John F. Kennedy, inaugural address, January 20, 1961; http://www.white house.gov/history/presidents/jk35.html.

[16]Grant, 57.

[17]Margaret Sanger, "An Answer to Mr. Roosevelt," *Birth Control Review*, December 1917.

[18]Lamson, 55.

[19]John Ray, "Eugenics and the Left," Frontpagemagazine.com, September 25, 2003; http://www.frontpagemag.com/Articles/Printable.asp?ID=10004.

[20]Ibid.

[21]Lamson, 55.

[22]Ibid., 62.

[23]The Emma Goldman Papers at the Berkeley Digital Library; http://sun site.berkeley.edu/goldman/exhibition/introduction.html.

[24]Lamson, 62.

[25]Emma Goldman, *Living My Life* (New York: Knopf, 1931), 83–88; http://historymatters.gmu.edu/d/99.

[26]See http://www.pbs.org/wgbh/amex/goldman/sfeature/sf_motherearth.html.

[27]See http://www.pbs.org/wgbh/amex/goldman/peopleevents/p_goldman.html.

[28]Ibid.

[29]See http://www.jwa.org/exhibits/wov/goldman/speech.html.

[30]Lamson, 58.

[31]Ibid., 58–59.

[32]Ibid., 62, citing Richard Drinnon, *Rebel in Paradise* (Chicago: University of Chicago Press, 1961), 140.

[33]Ibid., 63.

[34]Ibid., 63–64.

[35]Ibid., 94.

[36]Ibid., 67.

[37]Ibid., 71.

[38]Ibid., 86.

[39]Ibid., 86–88.

[40]Ibid., 107.

[41]Ibid., 88 and 106.

[42]Ibid., 109.

[43]Ibid., 116–17.

[44]Ibid., 117.

[45]Ibid., 125.

[46]Ibid., 192.

[47]Ibid., 140.

[48]Ibid., 138.

[49]See http://www.iww.org.

[50]"Freedom Is Why We're Here," ACLU position paper, 1999; http://www.nhclu.org/publications/freedom_is_why.htm.

[51]William Donohue, *The Politics of the American Civil Liberties Union* (New Brunswick, NJ: Transaction Publishers, 1985), 45.

[52]William Donohue, *Twilight of Liberty* (New Brunswick, NJ: Transaction Press, 2001), 7, citing Frederick R. Barkley, "Calls New Deal Communist 'Front,'" *New York Times*, September 7, 1939, 26.

[53]Lamson, 195.

[54]Donohue, *Politics*, 132, citing "Robert W. Dunn, 81, a Co-Founder of American Civil Liberties Union," *New York Times*, January 23, 1977, 28.

[55]Lamson, 141.

[56]Dan Michaels, "The Gulag: Communism's Penal Colonies Revisited," *Journal of Historical Review* 21, no. 1 (January/February 2002): 39.

[57]Donohue, *Politics*, 134.

[58]Daniel J. Popeo, "Not OUR America ... The ACLU Exposed!" Washington Legal Foundation, 10, 1989.

[59]Donohue, *Twilight of Liberty*, 7, quoting William H. McIlhaney II, *The ACLU on Trial* (New Rochelle, NY: Arlington House, 1976), 194.

[60]Popeo.

[61]Donohue, *Twilight of Liberty*, xi, citing Roger Baldwin, "Freedom in the U.S.A. and the U.S.S.R.," *Soviet Russia Today* (September 1934): 11.

[62]Donohue, *Twilight of Liberty*, xii.

[63]Ibid., 7.

[64]Ibid.

[65]Samuel Walker, *In Defense of Civil Liberties: A History of the ACLU* (New York: Oxford University Press, 1990), 118.

[66]Lamson, 201.

[67]Ibid., 232.

[68]Ibid., 224.

[69]Ibid., 231–32.

[70]Terry Chang, "Religious Employer Must Provide Contraceptive Coverage for Employees," *ACLU of Northern California News*, July/August 2001.

[71]Lamson, 164.

[72]Ibid., 163–64.

[73]Ibid., 164–65.

[74]Justice Paul E. Pfeifer, "The Scopes Monkey Trial." See www.sconet.state. oh.us/Public_Information/Justice_Pfeifer/JP12899.htm.

[75]Ibid., 164.

[76]Ibid.

[77]Ibid., 165.

[78]"Darrow Argues Law Is Unconstitutional"; http://www.law.umkc.edu/faculty/projects/ftrials/scopes/day2.htm.

[79]Lamson, 166.

[80]"The ACLU and the Supreme Court: 77 Years, 77 Great Victories"; www. aclu.org/library/75hits.html.

[81]*Everson vs. Board of Education of Ewing Township*, 330 U.S. 1 (1947).

[82]*Engel v, Vitale*, 370 U.S. 421, 436 (1962).

[83]*Abington School District vs. Schempp*, 374 U.S. 203, 226–27 (1963).

[84]*Epperson vs. Arkansas*, 393 U.S. 97 (1968).

[85]*Wallace vs. Jaffree*, 472 U.S. 38, 61 (1985).

[86]*Lee vs. Weisman*, 505 U.S. 577, 599 (1992).

[87]*Griswold vs. Connecticut*, 381 U.S. 479, 484 (1965).

[88]*Eisenstadt vs. Baird*, 405 U.S. 438, 453 (1972).

[89]*Roe vs. Wade*, 410 U.S. 113, (1973).

[90]http://www.nrlc.org/abortion/facts/abortionstats.html

[91]*Planned Parenthood of Southeastern Pennsylvania vs. Casey*, 505 U.S. 833 (1992).

[92]Ibid.

[93]Lamson, 63–64.

[94]*Jacobellis vs. Ohio*, 378 U.S. 184 (1964).

[95]*New York vs. Ferber*, 458 U.S. 747 (1982).

[96]*Romer vs. Evans*, 517 U.S. 620, 632 (1996).

[97]*Lawrence vs. Texas*, No. 02–102 (2003).

[98]Linda Greenhouse, "Supreme Court Paved Way for Marriage Ruling with Sodomy Law Decision," *New York Times*, November 19, 2003.

[99]John Quincy Adams, "The Jubilee of the Constitution: A Discourse," delivered at request of New York Historical Society, April 30, 1839.

[100]See *Miller vs. California*, 413 U.S. 15 (1973).

[101]See Article 1, Declaration of Rights, Section 5 Freedom of Speech, Constitution of the State of Washington.

[102]Russell L. Weaver and Donald L. Lively, "Understanding the First Amendment." See www.lexisnexis.com/lawschool/study/understanding/pdf/FirstAmendChl.pdf.

[103]Ibid.

[104]Dennis Prager, "The Left Thinks Legally, The Right Thinks Morally," *Creators Syndicate*, September 21, 2004.

[105]Robert Bork, *Coercing Virtue: The Worldwide Rule of Judges* (Washington, D.C.: AEI Press, 2003).

Chapter 2

[1]"Civil Liberties at Risk through Ballot Initiatives," ACLU press release, November 4, 1998. See http://archive.aclu.org/news/n110498c.html.

[2]Sir Winston Churchill, "Speech on Collective Security," April 30, 1938.

[3]"Legal Groups Say Denial of Marriage Licenses Violates State Constitution," ACLU press release, March 12, 2004; http://www.aclu.org/news/newsprint.cfm?ID=15254&c=101.

[4]"Lesbian and Gay Couples in San Francisco Are Granted Marriage Licenses," ACLU press release, February 12, 2004.

[5]William Donohue, *Twilight of Liberty* (New Brunswick, NJ: Transaction Publishers, 2001), 49.

[6]"Civil Liberties at Risk through Ballot Initiatives," ACLU press release, November 4, 1998; http://archive.aclu.org/news/n110498c.html.

[7]"Village Mayor in New York Says He Will Marry Gay Couples," Associated Press, February 26, 2004.

[8]Sir Winston Churchill, speech on collective security, April 30, 1938.

[9]"Couples Challenge Marriage Discrimination in California: Legal Groups Say Denial of Marriage Licenses Violates State Constitution," ACLU press release, March 12, 2004; http://www.aclu.org/lesbiangayrights/lesbiangayrights.cfm?ID=15254&c=101.

[10]Ibid.

[11]"ACLU to Sue Oregon Officials over Refusal to Recognize Same Sex Marriage," ACLU press release, March 19, 2004, and "A Second County in Oregon Votes to Issue Marriage Licenses to Same-Sex Couples; ACLU Urges Others to Do the Same," ACLU press release, March 17, 2004.

[12]"ACLU Asks New York Court to Let Marriages Continue," ACLU press release, March 5, 2004, and John Wiley, "ACLU Sues State Over Gay Marriage Ban," Associated Press, April 1, 2004.

[13]ADF News Alert, April 14, 2004.

[14]Ibid.

[15]Kevin G. Clarkson, David Orgon Coolidge, William C. Duncan, "The Alaska Marriage Amendment: The People's Choice on the Last Frontier," 16 Alaska Law Review, Revs. 213.

[16]Ibid.

[17]"Louisiana Residents: Oppose Writing Intolerance into the Louisiana Constitution"; http://www.aclu.org/lesbiangayrights/lesbiangayrights.cfm?ID=15628&c=23.

[18]"ACLU Files Challenge to Misleading Arkansas 'Marriage' Ballot Initiative," ACLU press release, August 26, 2004; http://www.aclu.org/lesbiangayrights/lesbiangayrights.cfm?ID=16316&c=101. "Arkansas Supreme Court Rebuffs ACLU, Marriage Amendment Will Remain on Ballot," ADF Press Release, October 7, 2004; http://http://www.alliancedefensefund.org/story/?id=514.

[19]"Judge Decides Not to Stop Vote on Gay Marriage Amendment," Associated Press, September 30, 2004.

[20]"Proposed Oklahoma Marriage Ban Draws Court Challenge"; http://www.advocate.com/new_news.asp?ID=12557&sd=05/26/04.

[21]"ACLU Helping Fight Amendment Banning Same-sex Marriages," Clarion-Ledger (Jackson, MS), September 8, 2004.

[22]ADF News Alert, January 19, 2005.

[23]Vaishali Honawar, "Lawmakers Fight Same-Sex Suit"; http://www.home townannapolis.com/cgi-bin/read/2004/09_12-53/govs.

[24]"ACLU and Lambda Legal File Federal Lawsuit to Strike Down Nebraska's Extreme Law Banning Any Recognition of Gay Couples," ACLU press release, April 30, 2003; http://www.aclu.org/news/newsprint.cfm?ID=12504&c=101.

[25]Citizens for Equal Protection, Inc., et al., vs. Attorney General Jon C. Bruning, et al. 4:03cv3155, May 12, 2005.

[26]"Federal Court Strikes Down Nebraska's Anti-Gay Union Law Banning Protections for Same-Sex Couples," ACLU press release, May 12, 2005. See http://www.aclu.org/LesbianGayRights/LesbianGayRights.cfm?ID=18233&c=101.

[27]"Why the Supreme Court Decision Striking Down Sodomy Laws Is So Important"; http://www.aclu.org/lesbiangayrights/lesbianrightsmain.cfm.

[28]Marie-Jo Proulx, "ACLU Marriage Discussion Lays Out Challenges," Windy City Times, June 9, 2004.

[29]"Why the Supreme Court Decision Striking Down Sodomy Laws Is So Important."

[30]Ibid.

[31]Franklin E. Kameny, "Deconstructing the Traditional Family," *The World and I* (October 1993): 394–95.

[32]John Adams, *The Works of John Adams, Second President of the United States,* Charles Francis Adams, ed. (Boston: Little, Brown, and Company, 1854), vol. IX, p. 229, October 11, 1798.

[33]"New CD *Marry Me* Supports the ACLU's Efforts to Win Marriage for Same-Sex Couples," ACLU press release, November 12, 2004.

[34]"ACLU Launches Marriage Campaign to Move Americans to Treat Families of Same-Sex Couples More Fairly," ACLU press release, May 16, 2005. See http://www.aclu.org/LesbianGayRights/LesbianGayRights.cfm?ID=18250&c=23.

[35]*Williams vs. Attorney General of Alabama,* 378 F.3d 1232, 1234-35, 1250 (11th Cir. 2004).

[36]Gene Edward Veith, "Doing without Marriage," *World,* April 29, 2000.

[37]Ibid.

[38]Stanley Kurtz, "Slipping toward Scandinavia," *National Review* online, February 2, 2004.

[39]Christine Winquist Nord and Nicholas Zill, "Non-Custodial Parents' Participation in Their Children's Lives: Evidence from the Survey of Income and Program Participation," prepared for office of Assistant Secretary for Planning and Evaluation, U.S. Department of Health and Human Services, August 14, 1996.

[40]Stanley Kurtz, "The Marriage Mentality," *National Review* online, May 4, 2004.

[41]Gene Edward Veith, "Wages of Sin: Marriage Benefits Are Starting to Go to Those Who Are Shacking Up," *World,* August 18, 2001.

[42]"Legal Recognition of Same-sex Marriage: A Conference on National European and International Law," King's College, University of London, July 1-9, 1999.

[43]Centers for Disease Control and Prevention, *Tracking the Hidden Epidemics: Trends in STDs in the United States 2000;* http://www.cdc.gov/nchstp/dstd/stats_trends/trends2000.pdf.

[44]Centers for Disease Control, *Sexually Transmitted Disease Surveillance 2001,* www.cdc.gov/std/stats/TOC2001.htm, cited in Brief in support of respondent on behalf of *amici curiae,* Texas Physicians Resource Council, Christian Medical and Dental Associations, and Catholic Medical Association, Glen Lavy, counsel of record, *John Geddes Lawrence and Tyron Garner vs. State of Texas,* 539 U.S. 558 (2003).

[45]Thomas C. Quinn, M.D., cited in brief in support of respondent, *John Geddes Lawrence and Tyron Garner vs. State of Texas,* 539 U.S. 558 (2003).

[46]Neil E. Reiner, M.D., et al., "Asymptomatic Rectal Mucosal Lesions and Hepatitis B Surface Antigen at Sites of Sexual Contact in Homosexual Men with Persistent Hepatitis B Virus Infection: Evidence for de facto Parenteral Transmission," 96 *Annals of Internal Medicine* (1984): 170, cited in brief in

support of respondent, *John Geddes Lawrence and Tyron Garner vs. State of Texas*, no. 02–102, U.S. Supreme Court.

[47]Centers for Disease Control, *Tracking the Hidden Epidemics.*

[48]John O.G. Billy, et al., *Family Planning Perspectives*, Alan Guttmacher Institute, March/April 1993.

[49]"1992 Policy Guide of the ACLU," 91A, p. 175.

[50]Stanley Kurtz, "Beyond Gay Marriage: The Road to Polyamory," *Weekly Standard*, August 4, 2003.

[51]Edward Leo Lyman, "Struggle for Statehood," *Utah History Encyclopedia*, see http://historytogo.utah.gov/statehood.html.

[52]Alexandria Sage, "Attorney Challenges Utah Polygamy Ban," Associated Press, January 26, 2004.

[53]Angie Welling, "Judge Dismisses Challenge to Utah Ban on Polygamy," *Deseret News*, February 17, 2005.

[54]"ACLU of Utah to Join Polygamists in Bigamy Fight," ACLU press release, July 16, 1999. See http://www.aclu.org/news/NewsPrint.cfm?ID =8318&c=142.

[55]Joe Crea, "Polygamy Advocates Buoyed by Gay Court Wins," *Washington Blade*, December 26, 2003.

[56]"ACLU Wants to Legalize Polygamy," *Christians and Society Today*, June 1990, 4, cited in Donohue, 44.

[57]Crystal Paul-Laughinghouse, "Leader of ACLU Talks on Agenda," *Yale Daily News*, January 19, 2005.

[58]Bruce Fein and William Bradford Reynolds, "Polygamy Stand Exposes ACLU's Agenda," *Legal Times*, May 22, 1989, 22, cited in Donohue, 45.

[59]George W. Dent Jr., "The Defense of Traditional Marriage," *Journal of Law and Politics*, vol. 15, no. 4 (Fall 1999): 628–37.

[60]Don Lattin, "Committed to Marriage for the Masses, Polyamorists Say They Relate Honestly to Multiple Partners," *San Francisco Chronicle*, April 20, 2004.

[61]Ibid.

[62]"ACLU Denounces Passage of Anti-Gay Initiative in Hawaii (and Alaska)," ACLU-NC press release, November 4, 1998.

[63]Debra Saunders, "One Man's Animal Husbandry," *Creators Syndicate*, March 21, 2001.

[64]"Marriage Amendment: Oppose Writing Intolerance into the Constitution," ACLU press release; http://www.aclu.org/lesbiangayrights/ lesbiangayrights.cfm? ID=9977&c=101.

[65]"Talking Points on the Federal Marriage Amendment," ACLU press release, February 25, 2004; http://www.aclu.org/lesbiangayrights/lesbiangay rights.cfm?ID=15071&c=23.

[66]Ibid.

[67]Ibid.

[68]"Testimony Submitted by Bob Barr, Former Member of Congress, to the House Judiciary Committee, Subcommittee on the Constitution on the

Defense of Marriage Act and the Federal Marriage Amendment," *ACLU Legislative Update*, March 30, 2004.

[69]Matthew Coles, "Don't Just Sue the Bastards! A Strategic Approach to Marriage"; http://www.aclu.org/lesbiangayrights/lesbiangayrightsmain.cfm.

[70]Letter to Rep. Charles Canady, May 15, 1996; http://archive.aclu.org/congress/defmarr.html.

[71]"Thinking of Getting Married in Massachusetts?" ACLU press release, November 25, 2003; http://www.aclu.org/lesbiangayrights/lesbiangayrights.cfm?ID=14455&c=101.

[72]"Following Passage of Gay Marriage Bans in 11 States, ACLU Vows to Continue Striving for Equality," ACLU press release, November 3, 2004.

[73]Stanley Kurtz, "The End of Marriage in Scandinavia," *Weekly Standard*, February 2, 2004, citing the work of British scholar Duncan W. G. Timms.

[74]Ibid.

[75]Ibid.

[76]Glenn Stanton, "No-Fault Fallout," *Focus on the Family*.

[77]"Covenant Marriages Tie a Firm Knot," ACLU press release, August 18, 1997; http://archive.aclu.org/news/w081897b.html.

[78]Marilyn Elias, "Divorce Is Likelier for Kids of Divorce," *USA Today*, May 14, 1991.

[79]David Popenoe, "Teen Pregnancy: An American Dilemma," testimony, House of Representatives, Committee on Small Business, Subcommittee on Empowerment, Washington, D.C., July 16, 1998; http://marriage.rutgers.edu/publications/print/printteen%20pregnancy.htm.

[80]Elias.

[81]Phillip Vassalo, "More Than Grades: How Choice Boosts Parental Involvement and Benefits Children," *Policy Analysis*, Cato Institute, October 26, 2000.

[82]"Back to School 1999: National Survey of American Attitudes: Substance Abuse vs. Teens and Their Parents," National Center on Addiction and Substance Abuse at Columbia University, September 1999; http://www.casacolumbia.org.

[83]Julie Cart, "Utah Paying a High Price for Polygamy," *Los Angeles Times*, September 9, 2001.

Chapter 3

[1]"In a Victory of Privacy Rights, Florida Supreme Court Strikes Down Parental Notification Law," ACLU press release, July 10, 2003. See http://www.aclu.org/news/NewsPrint.cfm?ID=13111&c=223.

[2]Excerpted from "In My Mommy's High Heels," lyrics by Paul Selig, music by Scott Killian, from *Cootie Shots: Theatrical Inoculations against Bigotry for Kids, Parents, and Teachers* (Theatre Communications Group, 2001).

[3]Diana Lynne, "Schools Sued over Pro-Homosexual Skits," Worldnetdaily.com, February 6, 2002.

[4]"Victory for Novato School District's Diversity Education Program," ACLU of Northern California press release, September 4, 2004; http://www.aclunc.org/pressrel/030904-cooties.html.

[5] *West Virginia State Bd. of Educ. vs. Barnette,* 319 U.S. 624 (1943).

[6] "Testimony on HB 1010 Regarding 'Parental Rights,'" *ACLU in the States;* http://www.archive.aclu.org/community/pennsyl/parent.html.

[7] *Prince vs. Massachusetts,* 321 U.S. 158, 166 (1944).

[8] *Wisconsin vs. Yoder,* 406 U.S. 205 (1972).

[9] *Prince,* 321 U.S. at 165.

[10] *Pierce vs. Society of Sisters,* 268 U.S. 510, 535–35 (1925).

[11] *Parham vs. J.R.,* 442 U.S. 584, 602 (1979).

[12] Larry O'Dell, "Judge Allows Virginia Law on Teen Nudist Camp," Associated Press, August 10, 2004.

[13] Christina Bellantoni, "Teen Nudist Law Faces Challenge," *Washington Times,* June 22, 2004.

[14] O'Dell.

[15] Bellantoni.

[16] O'Dell.

[17] Cheryl Wetzstein, "Sex Teacher Faces Suit for High School Performance," *Washington Times,* March 7, 1994.

[18] Cheryl Wetzstein, "Educator Gets Laughs, Lawsuit with Her Hot Talk About Safe Sex," *Washington Times,* March 20, 1994.

[19] Wetzstein, "Sex Teacher Faces Suit," March 7, 2004.

[20] Joe Heaney, "Massachusetts Students Lose Suit over School Sex Program," *Boston Herald,* March 5, 1996.

[21] Letter to Robert Dole, Senate majority leader, from Laura Murphy, director, and Elizabeth Symonds, legislative counsel, American Civil Liberties Union, January 25, 1996; http:// archive.aclu.org/congress/parrght.html.

[22] "S. 661/H.R. 1218 Threatens the Well-Being of Young Women," *ACLU in Congress,* June 29, 1999; http://archive.aclu.org/congress/ccpa_analysis.html.

[23] Martha Kleder, "School Counselor Guided Daughter Astray, Parents Claim," *Focus on the Family Citizen;* http://www.family.org/cforum/citizenmag/departments/a0007939.cfm.

[24] "ACLJ Announces Settlement in Pennsylvania School District Lawsuit Charging Secret Abortion for Minor Student: School District Required to Issue Directive Prohibiting Personnel from Aiding Students in Obtaining Abortions," American Center for Law and Justice press release, March 15, 2000.

[25] "Parental Rights Legislation," *ACLU Reproductive Rights;* http://archive.aclu.org/library/parentrt.html.

[26] Ibid.

[27] Ibid.

[28] *Lambert vs. Wicklund,* 520 U.S. 292 (1997).

[29] "In a Victory for Privacy Rights, Florida Supreme Court Strikes Down Parental Notification Law," ACLU press release, July 10, 2003; http://www.aclu.org/news/newsprint.cfm?ID=13111&c=223.

[30] ACLU briefing paper 7, "Reproductive Freedom: The Rights of Minors"; http://www.lectlaw.com/files/con16.htm.

³¹William A. Donohue, *The New Freedom* (New Brunswick, NJ: 1990), 119.
³²Letter to Sen. Dole.
³³Patrick F. Fagan and Wade F. Horn, Ph.D., "How Congress Can Protect the Rights of Parents to Raise Their Children," *National Fatherhood Initiative Issues Bulletin*, no. 227 (July 23, 1996).
³⁴Ibid.
³⁵Letter to Sen. Dole.
³⁶Ibid.
³⁷Ibid.
³⁸Ibid.
³⁹Ibid., citing National Commission on Children, final report, *Beyond Rhetoric: A New Agenda for Children and Families*, 1991.
⁴⁰"1992 Policy Guide of the ACLU," policy 211, p. 261.
⁴¹Ibid., policy 4d, p. 7, and policy 4g, p. 9.
⁴²Ibid., policy 2a, p. 3.
⁴³Ibid., p. 4.
⁴⁴"ACLU Defends Library Against Parent Seeking Internet Censorship," ACLU of Northern California press release, January/February 2000; http://www.aclunc.org/aclunews/news12000/library.html and "ACLU Defends California Library against Parent Seeking to Compel Internet Censorship," ACLU press release, June 10, 1998.
⁴⁵See http://www.caselaw.lp.findlaw.com/scripts/ts_search.pl?title=47&sec=231.
⁴⁶See 18 U.S.C., sec. 2257; http://www4.law.cornell.edu/uscode/18/2257.html.
⁴⁷See *American Library Association et al., vs. Reno, et al.*, 515 U.S. 1558, (1995)
⁴⁸"1992 Policy Guide of the ACLU," policy 2a, p. 4.
⁴⁹Ibid.
⁵⁰William Donohue, *Twilight of Liberty* (New Brunswick, NJ: Transaction Publishers, 2001), 39.
⁵¹Ibid.
⁵²*Flores vs. Morgan Hill Unified School District*, settlement fact sheet, January 6, 2004; http://www.aclu.org/news/NewsPrint.cfm?ID=14658&c=106.
⁵³Ibid.
⁵⁴"In Groundbreaking Settlement, School Agrees to Sweeping Anti-Gay Harassment Program," ACLU press release, August 13, 2002.
⁵⁵"ACLU Wins Settlement for Kentucky School's Gay-Straight Alliance," ACLU press release, February 3, 2004.
⁵⁶Ibid.
⁵⁷"View Homosexual Film, or School Faces Lawsuit," WorldNetDaily.com., November 28, 2004.
⁵⁸*Making Schools Safe: An Anti-Harassment Training Program from the ACLU Lesbian and Gay Rights Project's Every Student, Every School Initiative*, 2nd ed., May 2002.

[59]"Day of Silence" 2002 organizing manual, 13; http://www.dayofsilence.com/resources/manual.php.

[60]"The ACLU of Texas Position on School Vouchers"; http://www.aclutx.org/pubed/positionpapers/vouchers.htm.

[61]Justin Torres, "Conference: 'New Moment' in Homosexual Activism," cnsnews.com, October 4, 1999.

[62]Philip Vassallo, "More than Grades: How Choice Boosts Parental Involvement and Benefits Children," *Policy Analysis*, no. 383, October 26, 2000.

[63]"Cleveland Public Schools Performance Audit, Executive Summary," 2–3.

[64]*Zelman vs. Simmons-Harris*, 536 U.S. 639, 2002; http://www.supct.law.cornell.edu/supct/html/00-1751.ZS.html.

[65]"ACLU Victorious in Ending High School 'Pink Triangle' Zones for Homosexual Students"; see http://www.freerepublic.com/forum/a36d559fl68e5.html.

[66]"God Grants Victory for Life from the Ninth U.S. Circuit Court of Appeals," ADF weekly news alert, October 20, 2002.

Chapter 4

[1]Deroy Murdock, "No Boy Scouts," *National Review* online, February 27, 2004.

[2]Ibid.

[3]Julie Foster, "ACLU Defends Child-Molester Group," WorldNetDaily.com, December 13, 2000.

[4]Murdock.

[5]Ibid.

[6]Foster.

[7]Ibid.

[8]Murdock.

[9]Ibid.

[10]"ACLU Agrees to Represent NAMBLA in Freedom of Speech Case," ACLU of Massachusetts press release, June 9, 2003.

[11]Ibid.

[12]Deborah Mathis, "Many Share in the Hate-Filled Killing of Gay Student," *Orlando Sentinel*, October 15, 1998.

[13]Foster.

[14]"ACLU Mourns the Death of Matthew Shepard," ACLU news release, October 14, 1998; http://archive.aclu.org/news/n101498b.html.

[15]ACLU briefing paper 10, "Freedom of Expression"; http://archive.aclu.org/library/pbp.10.html.

[16]David Pitt, "Judge Strikes Down Iowa Sex-Offender Law," Associated Press, February 9, 2004.

[17]Paul Walfield, "Caring Less for Our Children," *Accuracy in Media*, July 10, 2003; http://www.aim.org/publications/guest_columns/walfield/2003/jul10.html.

[18]Ibid.

[19]Ibid.

[20]Murdock.

[21]See http://www.scouting.org/factsheets/02-516.html.

[22]Ibid.

[23]Murdock.

[24]William Donohue, "On the Front Line of the Culture War: Recent Attacks on the Boy Scouts of America," Claremont Institute; adnetsolfp2.ad netsol.com/ssl_claremont/publications/scouts.cfm.

[25]David Kupelian, "Pedophile Priests' and Boy Scouts," WorldNetDaily. com, May 8, 2002.

[26]Letter from Ireland Stevenson, NAMBLA, co-recording secretary to Ben Love, chief Scout executive, Boy Scouts of America, November 1992, cited by Steve Baldwin in "Child Molestation and the Homosexual Movement," *Regent University Law Review*, 14 (2001–2002): 270.

[27]Bill Morlin, "West Tied to Sex Abuse in the '70s, Using Office to Lure Young Men," *Spokane Review*, May 5, 2005.

[28]Ibid.

[29]Ibid.

[30]Ibid.

[31]Donohue, "Front Line of the Culture War."

[32]*Curran vs. Mount Diablo Council of the Boy Scouts*, 195 Cal. Rptr, 325 (Cal. Ct. App. 1983).

[33]"California State Supreme Court Upholds Discrimination by Boy Scouts," ACLU press release, March 23, 1998; http://archive.aclu.org/news/n032398b.html.

[34]*Boy Scouts of America vs. Dale* (99–699) 530 U.S. 640 (2000).

[35]ACLU press release, March 23, 1998.

[36]Donohue, "Front Line of the Culture War."

[37]See http://www.scouting.org/factsheets/02-503a.html.

[38]Donohue, "Discrimination by Boy Scouts Challenged in California," ACLU press release, December 31, 1997.

[39]ACLU press release, March 23, 1998.

[40]Peter Ferrara, "The War on the Boy Scouts: The ACLU Never Sleeps," *Weekly Standard*, September 29, 2003.

[41]Ibid.

[42]Ibid.

[43]Hans Zeiger, "Destroying Scouting the ACLU Way," cnsnews.com, August 5, 2003.

[44]Sam Kastensmidt, "San Diego Settles Boy Scout Suit—Gives ACLU $950,000"; http://www.reclaimamerica.org/pages/news/newspage.asp?story=1516.

[45]Bill O'Reilly, "Another Big Win for the ACLU," *Fox News*, January 12, 2004.

[46]Ibid.

[47]"Schools Must Pay ACLU in Case Involving Atheist, Scouts," Associated Press, July 14, 1992.

48"Chicago Ends Boy Scout Sponsorship," ACLU press release, February 4, 1998; http://archive.aclu.org/news/n020498a.html.

49Annette Scalise, "On the Recruiting Trail: The Boy Scouts Extend Their Efforts in Ethnic Communities," Newsday, May 24, 2002.

50Jim Trageser, "ACLU on Wrong Side against Scouts," North County Times, April 2, 2004; http://www.nctimes.com/articles/2004/04/02/news/columnists/trageser/4_1_0421_21_36.txt.

51Rich Lowry, "The Boy Scouts in the Cross Hairs," King Features Syndicate, March 11, 2004; http://www.townhall.com/columnists/richlowry/r120040311.shtml.

52"ACLU Says Rent-Free Leases to Boy Scouts Violate California Constitution," ACLU press release, January 16, 2001; http://archive.aclu.org/news/2001/n011601c.html.

53Ben Boychuk, "The ACLU versus Freedom of Assembly," Claremont Institute, September 29, 2000.

54"ACLU Threat Drives Scouts of Schools," WorldNetDaily.com, March 11, 2005.

55Art Moore, "Veterans Blast Pentagon for Giving in to ACLU," WorldNetDaily.com, November 18, 2004.

56Nat Hentoff, "The War Against the Boy Scouts," Jewish World Review, June 19, 2001.

57Donohue, "Front Line of the Culture War."

58Peggy Lamson, Roger Baldwin: Founder of the American Civil Liberties Union: A Portrait (Boston: Houghton-Mifflin, 1976), 63.

59Ibid., 231–32.

60Donohue, "Front Line of the Culture War."

61Boychuk.

62"Court Upholds Livermore Library's Uncensored Internet Access Policy," ACLU of Northern California press release, January 14, 1999.

63"ACLU Hails Victory as California Library Agrees to Remove Internet Filters from Public Computers," ACLU of Northern California press release, January 28, 1998.

64"Perseverance Pays Off, Another ADF-Assisted Victory for Families and Children at the U.S. Supreme Court," ADF weekly news alert, June 23, 2003.

65ACLU memo, "Library Filtering After U.S. vs. ALA: What Does It All Mean and What Should We Do," August 1, 2003; http://www.aclu.org/privacy/privacy.cfm?ID=13270&c=252.

66"ACLU Hails Victory."

67Miller vs. California, 418 U.S. 915 (1974).

68Herceg vs. Hustler Magazine, 814 F.2d 1017, April 20, 1987.

69"1992 Policy Guide of the ACLU," policy 4d, p. 7, and policy 4g, p. 9.

70New York vs. Ferber, 458 U.S. 747.

71James Dobson, final report, Attorney General's Commission on Pornography, v 1, pp. 75–76.

[72]William Donohue, *Twilight of Liberty* (New Brunswick, NJ: Transaction Press, 2001), 208.

[73]"Security Cameras: Why They Are an ACLU Issue," ACLU of Colorado press release; http://www.aclu-co.org/news/letters/paper_securitycameras. htm.

Chapter 5

[1]"ACLU: National Day of Appreciation for Abortion Providers," *ACLU Features*, March 10, 2002. See http://www.archive.aclu.org/features/031002a. html.

[2]"Who Will Remember Terri?" *The Wall Street Journal*, April 1, 2005.

[3]Alan Sears, speaking in Washington, D.C., at the National Day of Prayer, May 5, 2005.

[4]Brenda Pratt Shafer, R.N., 1996 hearing on partial-birth abortion before the House Committee on the Judiciary, Subcommittee on the Constitution, 104th Cong; http://www.house.gov/judiciary/215.htm.

[5]"Planned Parenthood of America, Reported Clinic Income, Estimated Abortion Income," STOPP International; http://www.all.org/stopp/ab_cl_in.pdf.

[6]Lydia Saad, "Americans Agree with Banning 'Partial-Birth Abortion,'" Gallup poll, November 6, 2003; http://www.gallup.com/content/login.aspx?ci=9658.

[7]"ACLU Calls Ban on Safe Abortion Procedures Dangerous Political Power Play, Promises to Sue," ACLU press release, March 26, 2003.

[8]Saad.

[9]"ACLU Promises Suit to Counter Ban on Safe Abortion Procedures," *ACLU Causes That Matter*, October 24, 2003.

[10]"Reproductive Rights Groups Hail First Ruling to Permanently Block Federal Abortion Ban," ACLU press release, June 1, 2004; http://www.aclu.org/reproductiverights/reproductiverights.cfm?ID=15875&c=148.

[11]"ACLU and the National Abortion Federation Hail Decision to Protect Women's Health," ACLU press release, August 26, 2004; http://www.aclu.org/reproductiverights/reproductiverights.cfm?ID=16317&c=148.

[12]"ACLU and National Abortion Federation Hail Third Ruling to Protect Women's Health," ACLU press release, September 8, 2004; http://www.aclu.org/reproductiverights/reproductiverights.cfm?ID=16385&c=148.

[13]ACLU press release, June 1, 2004.

[14]ACLU press release, August 26, 2004.

[15]ACLU press release, September 8, 2004.

[16]Mary Meehan, "ACLU vs. Unborn Children," *Human Life Review* (Spring 2001); http://www.humanlifereview.com/2001_spring/meehan_s2001.php.

[17]Nat Hentoff, "Pro-Choice Bigots," *New Republic*, November 30, 1992.

[18]"The ACLU and the Supreme Court: 77 Years, 77 Great Victories"; http://www.archive.aclu.org/library/75hits.html.

[19]Meehan;   http://www.humanlifereview.com/spring2001/meehan_s2001.
htm.
[20]"The ACLU . . . : 77 Years . . . ."
[21]Ibid.
[22]Meehan.
[23]Ibid., citing Harriet F. Pilpel, "Civil Liberties and the War on Crime,"
paper presented at ACLU Biennial Conference, Boulder, CO, June 21–24,
1964, pp. 7–8.
[24]Ibid.
[25]Ibid.
[26]Harriet Pilpel, "The Right of Abortion," *Atlantic Monthly*, June 1969.
[27]Meehan, citing Pilpel.
[28]Ibid.
[29]Ibid., citing Barbara J. Syska and others, "An Objective Model for
Estimating Criminal Abortions and Its Implications for Public Policy," *New
Perspectives on Human Abortion* (Frederick, MD, 1981), 164–81.
[30]Ibid., citing Cynthia McKnight, *Life without Roe: Making Predictions
about Illegal Abortions* (Washington, DC: 1992), 10–15.
[31]Ibid., citing Bernard Nathanson, *Aborting America* (Garden City, NY,
1979).
[32]"1992 Policy Guide of the ACLU," policy 263, p. 347.
[33]Ibid.
[34]Meehan, citing brief for appellants at 49, *Doe vs. Bolton*, 410 U.S. 179
(1973).
[35]Pilpel.
[36]Ibid.
[37]Aryeh Neier, interview by Thomas J. Balch, November 3, 1979.
[38]Meehan.
[39]Ibid., citing Norman Dorsen, ACLU Campaign for Choice fund-raising
letter, September 1979.
[40]Meehan, citing Eleanor Norton, memo to Alan Reitman, December 5,
1967, ACLU Archives, box 1145, folder 1.
[41]Meehan.
[42]Meehan, citing Special Committee Reviewing ACLU Abortion Policy,
May 19, 1986, minutes 6 & 11, ACLU Archives, box 155, folder 6.
[43]William Donohue, *The Politics of the American Civil Liberties Union*
(New Brunswick, NJ: Transaction Press, 1990), 102.
[44]Ibid., 104.
[45]Ibid., 103–104.
[46]Ibid., 103.
[47]Ibid.
[48]"ACLU: National Day of Appreciation for Abortion Providers,"
ACLU features, March 10, 2002; http://archive.aclu.org/features/f031002a
.html.

[49]Nat Hentoff, "The Awful Privacy of Baby Jane Doe"; http://web.syr.edu/~sndrake/hentoff.htm.

[50]Ibid.

[51]Ibid.

[52]Nat Hentoff, "The Indivisible Fight for Life," presented at AUL Forum, October 19, 1986; http://www-swiss.ai.mit.edu/~rauch/nvp/consistent/indivisible.html.

[53]Ibid.

[54]"President Bush Signs Unborn Victims of Violence Act"; http://www.whitehouse.gov/news/releases/2004/04.

[55]Nat Hentoff, "Abortion by Any Means," *Doctors for Life*, June 5, 2001.

[56]"ACLU Urges House to Defeat 'Unborn Victims of Violence Act,' Says Bill Seeks to Erode Reproductive Freedom," ACLU press release, April 25, 2001.

[57]Hentoff, "Abortion by Any Means."

[58]"The Right to Choose at 25: Looking Back and Ahead," *ACLU Reproductive Rights Update*; http:/archive.aclu.org/issues/reproduct/rrujan98.html.

[59]Robyn Blumner, "ACLU Backs Free Speech for All—Except Pro-Lifers," *Wall Street Journal*, February 10, 1999.

[60]Meehan.

[61]Ibid.

[62]Ibid.

[63]"Reproductive Rights: A Guide for Women in North Carolina," ACLU of North Carolina press release, July 17, 2003; http://www.acluofnorthcarolina.org/reproductiverights.html.

[64]Meehan.

[65]See *Scheidler vs. National Organization for Women*, 510 U.S. 249 (1994).

[66]Ibid.

[67]John Leo, "Protection for Protesters," *U.S. News & World Report*, March 10, 2003.

[68]Meehan.

[69]Nat Hentoff, "Was Terri Schiavo Beaten in 1990?" *Village Voice*, November 14, 2003 and David Thibault, "Governor Bush Mulls 'Limited' Options to Save Terri Schiavo," cnsnews.com, September 24, 2004.

[70]"Schindler Family's Statement in Response to Florida Supreme Court Ruling," cnsnews.com, September 24, 2004.

[71]E-mail from Robert Schindler to ADF Ministry Friends, January 5, 2005.

[72]Thibault.

[73]Ibid.

[74]"ACLU Backs Husband in Terri Schiavo Case," *Miami Herald*, October 25, 2003.

[75]"ACLU Asks a Pinellas Judge to Strike Special Law That Reverses Court Order, Violates Patient's Privacy Rights," ACLU of Florida press release, October 29, 2003; http://www.aclufl.org/news_events/archive/2003/schiavo release.cfm.

[76]Randy Hall, "ACLU Joins Dispute Over Terri Schindler Schiavo," cnsnews.com, October 24, 2003.

[77]"A Second County in Oregon Votes to Issue Marriage Licenses to Same-Sex Couples; ACLU Urges Others to Do the Same," ACLU press release, March 17, 2004.

[78]Hall.

[79]"Who Will Remember Terri?" The Wall Street Journal, April 1, 2005.

[80]Ibid.

[81]Nat Hentoff, "Lying about Terri Schiavo," Village Voice, November 10, 2003.

[82]Ibid.

[83]"Schiavo Case Heads to Court," Associated Press, August 31, 2004.

[84]"Unanimous Florida Supreme Court Strikes Down Special Law That Overrides Medical Decisions in Terri Schiavo Case," ACLU press release, September 23, 2004.

[85]"Schiavo Case Heads to Court."

[86]ACLU press release, September 23, 2004, and "Florida Court Nixes Law Keeping Woman Alive," Associated Press, September 23, 2004.

[87]ACLU press release, September 23, 2004.

[88]Nat Hentoff, "Terri's Tragedy," Washington Times, March 25, 2005.

[89]John Leo, "A Regrettable Limit on Life," U.S. News and World Report, April 4, 2005.

[90]"ACLU of Florida Welcomes Judge Whittemore's Ruling in Schiavo Case," ACLU of Florida press release, March 22, 2005.

[91]Marie McCain, "Senator: Bill to Ban Assisted Suicide Due This Fall," Sentinel (Holland, MI), September 3, 1997.

[92]"Debate Shifting to Eligibility for Assisted Suicide," ACLU press release, August 27, 1996; http://www.archive.aclu.org/news/w082796a.html.

[93]"ACLU Asks Supreme Court to Hear Assisted Suicide Case; Michigan Case Had Been Filed on Behalf of Cancer Patients, Doctors," ACLU press release, March 3, 1995; http://www.archive.aclu.org/news/n030395a.html.

[94]"Civil Liberties at Risk through Ballot Initiatives," ACLU press release, November 4, 1998; http://archive.aclu.org/news/n110498c.html.

[95]"Michigan Lawmakers Ban Assisted Suicide," NurseWeek, July 13, 1998; http://www.nurseweek.com/news/98-7/13e.html.

[96]ACLU press release, August 27, 1996.

[97]John Leo, "Dancing with Dr. Death," U.S. News and World Report, March 22, 1999.

[98]Vacco vs. Quill, 521 U.S. 793 (1997); Washington vs. Glucksberg, 521 U.S. 702 (1997); http://www.archive.aclu.org/court/quill.html.

[99]Ibid.

[100]"Arguments Made in Right-to-Die Case," CNN, August 31, 2004.

[101]"Assisted Suicide in Michigan"; http://www.rtl.org/html/assisted_suicide_in_mi.html.

[102]Nat Hentoff, "Expanding the Culture of Death," *Jewish World Review*, January 2, 2001.

[103]*Vacco vs. Quill*, 521 U.S. 793 (1997).

[104]"Blessed Titus Brandsma"; http://carmelnet.org/titus/titus.htm.

[105]"Over 40 Million Abortions in U.S. since 1973"; http://www.nrlc.org/abortion/aboramt.html.

[106]The Pro-Life Majorities"; http://www.nrlc.org/abortion/major.html.

[107]Kevin Belmonte, "Wilberforce Biography"; http://www.pfm.org/am/template.cfm?section=william_wilberforce&template=/taggedpage/taggedpagedisplay.cfm&TPLID=13&ContentID=3055.

[108]Ibid.

Chapter 6

[1]Don Feder, "One Nation Under . . . ," *FrontPageMagazine.com.*, April 30, 2004.

[2]Dwight D. Eisenhower, as quoted by President Gerald Ford, December 5, 1974, in National Day of Prayer Proclamation 1974, Proclamation 4338.

[3]David McCullough, *John Adams* (New York, NY: Simon and Schuster, 2001), 554.

[4]Adam Nossiter, "ACLU Asks Jail for Tangipahoa School Officials," Associated Press, May 18, 2005.

[5]E-mail from Gena Chieco, ACLU of the National Capital Area paralegal, to Joe Alston, National Park Service, February 28, 2003.

[6]"Park Service Removes Grand Canyon Plaques Containing Bible Verses," Associated Press, July 17, 2003.

[7]Dennis Prager, "A Grand Victory at the Grand Canyon," *Creators Syndicate*, August 5, 2003.

[8]"Secular Absolutism," *The Wall Street Journal*, March 10, 2004.

[9]Mark Kellner, "Out in the Cold?" *Christianity Today*, May 2004.

[10]Seth Lewis, "Court Lets Homosexuals Sue for Access to Married Housing," cnsnews.com, July 2, 2001.

[11]"1992 Policy Guide of the ACLU," policy 84a, p. 166.

[12]Brief of Americans United for the Separation of Church and State, American Civil Liberties Union, and Americans for Religious Liberty in Support of Affirmance, 2004 WL 298118 (February 13, 2004).

[13]"Vast Majority in U.S. Support 'Under God,'" cnn.com, June 29, 2002.

[14]*Newdow vs. U.S. Congress*, 292 F.3d 597 (9th Cir. 2002), rev'd *Elk Grove Unified School District vs. Newdow*, 124 S.Ct. 2301 (2004).

[15]Michael Novak, "The Atheist—Civil Liberty Union?" *National Review* online, July 12, 2002.

[16]Carl G. Karsh, "The Rector Who Changed His Mind," Independence Hall Association; http://www.ushistory.org/carpentershall/history/tour/rector.htm.

[17] George Washington, July 9, 1776, general orders, George Washington Papers, Library of Congress. From John C. Fitzpatrick, ed., *The Writings of George Washington from the Original Manuscript Sources*, 1745–99; http://memory.loc.gov/cgi-bin/query/r?ammem/mgw:@field(DOCID+@lit(gw050 226).

[18] George Washington, March 6, 1776, general orders, George Washington Papers, Library of Congress. From Fitzpatrick; http://memory.loc.gov/cgi-bin/query/r?ammen/mgw:@field(DOCID+@lit (gw040313)).

[19] *Mellen vs. Bunting*, 327 F.3d 355 (4th Circuit. 2003).

[20] Samuel E. Kastensmidt, "ACLU Attacks Prayer at Naval Academy," January 6, 2004; http://www.reclaimamerica.org/pages/news/newspage.asp?story=1503.

[21] Declaration of Independence, adopted July 4, 1776; http://www.archives.gov/national_archives_experience/charters/declaration_transcript.html.

[22] Congress, Proclamation for Fasting and Humiliation, December 11, 1776; http://lcweb2.loc.gov/cgi-bin/query/r?ammem/bdsdcc:@field(DOCID+@lit(bdsdcc018a1))

[23] Novak.

[24] Paris Peace Treaty, 1783; http://www.law.ou.edu/hist/paris.html.

[25] George Washington, Farewell Address, September 19, 1796; http://gwpapers.virginia.edu/farewell/transcript.html.

[26] Thomas Jefferson, letter to Danbury Baptists, January 1, 1802; http://www.loc.gov/loc/lcih/9806/danpre.html.

[27] "The First Forty Years of Washington Society"; http://lcweb2.loc.gov/gc/gcmis/chesapeake/dcgcl028/40262/40262.sgm.

[28] Northwest Ordinance 1787, Article 3, see http://usinfo.state.gov/usa/info usa/facts/democrac/5.htm.

[29] Constitution of the Commonwealth of Massachusetts; http://www.mass.gov/legis/const.htm.

[30] First Amendment, U.S. Constitution; http://www.usconstitution.net/const.html#Am1.

[31] Ronald D. Rotunda and John E. Novak, eds., *Joseph Story: Commentaries on the Constitution of the United States* (Durham, NC: Carolina Academic Press, 1987), sec. 988, p. 700.

[32] *Joseph Story: Commentaries on the Constitution*, 3:sec. 1867; http://press-pubs.uchicago.edu/founders/print_documents/amendI_religions69.html.

[33] Novak, p. 701, sec. 990.

[34] Rotunda and Novak, 990, p. 701.

[35] Joseph LoConte, "The Wall Jefferson Almost Built," December 27, 2001; http://www.heritage.org/Press/Commentary/ed122701c.cfm.

[36] Daniel Dreisbach, *Thomas Jefferson and the Myth of Separation* (New York: New York University Press, 2002), 29.

[37] Ibid.

[38] Joseph LoConte, "The Wall Jefferson Almost Built."

[39] Ibid.

[40]*Everson vs. Board of Education of Ewing Township*, 310 U.S. 1, 18 (1947.

[41]Lino A. Graglia, "Our Constitution Faces Death By 'Due Process,'" *Wall Street Journal*, May 24, 2005, A12.

[42]Dr. Robert P. George, "Judicial Activism and the Constitution: Solving a Growing Crisis," Family Research Council, May 26, 2005, citing Thomas Jefferson letter to Abigail Adams, September 11, 1804, in *11 Writings of Thomas Jefferson* (Albert E. Bergh, ed. 1905), 311–13.

[43]David Asman, "Battle to Tear Down a Tribute," Fox News, June 2, 2005.

[44]See http://www.sandiegohistory.org/bio/serra/serra.htm.

[45]John Antczak, "ACLU Demands Removal of Cross from Los Angeles County Seal," Associated Press, May 25, 2004.

[46]"Proposed L.A. County seal lacks cross," Associated Press, September 9, 2004.

[47]Ibid.

[48]Ibid.

[49]Ibid.

[50]Troy Anderson, "Cross Cave-In Sparks Furor," *Pasadena Star-News*, June 3, 2004.

[51]Ibid.

[52]Ibid.

[53]Ibid.

[54]Dennis Prager, "Taliban Come to Los Angeles," *Creators Syndicate*, June 8, 2004.

[55]Mike Cassidy, "San Jose Churches Battling Plan for Aztec God Statue," *San Jose Mercury-News*, September 17, 1993.

[56]Rebecca Villaneda, "History Depicted through San Jose's Art," *The Daily Spartan*, April 4, 2005.

[57]Leo Morris, "ACLU's Seal of Approval," *Fort Wayne News-Sentinel*, June 16, 2004, and Baird Helgeson, "Monument Debate Heads to Court," *Duluth News-Tribune*, April 14, 2004.

[58]Rusty Pugh, Bill Fancher, and Jenni Parker, "ADF Attorney Says ACLU Threatens to Censor Religious Heritage," *AgapePress*, July 24, 2003.

[59]"Good News in the Midst of a Storm," ADF weekly news alert, July 7, 2003.

[60]Morris.

[61]Phyllis Schlafly, "ACLU Finds Pot of Gold at the Foot of the Cross," *Copley News Service*, June 21, 2004.

[62]Ibid.

[63]Ibid.

[64]Ann Coulter, "When Blue States Attack," anncoulter.com, December 24, 2003.

[65]Ibid.

[66]Harry S. Truman, Speech at attorney general's Conference on Law Enforcement Problems, February 15, 1950; http://www.trumanlibrary.org/publicpapers/index.php?pid=657&st=exodus&st1=matthew.

[67]Felix Hoover, "ACLU Aims to Halt Concert Gospel Event Planned by Children Services Likely Would Violate Law, Legal Agency Says," *Columbus Dispatch*, August 17, 2004.

[68]"Another Victory over the ACLU," ADF weekly news alert, September 24, 2001.

[69]*Hughes vs. Warrington*, 74 F.3d 1249, January 4, 1996.

[70]"High School's Pre-Game Prayer Called 'Un-American and Immoral,'" WKYC.com., April 6, 2005.

[71]Adam Nossiter, "ACLU Asks Jail for Tangipahoa School Officials," Associated Press, May 18, 2005.

[72]Jim Brown, "ACLU Focuses Crosshairs on Louisiana Schools for Religious Activities," *AgapePress*, April 20, 2004.

[73]"Agreeing with ACLU Arguments, Tennessee Court Overturns Local Ban on Fortune-Telling," ACLU press release, June 7, 2004.

[74]Michael Novak and John Templeton, "God Bless the ACLU," *Washington Times*, December 31, 2003.

[75]*Bronx Household of Faith vs. Bd. of Education of the City of New York*, 331 F.3d 342 (2nd Cir. 2003) and *Amandola vs. Town of Babylon, New York* 251 F.3d 339 (2nd Cir. 2001).

[76]Eva-Marie Ayala, "Seniors Win Back Religious Activities," *Fort Worth Star-Telegram*, January 9, 2004.

[77]Amy Hetzner, "School Rejected Girl's Religious Cards, Suit Says," *Milwaukee Journal-Sentinel*, March 21, 2001.

[78]Howard Fisher, "Court Says God Is OK on School Tiles," *East Valley Tribune*, August 3, 2004.

[79]ADF news alert, March 14, 2005.

[80]Charles Haynes, "Public School Sponsored Baccalaureate Service Poses Problem"; http://www.firstamendmentcenter.org/commentary.aspx?id=2356.

[81]*Santa Fe Independent School District vs. Doe*, 505 U.S. 290 (2000); brief filed by ACLU at http://www.archive.aclu.org/court/santafe.html; and *Santa Fe Independent School District vs. Jane Doe, et al.*, 530 U.S. 290 (2000).

[82]*Lee vs. Weisman*, 505 U.S. 577 (1992).

[83]"Chalk Up Another God-Given Win against the ACLU in the Battle for Religious Speech," ADF weekly news alert, September 8, 2003.

[84]Ibid.

[85]"ADF Steps In to Protect Graduation Speech," ADF weekly news alert, May 24, 2004.

[86]Ibid.

[87]Terry Chang, "Religious Employer Must Provide Contraceptive Coverage for Employees," *ACLU of Northern California News*, July/August 2001.

[88]Bob Egelko, "High Court Declines Religious Dispute over Contraceptives, Catholic Charities Challenged Law on Drug Coverage," *San Francisco Chronicle*, October 5, 2004.

[89]Alan Sears, quoting *Bob Jones vs. United States*, 461 U.S. 574 (1983).

[90]"B.C. Lesbians Fight to Hold Wedding Reception in Catholic Hall," CBC News, January 25, 2005.

[91]Pete Vere, "An Impending Religious Persecution in Canada," see http://www.enterstageright.com/archive/articles/0803/0803relper.htm.

[92]Robert B. Bluey, "Marriage Changes May Shake Churches' Tax Exemption," CNSNews.com., February 23, 2004.

[93]Ibid.

[94]*Newport Church of the Nazarene vs. Hensley,* 56 P.3d 386, May 15, 2000 (Or. 2002).

[95]Ibid.

[96]Novak, July 12, 2002.

Chapter 7

[1]John Leo, "Merry C******S to All," *U.S. News & World Report* (used with permission), December 23, 2002.

[2]Ibid.

[3]"Merry Christmas? Not for Many Americans Who Believe the Holiday Has Lost Its Focus," Gallup Poll, December 15, 2000.

[4]John Leo, "Seasonal Symbols Make Some People See Red," *U.S. News & World Report,* December 17, 2001.

[5]Ibid.

[6]ADF news alert, December 20, 2004.

[7]Leo, "Seasonal Symbols."

[8]Rob Moll, "Censoring Christmas," *Christianity Today,* December 11, 2003.

[9]John Leo, "Foiling Those Evil Grinches," *U.S. News & World Report,* December 29, 2003.

[10]"Parents to Speak Out on Christmas Music Ban," ADF press release, December 6, 2004.

[11]Leo, "Foiling Those Evil Grinches."

[12]"Victory in Wisconsin! 'God Bless America' Can Hang on So-Called 'Holiday' Tree," ADF weekly news alert, December 3, 2001.

[13]"It Might Only Be May . . . but ADF Continues Defending Christmas Year-Round," ADF weekly news alert, May 2, 2004.

[14]Letter from Randall C. Wilson to Lee Beine, Cedar County, Iowa, attorney, November 4, 2003.

[15]Daniel Barbarisi, "After Last Year's Flap, City Hall's 2004 Display is Decidedly Tamer," *Providence Journal,* December 14, 2004.

[16]Ibid.

[17]Ibid.

[18]"Students Threatened by Christmas? ACLU Warns of Lawsuit Unless Principal Censors Celebration," WorldNetDaily.com, November 21, 2003, and Don Feder, "Public Schools and the ACLU Play Scrooge This Christmas," frontpagemagazine.com, November 24, 2004.

[19]Moll.

[20]Ibid.

[21]"Students Threatened by Christmas."

[22]Leo, "Foiling Those Evil Grinches."

[23]Nadine Strossen, "The Real Christmas Spirit"; http://www.aclu-em.org/newsletter/1998liberties/november1998/realchristmasspirit.htm.

[24]*Lou Dobbs Tonight*, December 19, 2003; http://www-cgi.cnn.com/transcripts/0312/19/ldt.00.html.

[25]Don Feder, "Public Schools and the ACLU Play Scrooge This Christmas." Documentation also available on request from ADF.

[26]This case is being handled by Kevin Theriot, an ADF staff attorney.

[27]Documentation on this case available from the Alliance Defense Fund on request.

[28]Barbarisi.

[29]"Groups Push for Christmas to Get Religion," Associated Press, December 15, 2004.

[30]*Florey vs. Sioux Falls School District*, 619 F.2d 1311, 1319 (8th Cir. 1980).

[31]*Lynch vs. Donnelly*, 465 U.S. 668, 676 (1984).

[32]*Tinker vs. Des Moines Independent Community School District*, 393 U.S. 503, 506, (1969).

[33]*School District of Abington Township vs. Schempp*, 374 U.S. 203, 225–26. (1963).

[34]*Stone vs. Graham*, 449 U.S. 39, 42 (1981).

[35]*Lynch*, 465 U.S. at 681.

[36]*Lynch*, 465 U.S. at 679.

[37]*Lynch*, 465 U.S. at 679 (citing *Lemon vs. Kurtzman*, 403 U.S. 602, 612–13 (1971).

[38]*Adland vs. Russ*, 307 F.3d 471, 479 (6th Circuit. 2002).

[39]Moll.

[40]Barbarisi.

[41]Charles Colson, *Breakpoint*, vol. 3, no. 20, December 1998.

[42]*Lou Dobbs Tonight*, December 19, 2003.

[43]Colson.

[44]Rabbi Daniel Lapin, "Religious Freedom Is for Everyone—Not Just Minorities," orthodoxytoday.org, August 3, 2004; http://www.orthodoxy today.org/articlesprint4/LapinChristmasP.shtml.

[45]Don Feder, "Schools Play Scrooge at Christmas," www.donfeder.com.

[46]Meghan Cox Gurdon, "Post-Season's Greetings!" *National Review* on-line, January 9, 2004.

Chapter 8

[1]*Lawrence vs. Texas*, 539 U.S. 558, 579 (2003).

[2]Harris Meyer, "Justice Kennedy Wades into International Waters Again," *Daily Business Review*, May 17, 2005.

[3]Richard John Neuhaus, "The Public Square: The Culture Wars Go International," *First Things*, January 2004 citing Robert Bork, *Coercing Virtue: The Worldwide Rule of Judges* (Washington, DC: AEI Press, 2003).

[4]Tom Brokaw, *The Greatest Generation* (New York, NY: Random House, 1998).

[5]Staff Sgt. Elaine Aviles, "Bataan Recalled," *Airman*, July 2001; http://www.af.mil/news/airman/0701/bataan.html.

[6]U.S. National Archives, Bataan Death March; http://history.acusd.edu/gen/st/~ehimchak/death_march.html.

[7]Aviles.

[8]Ibid.

[9]"Training on International Law in U.S. Courts"; http://www.hrea.org/lists/hr-education/markup/msg01207.html.

[10]"ACLU Convenes First National Conference on the Use of International Human Rights Law in the U.S. Justice System," ACLU press release, October 8, 2003; http://www.aclu.org/International/Interntational.cfm?ID=13994&c=36.

[11]Ibid.

[12]"Human Rights at Home: International Law in U.S. Courts," October 9–11, 2003, Carter Center, Atlanta, GA.

[13]Lawrence Morahan, "Judge Gives Moore 15 Days to Remove Ten Commandments," cnsnews.com, August 6, 2003.

[14]*Lawrence vs. Texas*, 539 U.S. 558 (2003).

[15]Ibid., item C.

[16]*Bowers vs. Hardwick*, 478 U.S. 186 (1986).

[17]*Lawrence vs. Texas*, 539 U.S. 558, 572–72 (2003).

[18]Justice Anthony Kennedy, majority opinion, U.S. Supreme Court, No. 02–102, John Geddes Lawrence and Tyron Garner vs. Texas.

[19]Ruth Bader Ginsburg, "Remarks for the American Constitution Society Looking beyond Our Borders: The Value of a Comparative Perspective in Constitutional Adjudication," August 2, 2003.

[20]Remarks by Associate Justice Sandra Day O'Connor, Southern Center for International Studies, Atlanta, GA, October 28, 2003.

[21]Keynote address, Associate Justice Sandra Day O'Connor, ninety-sixth annual meeting, American Society of International Law, March 16, 2002.

[22]*Atkins vs. Virginia*, 536 U.S. 304, 316 n. 21 (2002).

[23]*Atkins vs. Virginia*, 536 U.S. 304, 347–48 (2002).

[24]Associate Justice Stephen Breyer "The Supreme Court and the New International Law," ninety-seventh annual meeting, American Society of International Law, April 4, 2003.

[25]Justice Stephen Breyer, *ABC News This Week with George Stephanopoulos*, July 6, 2003.

[26]Ginsburg.

27Richard John Neuhaus, "The Public Square: The Culture Wars Go International," *First Things*, January 2004, citing Robert Bork, *Coercing Virtue: The Worldwide Rule of Judges* (Washington, DC: AEI Press, 2003).

28"ACLU Cheers Massachusetts High Court Decision Not to Deny Same-Sex Couples Right to Marry," ACLU press release, November 18, 2003; http://www.aclu.org/news/newsprintcfm?ID=14413&c=101.

29*Goodridge vs. Department of Public Health*, 798 N.E. 2d 941, 969 (Mass. 2003).

30The Constitution of the Commonwealth of Massachusetts, Part the First Part.

31"ACLU Files Complaint with United Nations in Geneva Seeking Justice for Immigrants Detained and Deported After 9/11"; http://www.aclu.org/safeandfree/safeandfree.cfm?ID=14804&c=206.

32Ann Beeson and Paul Hoffman, 2003 ACLU International Civil Liberties Report, 1–2.

33"New Report on Human Rights in the United States Analyzed," Stanford University News Service, May 2, 1995; http://www.stanford.edu/dept/news/pr/95/950502Arc5252.html.

34"U.N. Group in 'Showdown with Religion,'" WorldNetDaily.com, August 8, 2003.

35Ibid.

36Ibid.

37Charles Lane, "Thinking outside the U.S.," *Washington Post*, August 4, 2003.

38See http://www.aclu.org/International/Internationalmain.cfm.

39"Canada's Anti-Gay Violence Law Worries Some," FoxNews.com, May 18, 2004.

40"The Bible and Hate Propaganda: Bill C-250," *Focus on the Family Canada Action Guide*.

41Joanne Laucius, "Bible Had Role in Exposing Gays to Hatred," *Ottawa Citizen*, June 20, 2001.

42Ibid.

43*Owens vs. Saskatchewan* (Human Rights Commission), [2002] SKQB 506.

44Bob Kellogg, "Sweden Moves to Criminalize Opposition to Homosexuality," *Family News in Focus*, June 10, 2002.

45"Swedish Pastor Sentenced to One Month's Jail for Offending Homosexuals," *ENI News*, June 2004.

46 "Swedish Court Reviews 'Hate' Case," *BBC News*, May 9, 2005.

47"France to Outlaw Homophobia," *Australia Herald Sun*, June 23, 2004; http://www.freerepublic.com/focus/f-news/1158575/posts.

48"U.S. Church Sermons Being 'Monitored' for Anti-Homosexual Views," *LifeSite Daily News*, July 30, 2004. See http://www.lifesite.net/ldn/2004/july/04073001.html and Abe Levy, "Debate Rages on Faith's Role in Politics," *Wichita Eagle*, October 25, 2004.

[49]Beeson and Hoffman.

[50]ACLU press release, October 8, 2003.

[51]"Legal Recognition of Same-sex Marriage: A Conference on National European and International Law," King's College, University of London, July 1–9, 1999.

[52]*Knight vs. Florida*, 528 U.S. 990 (1999) (Breyer dissenting).

[53]"ACLU Welcomes Landmark Supreme Court Ruling Striking Down Death Penalty for Juveniles," ACLU press release, March 2, 2005. See http://www.aclu.org/court/court.cfm?ID=17592&c+286.

[54]*Roper vs. Simmons,* Slip Opinion, No. 03.

[55]*Roper,* Scalia, J. dissenting.

[56]*Roper,* O'Connor, J. dissenting.

[57]"The Blue State Court," *Wall Street Journal,* March 2, 2005.

[58]Transcript of Discussion between U.S. Supreme Court Justices Antonin Scalia and Stephen Breyer, American University Washington School of Law, January 13, 2005.

[59]President George Washington Farewell Address, September 17, 1796; http://www.law.ou.edu/hist/washbye.html.

Chapter 9

[1]Dwight D. Eisenhower, first inaugural address, January 20, 1953; http://www.yale.edu/lawweb/avalon/presiden/inaug/eisen1.htm.

[2]Ronald Reagan, farewell address to the nation, January 11, 1989; http://www.reaganlibrary.net.

[3]"The Pro-Life Majorities"; http://www.nrlc.org/abortion/major.html.

[4]See http://www.worldhistory.com/worldwarii.htm.

[5]Eisenhower.

[6]Ibid.